W9-BFL-025

PROTESTANT NATIONALISTS IN REVOLUTIONARY IRELAND: THE STOPFORD CONNECTION

Other works by León Ó Broin
also published by Gill and Macmillan
Michael Collins (Gill's Irish Lives)
In Great Haste:
    The letters of Michael Collins to Kitty Kiernan

LEÓN Ó BROIN

PROTESTANT NATIONALISTS IN REVOLUTIONARY IRELAND:

THE STOPFORD CONNECTION

GILL AND MACMILLAN

BARNES & NOBLE BOOKS
Totowa, New Jersey

Published in Ireland by
Gill and Macmillan Ltd
Goldenbridge
Dublin 8
with associated companies in
Auckland, Dallas, Delhi, Hong Kong,
Johannesburg, Lagos, London, Manzini,
Melbourne, Nairobi, New York, Singapore,
Tokyo, Washington
© León Ó Broin 1985
7171 1413 9
Print origination in Ireland by Galaxy Reproductions Ltd, Dublin
Printed in Great Britain by
Biddles Ltd, Guildford and King's Lynn
All rights reserved. No part of this publication may be copied,
reproduced or transmitted in any form or by
any means, without permission of the publishers.

First published in the USA 1985 by
Barnes & Noble Books
81 Adams Drive
Totowa, New Jersey, 07512

Library of Congress Cataloging in Publication Data
Ó Broin, León, 1902-
Protestant Nationalists in revolutionary Ireland.
1. Ireland — History — 1901-1910.   2. Ireland — History — 1910-1921.
3. Ireland — Intellectual life.   4. Nationalists — Ireland — Biography.   5. Pro-
testants — Ireland — Biography.   6. Stopford family.   I. Title.
DA960.B69 1965   941.5082'1   85-2745
ISBN 0-389-20569-9

British Library Cataloguing in Publication Data
Ó Broin, León
Protestant Nationalists in Revolutionary Ireland:
The Stopford Connection.
1. Nationalism — Ireland — History
2. Protestants — Ireland — Political activity — History
322.4'2'09415   DA959
ISBN 0-7171-1413-9

CONTENTS

ACKNOWLEDGMENTS

I am most grateful to the libraries and staffs of the National Library of Ireland, the Royal Irish Academy, the Libraries, Folklore and Archives Departments of University College and Trinity College, Dublin and to the persons I list below, living and dead, for all their help to me in compiling the material for this book over the years:

Hilda Allan, Stephen Barcroft, Flor Begley, Dan Bryan, George R. Chapman, Robert Childers, Saive Coffey, John Cowell, Denis, Margaret and Nora Crowley, Declan Cullen, Liam Deasy, Christopher Dillon, Siobhan de hOir, John P. Duggan, Alan Eager, Doreen Farrington, Sean Fawsitt, Dolores Flynn, Dorothy Mary and Douglas Gageby, R. J. Going, Geoffrey Hand, Patrick Henchy, Stephen Hilliard, Michael Laffan, Denis Lordan, A. T. Lucas, Bridget Lunn, Kenneth Milne, Michael McCarthy, Brian McKenna, N. D. McLachlan, Maire MacNeill, Eamon MacSuibhne, James Meenan, Coilin Ó Broin, Risteard Ó Glaisne, Seán Ó Lúing, Trevor Parkhill, Elizabeth Pim, Sheila Pim, Evelyn S. Price, Leslie Price, Helen Roe, Leo Sexton, Mary K. Smith, Mark Tierney, Fergal Tobin, Mollie Walsh, Jack Whelan, C. J. Woods.

Chapter One

FAMILY AND FRIENDS

The phenomenon of men and women of English stock becoming more Irish than the Irish themselves was repeated many times during the last hundred years. In this book the process can be seen at work within a family and in individuals. All the people involved were eccentrics in the strict sense of that word, that is to say that they had deviated from the centre, from the common line pursued by people of similar origin and class. Though numerically small, their influence on the development of Irish nationalism was very considerable.

We begin with the family. These were the Stopfords, whose Irish base was laid by enterprising men who, in the forties of the seventeenth century, obtained some forfeited Ulster land and added to it by speculation. In the next century an Edward Stopford was rewarded for his services in defence of the privileges of the established Anglican Church of Ireland by being made Bishop of Meath; and he appointed his second son Edward Adderly to be the rector of Kells and Archdeacon of Meath. When the disestablishment of the Church became an issue, the Archdeacon was the only leading ecclesiastic to support the government's measure. He told Gladstone that he wholly disapproved of disestablishment but since it was bound to come and had to be done, it should be done as well and as justly as possible. He claimed to have the confidence of the clergy and laity, though he was greatly pained by the way the bishops fumbled with the problem. At the same time, he was a vain man, full of his own importance, and entertained a notion of winning a see in England as a colleague of his in the Irish anti-episcopal cabal had done. Gladstone was wary of Stopford's intervention but he realised that the Archdeacon had stepped in to fill a breach, and that if others followed his lead, it would, in his thinking, be of great service to the Irish Church in the hour of need. He therefore invited Stopford to visit Hawarden, and his hesitation about making use of him was soon overcome by the Archdeacon's personality. In the upshot, Stopford's work considerably benefited the Church of Ireland, obtaining for it concessions that would not otherwise have been granted.

Archdeacon Stopford, of course, believed that the mission of his Church, established or otherwise, was to convert the Irish masses to Protestantism, and so his offspring of nine were set, on Sunday mornings, to writing out texts on pieces of card which were scattered by the roadside in the hope that some benighted Roman Catholics would pick them up and be converted. Two of these children were Jemmett Stopford, the Archdeacon's fifth son, and Alice Stopford, his third daughter.

Alice was born at Kells in 1848, a year in which the collapse of Smith O'Brien's attempted rising and the mad flight of tens of thousands of half-starved peasants to the emigrant ships appeared to justify the belief that the Celt 'was going with a vengeance'. She lived a moderately happy life in Kells for the first twenty-six years of her life and strove to teach herself German, Greek and metaphysics. In 1874 her father died, and her mother went to live in Chester with Alice and another unmarried daughter. Alice and her mother were not very compatible. Mrs Stopford was even more perfervidly evangelical than the Archdeacon had been and, in reaction to the strict atmosphere of the household, Alice's early faith gave way to a broad undogmatic Christianity. Her mother was otherwise highly conventional: she thought young ladies should not waste time on books, which Alice tended to do, but should make themselves agreeable to young gentlemen among whom they might find a spouse. We do not know how presentable Alice made herself but, in the course of enjoying the busy social round, this 'untrained intellectual', as R. B. McDowell calls her, tall, red-haired, elegant and vital, who was known to be writing a novel, met in the London house of her cousin Stopford Brooke, a small dark good-looking middle-aged slightly stooped cleric. This was John Richard Green,

who had managed to combine the core of a couple of East-
End parishes with the writing of historical articles for the
Saturday Review. He had become a consumptive, however,
and with all active work impossible as a consequence, he
devoted himself, with advances from the publisher Alexander
Macmillan, to the composition of what was to be the first
social history of England, a *Short History of the English
People*. In the later stages of producing this work Alice was
to be his collaborator, but at their first meeting the burden
of John Richard's conversation was not the history of
England but an aspect of his own history, how from being a
rationalist he had entered Holy Orders, returning to the High
Church position in which he had been brought up and even
turning Romeward for a time under the influence of John
Henry Newman. There were subsequent conversations and a
visit to the British Museum when he noted, as a point in
Alice's favour, that she did not say that the Elgin marbles
were nice and that there were a great many of them. They
married in 1877 but his precarious health shortened their life
together. He died at Mentone in 1883, leaving *The Conquest
of England* on which he had been engaged to be edited by
Alice.

Though her loss was profound, Alice rallied and, employing the skills she had learned from John Richard, set about
producing a new edition of the *Short History* which had
made him famous. There were to be twenty editions by 1920.
She then wrote a life of *Henry II* and a study, in two volumes,
of *Town Life in the Fifteenth Century*. She came to London,
bought herself a house on Kensington Square, employed a
cook, butler and maid, and, through entertainment, began to
create a wide circle of acquaintances, many of them Liberal
politicians. She profoundly believed in the value of a good
meal as a means of making and retaining the friendship of
people whose help she needed in whatever cause she happened
to be promoting, and these were numerous. She loved company, especially the company of men and, having been left so
well off by her husband — she had an income of about £1800
a year in the currency of the time — was able to entertain on
a fairly lavish scale. Even her nieces, who were well used to
her generosity, could be astonished when they saw as many

as fourteen places laid for dinner. She was an unusually diligent woman, beginning her reading, writing and researching at five in the morning and working steadily until lunchtime, when she would also have guests to suit her varied interests.

An early acquaintance of hers in London was the wealthy social scientist Beatrice Potter, who was to marry Sidney Webb, socialist founder of the *New Statesman*, a minister in a Labour government and ultimately a Labour peer. The friendship that ensued would hardly have endured, however, had Alice by any chance read Beatrice's first impression of her. 'Mrs Johnny Green,' she had entered in her diary, 'the historian's widow (and a lady of intellectual as well as social distinction) is courting me! poor little me! She has called twice in one week and seems to wish to see me every day and suggests I should live with her. She has a wizened face – ugly usually, attractive at times – reminds me of a medieval picture; only, unfortunately, one knows it is not only 'bad drawing' that distorts her features. Colourless hair and an acid expression, perpetual discontent written on her face, the rest of her nature an enigma. She has a weird mind, seldom speaks well of her friends, describes their faults with more sharpness of outline than is charitable and submerges their virtues in sentences implying personal affection as the origin of her appreciation'. And she gathered from a Frenchman who had been for a time an intimate friend of Mrs Green, but had broken with her, that she had only one characteristic – vanity (Webb, 1, 271-2).

Some months later Beatrice wrote:

Mrs Johnny Green has been here for the last fortnight. In appearance she is a slight woman with a neat figure and, if only she had more freedom of movement, with a graceful bearing. Her hands are small, white and well formed; her dress is natty though with the negligence of a woman with intellectual pretensions. Her hair and complexion are colourless, the colour worn from out of them by a strained and excited life. . . . She has the originality which springs from a lonely, unhappy and self-absorbed youth, from the enforced independence of a friendless womanhood. Bred in a remote part of Ireland in a poverty-stricken home, she struggled at self-culture against every imaginable adverse circumstance. A brief married life with a man of talent and she was left without a friend but with a distinguished name. Now she has climbed up the social ladder, but social success based on her husband's achievements does not satisfy her. She aims at the position to be gained by personal merit. But she does not love her work for its own sake, but only for what it brings her, not for what it may bring to others. . . .

During the fortnight's companionship she has taken the inventory of my mental experiences and has found something which suits her. She is in search of a confidential friend who will be a stay and support to her intellectual aims, who will encourage her to believe that she is governed and controlled by great motives (Webb, 1. 288-9).

Some months later Beatrice's attitude changed considerably. She had passed through a period of strain, and 'Alice Green with her extraordinary vivacity of intellect and brilliant powers of expression helped me over it, unknowing of the service she was rendering. . .' (Webb, 1. 301). Their friendship ripened and Beatrice, a year or two further on, could speak of 'A really enjoyable six weeks with Alice Green. I believe further back I have an entry describing her from the unfavourable point of view. . . . Now I see her differently, and certainly with more real knowledge. She is first, a brilliant woman with a veritable fund of intellectual curiosity. Warmhearted, full of divine pity for suffering, more especially mental suffering, ready to sacrifice herself, to give herself away. If there is a moral flaw in her character it is the intensely personal aspect in which all things clothe themselves — her judgment warped by the opinion of her, the treatment of herself. She is in fact extremely *feminine* in her character, with a grand capacity to be "a nasty enemy". A good woman, a sincere friend who encourages and also criticises' (Webb, 1. 355).

Alice by this time had met Sidney Webb, and made her house available for 'a queer party' he was organising. Haldane, M.P. a lieutenant of John Morley's, the Irish Chief Secretary,

was trying to arrange an alliance between progressive liberals
and the Fabian socialists, so five of the young Liberal Radicals
— Asquith, Haldane, Grey, Buxton, Acton — were there, with
five Fabians — Massingham, Webb, Clarke, Olivier and Bernard
Shaw. It was not successful, though not a failure, since all
were pleasant and cordial. Asquith spoilt it. He was the ablest
of the lot, and determined that it should not 'go'. 'Haldane
made himself most pleasant, and is really playing up. But the
machine — the Liberal party — is slow to move' (Webb, 1.
356). That may have been the first political gathering in
Alice's house. It was the forerunner of many. It took place in
December 1890, the very month when the world of politics
was shattered by the revelation in a London divorce court of
the adultery of perhaps the greatest Anglo-Irishman of all
time, Charles Stewart Parnell, with the wife of a former
member of his party. But none of this, surprisingly, is mentioned in the Stopford or Stopford Green papers.

Alice Green introduced a new friend to her London circle
and took him down with her for three days to Beatrice
Potter's place in Surrey. This was John Francis Taylor,
Alice's 'devoted Irish lawyer' in Beatrice's phrase. At this
time, October 1894, Alice, according to Beatrice, was in a
changing mood. 'She is, I fear, disillusioned about us, her
disillusionment taking the form of an almost irritable criticism of our ways of life, with our sordid simplicity, lack of
culture and general lower-middle-class-ness. . . . If she cared
to go on seeing me I should like to be friendly with her, for
she is an open window to other ways of thought and feeling,
to other emotional and intellectual interests, new outlooks
which amuse and entertain and rest me. But unless we
speedily become "distinguished" that is, thought well of by
London Society I fear we shall see little more of Alice
Green . . .' (Webb, 2. 58-9).
   Alice was undoubtedly acquiring other 'emotional and
intellectual interests' through John Francis Taylor, and we
shall hear presently about some of these, but they were
unlikely to have included a preference for London society
as against any other. Another suggestion that Alice had become society conscious arises shortly after this in Beatrice

Webb's diary. Discussing one of London's great hostesses she says that to Alice Green, 'with her fortuitous mind and uncertain ways', the lady is anathema, "though possibly now that she is the wife of the Bishop of London" Alice may see "quality" in her' (Webb, 2. 102).

Alice continued to visit Beatrice, however, and is described in June 1897 as 'withering up into a strange sort of uneasy conventionality but pathetic in her utter loneliness and drifting intention'. 'There is', Beatrice said, 'a multitude of tragedies in that woman's life — always in the process of being deserted and of deserting — and yet withal a certain faithfulness and persistency of disposition, never daring to let go a friendship lest the friend should turn out after all trumps. So she keeps us up, gazing on us with that weird veiled look, uncertain whether to hold on or let go, but giving us only her leavings. Even the clothes she comes in are always her shabbiest! Poor Alice! She chose me as a friend and not I her, but she was good to me in the early springtide of my good fortune and she was one of the first to appreciate and like Sidney . . .' (Webb, 2. 116-17).

The tragedy of Alice's life soon became startlingly clear in a subsequent diary entry:

14 January 1898. Poor Alice Green! For the last month or so she has become friendly to us and the other evening when I was alone with her and she broke down and wept bitterly in my arms. Arthur Strong, after using her money and her influence to climb into the position of Librarian to the House of Lords, marries a brilliant and beautiful Greek scholar — Eugenie Sellers. For eighteen months the poor woman has been eaten into with bitterness; when at times I have watched her unawares she has looked like a lost soul. And a certain lack of dignity and the extreme unhappiness of her expression has alienated some of her old friends, and even Society is becoming cold to her. The world gets impatient of her restless unhappiness: at fifty years of age, with a good income, distinguished position, a woman ought to settle down contentedly. But some women never grow too old to be in love, or at least to require love. And, why should they? With intellectual persons love is the passion for warm enduring affection and intimate mental companionship. Only religion can take its place. And Alice Green has no religion, no conviction, not even a cause she believes in (Webb, 2. 128).

We now turn to the first in the gallery of individual deviationists. This man, Douglas Hyde, was some years younger than Alice Green but shared with her a clerical background. His father was the Rector of Frenchpark, Co. Roscommon and his mother the daughter of the Church of Ireland Archdeacon of Elphin. Frenchpark is not far from the Roscommon-Mayo border and there young Hyde heard his father's servants speaking what he understood was the old Irish language. James Hart, 'the keeper of the bogs', spoke it, so did Mrs William Connolly when she came to milk the cows in the evening, 'so too did John Lavin and his wife, and other people I met out fowling'. He began keeping a diary in 1874 shortly after his fourteenth birthday, and within the first month his faltering effort at Irish appeared in it. The second volume was almost entirely in Irish. By that time (1879) he was a student in Trinity College, Dublin, and attending the debates at the Contemporary Club. He was fiercely anti-English, favoured the use of physical force to regain the freedom of Ireland, and wrote a toast in verse to the rebel O'Donovan Rossa, whom he made it his business to meet when some years later he went to America. He was strongly influenced by John Lavin who was a Fenian, and by the sentiments he heard expressed in a society he joined when at Trinity. This was the Young Ireland Society, a front for the Irish Republican Brotherhood (IRB), which met in the lecture hall of a workmen's club at 41 York Street with the former Fenian leader John O'Leary for President. O'Leary had recently returned to Ireland after five years imprisonment and fifteen years exile. 'There', said William Butler Yeats, 'four or five University students and myself, and occasionally John Francis Taylor, spoke on Irish History or Literature' (*Autobiographies*, 99) and listened to O'Leary orating on the subject of Thomas Davis.

'Hyde was a very dark young man, who filled me with surprise' Yeats said when he met him first in college rooms, 'partly because he had pushed a snuff-box towards me, and partly because there was something about his vague serious eyes and his high cheek-bones, that suggested a different civilisation, a different race. I had set him down as a peasant, and wondered what brought him to college, and to a Protestant college, but somebody explained that he belonged to some branch of the Hydes of Castle Hyde. . . . He had much frequented the company of old countrymen, and has so acquired the Irish language, and his taste for snuff, and for moderate quantities of a detestable species of illegal whiskey. . .'. He took snuff like those Mayo people whose stories and songs he was writing down, and which he dispensed so freely to his friends. He gave Yeats the best tale in his book on *Fairy and Tolk Tales* and, in return, Yeats helped to find him a London publisher for his *Beside the Fire*, a book which Yeats said 'was written in the beautiful English of Connacht which is Gaelic in idiom and Tudor in vocabulary'. This contained an English translation of about half the stories he had already presented in Irish in an earlier book, together with some half-dozen other traditional tales in the original Irish with English renderings. Hyde's first impressions of Yeats were not so complimentary. He had no sympathy with his occult interests and was 'bored to death with his blather'.

As time went on Hyde's nationalist views underwent a change; he became convinced that cultural regeneration was more important for Ireland than political autonomy. In 1892, on taking over the presidency of the National Literary Society from O'Leary, he lectured on 'the necessity for de-anglicising the Irish Nation'. The real Irish, he pointed out, were not the upper classes of the ascendancy, whose ancestors had come in with Cromwell and with William and had once sat in the parliament in College Green. The life and soul of Ireland did not belong to these people, but to those whom Dean Swift had called the hewers of wood and drawers of water. These were the Irish nation, to whom the Irish language belonged. They had advanced very far towards complete anglicisation; the problem was to reverse the process, and this must be done through the language, music and national games, but especially through the language and speaking it. 'I believe,' said Hyde, 'it is our Gaelic past which is really at the bottom of the Irish heart. Do what the Irish race may do, it cannot wholly divest itself from the mantle of its past.' When an Irishman lost his native language he lost much more than a medium of communication; he cut himself off from his cultural roots and suffered a deterioration of his national character.

In 1930 Hyde recalled in an autobiographical book, *Mise agus an Connradh*, the night when he had spoken those words: 'There was an audience of a hundred or a hundred and fifty but what I had to say did not seem to impress them particularly. A friend of mine heard two young men talking as they left the hall. One said to the other: "Do you think that anything of that kind would ever catch on in Ireland?" "No," his companion replied. "It's just a lot of rubbish".' At the Contemporary Club that night when the discussion tended to turn towards what Hyde had said earlier, the Land Commissioner W. F. Bailey, who was in the chair, quickly intervened to get the members to talk about something more substantial, and more likely. And the *Irish Times*, 'the paper of the English in Ireland', as Hyde called it, commented that there was no country in the world where such a speech could have been made and an audience found to pretend they liked its content. That reflected the mood of many nationally-minded people, too. At a large meeting in Cork early in 1893 which Hyde and W. B. Yeats attended, the chairman, Denny Lane of Young Ireland renown, said that if we had to have about us the chain of a foreign language he was happy it would be English, 'the jewelled key that opened to us the storeroom containing the wealth of centuries from the time of Chaucer and Shakespeare down to the present day'. Hyde reacted as he had done in Dublin. He said that the G.A.A. had done more for Ireland in the five years since it was established than speakers like Lane had done in sixty.

That same year Hyde on his honeymoon visited in Nice Charles Gavan Duffy, another of the Young Irelanders and one-time editor of *The Nation*, spent a whole day with him, and kept his children breathless as he told them the folk story of the King of Ireland's son. Duffy told an intriguing story too, how as a child he had pressed his mother to tell him just one story more only to be told that she had no more stories unless she turned to Irish and that was a closed book to Charles. She had not passed her Irish on to him, and he in turn, had not seen fit to have it taught to his children. Louise, his youngest daughter, one day came across a reference to O'Growney's *Simple Lessons in Irish* in a catalogue of second-hand books. It was the first time she had heard of an Irish language. She quizzed her father about it. Yes, there was such a thing; his mother knew it, he didn't, and Davis was the only one of his Irish political colleagues who was interested in the subject.

There were, however, in 1893 some Irishmen who shared Hyde's line of thinking, among them the civil servant Eoin MacNeill who, nine months later, called a meeting which led to the foundation of a League which aimed at doing what Hyde had recommended in his speech at the National Literary Society. Hyde had met MacNeill in the library of the Royal Irish Academy and had been surprised to find him reading the Book of Leinster which was something he could not do. In his diary for 31 July 1893 Hyde entered in Irish 'We established a Gaelic League to keep the language being spoken among the people. There were present about ten or twelve people, among them MacNeill, O'Neill Russell, Cogan, O'Kelly, Father Hayden, S. J., and Quinn. I was in the chair. I made a long statement in Irish and English, and everything went off well'. On 3 August he went to the Literary Society and induced them to let two rooms for one night in the week to the League, and his next diary entry reads: '*4 August* — I wrote many letters. I went to the Gaelic League. I was in the chair and they made me President. I spoke in Irish and English. I stood Sigerson and O'Neill Russell a drink. I spent the night in P. J. McCall's rooms in Patrick Street drawing up an account of the proceedings of the Literary Society for the previous year'. He was surrendering office there, so as to be able to give more time to the new League.

Hyde and MacNeill made a formidable contribution. Hyde inspired the many with enthusiasm, P. H. Pearse said; MacNeill expounded the philosophy of the League to the few. Between them the League became much more than a language or literary organisation. It promoted the language primarily of course and it inspired literature, but it lifted the national morale by propagating self-reliance and self-respect. It became a well organised, nation-wide pressure group, and one of its many achievements was to secure for Irish a prominent place in every branch of education. Its appeal was surprisingly wide. Even some unionists were drawn to it. Sir Horace Plunkett, the most eminent of them perhaps, praised how it had invigorated every department of Irish life, thus adding to the intellectual, social and moral well-being of the people.

In 1893, the year the League began and that Hyde married, his *Love Songs of Connacht* were published with a dedication to George Sigerson whose earlier work to preserve the oral tradition Hyde greatly admired. The *Love Songs* is regarded as a primary source-book of the literary revival largely through the medium of English, but Hyde's interest, first and last, was the preservation of Irish and the culture enshrined in it. He was a language revivalist as, to a degree, was Yeats. Yeats would tell his friends that he would prefer to see them in the Gaelic movement and learning Gaelic than in any other Irish movement he could think of. His mind, like many others, was in revolt against politics since 'Parnell had been dragged down, his shattered party given up to vituperation, and Irish imagination driven from the sordid scene'. He wanted people to turn to the important matter of preserving that which was living, and help to unite the two Irelands, Gaelic Ireland and Anglo-Ireland, so that neither would shed its pride (*Explorations*, 322). When he first went to London, in 1887, at the age of 22, Yeats already felt himself a stranger. His mind was filled with Irish images; yet the Ireland he had left was also strange to him. He was separated from the Catholic majority because he did not share their faith and deplored their tastes. He did not altogether like the Irish Protestants either. They seemed to think of nothing but getting on in the world.

Yeats's father, the painter J. B., described with great frankness the position of the Anglo-Irish class to which the Hydes and the Yeatses then belonged. 'Our feelings', he wrote, 'were curious and though exceedingly selfish not exclusively so. We intended as good Protestants and Loyalists to keep the Papists under our feet. We impoverished them, though we loved them; and their religion by its doctrine of submission and obedience unintentionally helped us; yet we were convinced that an Irishman, whether a Protestant or Catholic, was superior to every Englishman, and that he was a better comrade and physically stronger and of greater courage' (Stanford, 120). In other words, the Anglo-Irish were English, yet superior to the English; Irish and yet a special sort of Irish. They were what Mahaffy, a Provost of Trinity College, liked to describe as 'splendid mongrels' whose intellect was more versatile and, when trained, superior to the pure English intellect. But in the matter of fundamental political allegiance these mongrels were rarely in doubt. They were Anglo, English, British as well as being Irish, but they knew where their centre of gravity lay, and what they should do when it came to making a political choice. Dublin might hold their attention sporadically but the totality of their individual lives was focused on the Empire, on London. Through London and what that meant, many, if not most, of them would find occupations and continuing interests. The few that veered away from the centre of gravity were oddities.

W. B. Yeats acknowledged that two-sidedness of his own make-up. His forbears, Yeatses and Pollexfens, were originally of planter stock; what was Irish about them had been acquired by long residence in the country. Outlining his background, he claimed that one ancestor had been a general under the Duke of Marlborough; one saved the life of Sarsfield in battle; another, taken prisoner by King James's army, owed his life to Sarsfield gratitude; another still, a century later, roused the gentlemen of Meath against some local Jacquerie and was shot dead upon a country road; and yet another, having chased the United Irishmen, fell into their hands and was hanged. He added that the notorious Major Sirr, who gave Lord Edward Fitzgerald the bullet wound he died of in jail, was godfather to several of his great-great grand-father's children, while, to make a balance, his great-grandfather had been Robert Emmet's friend (*Autobiographies*, 20-21). He adhered for a longer time than did Hyde to the physical force tradition, though never considered a serious revolutionary; between 1895 and 1900 he was a member of the secret Irish National Brotherhood (INB), a breakaway from the Irish Republican Brotherhood (IRB), being introduced by T. W. Rolleston, the founder of the *Dublin University Review*, who was an early Protestant member of the IRB and inspired the Young Ireland Society. Towards the end of his days, he enjoyed being considered a Fenian by men like Dr Pat Mc Curtain (Ó Broin, *Revolutionary Underground*, 1963, and 'Yeats the Fenian' in *Dolman Press Papers* 1965).

Although he had connexions with other parts of Ireland, Sligo was Yeats's real home. A great-grandfather Yeats had been rector of Drumcliff, and there were Middletons and Pollexfens who intermarried with their co-religionists to maintain their relative strength and their ascendancy status. They formed a colony of townies and country people, the latter rarely having anything to do with the former. Yeats, belonging to the merchant class, was treated exceptionally. He was after all a poet, a superior person, and that enabled him to speak to the land-owning Gore-Booths, for example. There were two Gore-Booth girls. One of them Constance or Con all through his childhood had been romantic to him; more than once he had looked over the grey wall of Lissadell in the hope of seeing her. She passed by sometimes on horseback, going or coming from the hunt. She was the acknowledged beauty of the county and there were many stories of her reckless riding. When Yeats first met her he was surprised by some physical resemblance to another girl to whom he had been indirectly introduced by John O'Leary. Her voice, too, was exactly similar; but it changed, as he noted in the critical lines he wrote about her when she was undergoing a life sentence in 1916.

> That woman's days were spent
> In ignorant good will,
> Her night in argument
> Until her voice grew shrill.
> What voice more sweet than hers
> When young and beautiful,
> She rode to harriers?
>   (*Easter 1916*)

Even more critical was his view of her when she was in prison for a second time in 1917. She was 'blind and leader of the blind', and 'drinking the foul ditch where they be.' Yeats was in closer sympathy with Eva: her delicate gazelle-like beauty reflected a mind far more subtle and distinguished than Con's. For a couple of happy weeks she was his close friend, and he briefly thought of asking her to marry him, but he rejected the idea. 'That house would never accept so penniless a suitor', he decided, 'and besides I was still deeply in love with that other'. That other was the English girl Maud Gonne who, through her father being an army officer stationed in Ireland, had been introduced to the Viceregal Court. She was now an extreme nationalist and came under police notice. They reported in February 1891 that the Irish Party looked on her as a fanatic: they might use her for electioneering purposes but nothing more (S.P.O., C.B.S. 1833/S) Yeats was enraptured by her: 'I had never thought to see in a living woman so great beauty', he wrote. 'It belonged to famous pictures, to poetry, to some legendary past. . . . She, like myself, had received the political tradition of Davis, with an added touch of hardness and heroism, from the hand of O'Leary', the Fenian leader. They dined together every day for a week. She spoke of her wish for a play in Dublin that she could act in, and Yeats told her of a story he had found when compiling his *Fairy and Folk Tales of the Irish Peasantry*, and offered to write for her the play about it that he called *The Countess Cathleen* (*Memoirs*, 40-41). Hyde had already made her acquaintance in December 1888. He first saw her at George Sigerson's and wrote in his diary that she was 'the most dazzling woman I have ever seen'. She drew every male in the room around her. She was wonderfully tall and beautiful. We stayed talking until 1.30 a.m. My head was spinning with her beauty.' He went to her place several times afterwards to give her lessons in Irish, but invariably, as he recorded, 'we did not do much Irish'. Indeed, it looked as if Miss Gonne's beauty would bring to an end Hyde's assiduous courtship of Frances Crofton, a fellow student (Daly, 95-7).

Maud was in France on and off from 1887 to 1904 and in a sanatorium in the Auvergne came to know Lucien Millevoye, who became her lover and the father of two of her children. Millevoye was a prominent member of Boulanger's National

Party and Maud's association with him facilitated her propagandist work for Ireland in Paris where they joined in pro-Boer demonstrations and in the circulation of a news sheet she called *L'Irlande Libre*. The liaison had not long ended when another man came into Maud's orbit. This was John MacBride who had fought for the Boers. She travelled with him to the United States on a lecturing tour, and when he fell in love with her, the Irish Joan of Arc, and asked her to marry him, she agreed to do so, despite warnings from Arthur Griffith and from her sister Kathleen. Griffith told her: 'for your own sake and for the sake of Ireland, don't get married. I know you both, you Maud are so unconventional, a law unto yourself, John so full of conventions. You will not be happy for long.' Kathleen disapproved of MacBride and questioned his social and economic position. She also raised objections based on rumours she had heard about MacBride, probably to do with his drinking. She suggested an alternative, that Maud should marry Yeats who was such a persistent suitor, but Maud said no. 'As for Willie Yeats', she told Kathleen, 'I love him dearly as a friend, but I could not for one moment imagine marrying him. I think I will be happy with John. Our lives are exactly the same and he is so fond and thoughtful that it makes life very easy when he is there, and besides we have a vitality and joy in life which I used to have once, but which the hard life I have had wore out of me. With him I seem to get it back again a little' (Balliett, *Eire-Ireland*, Autumn 1979).

The marriage to MacBride did not last long. Griffith's prediction came true. There were legal proceedings and a form of separation based on what happened one winter night when, allegedly, MacBride came home drunk and out of control, upsetting their baby son, Jean Seaghan (Sean), and terrifying the household. MacBride subsequently, in an attempt to rescue his reputation, sued the *Independent* newspaper in Dublin for libellously accusing him of cruelty, infidelity and drunkenness. He got a technical decree in his favour and an insulting £1 damages (Balliett, *Eire-Ireland*, 1979). These happenings caused public dissent and division. IRB men like John O'Leary took MacBride's side, while Yeats thought that Maud would now assuredly marry him. He was seen a lot in her company; and one night when they entered the Abbey together there was hissing, and a shout was raised of 'Up John MacBride'.

Jemmett Stopford's career took a very different course from that of his sister Alice. Being the son of a man who had acquired distinction in connexion with the disestablishment of the Church of Ireland, he was well placed to join a class of Civil Servants that was recruited specifically to implement the financial aspect of the subsequent legislation and, working up through the ranks of the so-called Church Temporalities organisation, he became its accountant in 1902. He was then 53 years of age and, like Alice originally, a firm supporter of the British connexion. After a courtship of ten years' duration, he succeeded in marrying Constance Kennedy, the daughter of a Master of the Rotunda Hospital. She, too, was descended from planter stock, and brought up in the Irish Protestant way of life. Like the vast majority of her class, these Kennedys, however, never veered towards Irish nationalism. They were Anglo-Irish, and saw no reason to change the fundamentals of the society in which they found themselves. By his marriage to Constance, Jemmett had four children, Alice, Edie, Dorothy and Robert. It was a typical Anglo-Irish family which Edie was later to describe.

She, her sister and brother, she said, had been brought up in 'the Irish Protestant social and cultural tradition'. They went to church with their governesses or parents. They consorted only with young Protestants, the children of their parents' friends. To preserve their accents from any trace of Irish brogue, the governesses were imported from England; and they learned only English history, never that of Ireland. During the Boer War they wore in the lapels of their coats buttons with portraits of their favourite British generals, Roberts, Kitchener or Hunter, and they improvised a fortress in the garden which they christened Ladysmith, as distinct from the Mafeking fortress of a neighbouring family. They celebrated the relief of the real Mafeking by dancing and cheering round a bonfire, scarcely noticing the booing of the local population which, pro-Boer to a man, lined a low park wall hundreds of yards away. On the Day of Queen

Victoria's funeral, Alice, Edie, and Dorothy, thirteen, twelve
and eleven years of age respectively, were put into black
mourning coats and skirts, the blinds of the house were drawn,
and Edie was moved to compose an elegy which began:

> Our hope, our strength has passed away,
> Oh England, weep for her.

These children, Edie insisted, were singularly unaware of
any Irish problem, or of any hostility by Irishmen to British
rule which was regarded as perfect. They were class-conscious,
however: dominant Protestants seemed to them necessarily
the upper, and Catholics the lower, classes. On her first visit
with her parents to London she was staggered to learn, as
they drove from Euston, that the ragged women sitting in the
doorways and the barefoot children were Protestants, not
Catholics; this seemed to contradict a law of nature. And
when their Aunt Alice Green came over in 1902 to be near
John Francis Taylor, who was chronically ill, Edie sensed
that her parents disliked his association with a Roman Catholic
who was, *ipso facto*, a person of inferior rank. To this friendship they attributed a change they had noticed in Alice, her
criticism of British colonial policy and her concern for the
welfare of Boer prisoners. She had actually gone to the
trouble of visiting them on the island of St Helena.

The Stopfords of Bushy Park Road might think there was
no Irish problem, but the opposite had quite recently been
manifested in three separate outbursts of disaffection. In
1897 various extreme groups led by Maud Gonne, who
dragged Yeats everywhere after her, and James Connolly of
the Irish Republican Socialist Party, set about upsetting the
arrangements for the celebration of Victoria's Jubilee.
Through a magic lantern statistics were projected on to a
public screen showing the evictions and deaths that had
occured during the reign of 'the Famine Queen'. In a mock
funeral a coffin with 'The British Empire', painted on it was
paraded through the streets, and black flags carried by the
'mourners' bore the names of Irishmen who had been hanged
for treason. When the police drew their batons and charged,
Connolly ordered the coffin to be thrown into the Liffey
nearby. In the following year the centenary of the Rebellion

of 1798 was celebrated from one end of the country to the other, culminating in a Wolfe Tone demonstration in Dublin, which was said to have been the biggest thing of its kind seen in Dublin. Even the police were impressed by its size, and by the ability of the secret IRB to organise it. In 1899, when the Boers went to war for the second time in protest against British colonial policy, 'it was something so wonderful, so unexpected, so unheard to', Hyde said, 'that the English empire should be held up by a handful of farmers that it gave every Irishman a thrill of joy' (Hyde Memoir). Two Irish Brigades went to the aid of the Boers and were sustained by a Transvaal Committee at home. When the brigades were disbanded towards the end of the War in 1902, the Irish, who were British subjects, had to find shelter in foreign lands. Thus it was that John MacBride, an IRB man who had been second in command of one of the brigades, arrived in Paris and was met by his friend Arthur Griffith and by Maud Gonne.

1902 was a tragic year for the Stopfords. Out of the blue, Jemmett contracted typhoid and died. He had been overworked, it was said, but he had nevertheless enjoyed a full social life and lived to the limit of his means, so that his wife Constance was left so badly off that she had to sell Wyvern, their house on Bushy Park Road, and bring the children over to England where they had a number of relations. Besides Alice Green, there were two other aunts and two uncles, and Constance reckoned they could get a better and cheaper education in London than was possible in Dublin. They settled in 65 Campden Gardens, West Kensington. A governess was somehow found for the eldest child, Alice, and the others went to the St Paul's schools on foundation scholarships. There, Edie said, they were quite conventional – neither politically-minded nor politically educated – so that they could receive with equal boredom Aunt Alice's exposition of Irish nationalism and their teacher's occasional outbursts on women's suffrage which was then a burning question.

Time passed, and one by one the three girls put their hair up. It was Christmas time 1909 when Dorothy did this and, in a diary she started to keep, she wrote that this single action brought her great ideas of dignity, of womanhood, and of behaviour. We do not know whether the change meant so much for Alice and Edie. It had been decided, presumably by her mother, that Alice needed no further education; she was to be 'the Daughter at Home'. And, although only a year older than Dorothy, Edie, at the age of nineteen, in 1908, regarded herself as fully mature, when she went up to Cambridge on a scholarship. She was there at Newnham College for three years, and without apparent difficulty obtained a double first in English and a triple blue at games. Dorothy, though also brilliant, decided on a different sort of career, going to work with the Charitable Organisation Society to study what we would now call social science. This sent her visiting 'cases' in their homes, gave her a certain amount of business training, and made her read authoritative books about the problems of the poor. Her objective was to become an almoner at one of the London hospitals, and the purposeful Aunt Alice Green helped her by inviting social workers of importance to meet her at dinner. Among these was a Mrs Anstruther who, after their talk, invited Dorothy down to a Tuberculosis Day at Walworth where it was explained to her that money was needed to build a sanatorium in the region. This was hardly the first time the problem of tuberculosis impacted on Dorothy: she would have known, I am sure, that John Richard Green, the remote source of all Aunt Alice's entertaining, had died of this disease. In time the problem of TB as it gravely manifested itself in Ireland was to dominate Dorothy's life.

Neither social science in general nor tuberculosis in particular was Dorothy's original idea of a career, however. Art, especially design and ornamentation, first attracted her. She passed an examination into the Regent Street Polytechnic to study these subjects, and later, again by examination, she put herself in a position to enter the Royal College of Art. She kept that option open, while she was doing the rounds of the museums and galleries, with Aunt Alice sometimes at her elbow. These studies kept Dorothy in the South Kensington Museum for long stretches. 'I work very hard in the museum', she wrote 'and also at home in the evenings. One day I did 11 hours, one day 10, and most of the others 9. I am so absorbed in the work that I can hardly think of anything else.' This was a real deprivation for her, because she loved to have time for reading, and to go to the theatre and concerts. Her notes suggest that earlier she had read most of Scott's novels, as well as Lockhart's *Life of Scott*. She also read Robert Louis Stevenson, and the poets Shelley and Tennyson, and she confesses in her diary that once she broke away from the talk of Aunt Alice's dinner table to read Samuel Butler's *Erewhon* in the study. She had not much money but for a shilling she got a seat in the Coronet Theatre where Bernard Shaw's *Arms and the Man* was being produced, and for little more no doubt she was able to see Martin Harvey in *The Only Way*. She heard London orchestras under visiting German conductors and, at a concert in the Aeolian Hall she attended, Herbert Hughes introduced songs he had composed to words by Padraic Colum. Both of these men were friends of Aunt Alice's and to some degree benefited from her patronage.

Aunt Alice — the Widow Green, as Augustine Birrell and others used to call her — was more Irish every time her nieces met her. When she first married, John Richard would ask her searching questions about Ireland, the answers to which she did not know. When he enquired about the Irish Roman Catholic priesthood, she had to confess that although she had lived for so long in the heart of the Catholic County of Meath, she had never spoken to a priest. Her vision of Ireland, Irishmen and Irish affairs was to widen speedily after John Richard's death, primarily under the influence of John Francis Taylor, the Irish correspondent of the *Manchester Guardian*, author of a compact biography of Owen Roe O'Neill and in Hyde's estimation, a King among men. Brilliant but disorganised, awkward lover and exacting friend, Taylor thought for a time that Alice had accepted to marry him. But she had other ideas. However, a happy relationship endured between them till he died in 1902. She had benefited from his keen questing mind and his vast erudition; through him her thinking about Irish nationalism deepened considerably and from him she acquired a distrust of accepted political orthodoxies and established political leaders (McDowell, 54-5).

From W. B. Yeats we get a picture of this son of a watchmaker in a country town who, though only a shop assistant, had put himself to college and to the Bar, had become a

Queen's Counsel, had learned to speak at divers societies, and had won a reputation through his defence of criminals whose cases seemed hopeless. Yeats raved about his splendid voice, and his gift of oratory: in that respect 'he was', said Yeats, 'the greatest I ever listened to. I was not his match with the spoken word and barely reached him with the written word'. Yeats wondered whether Taylor was happy in his loves: his powerful intellect could fascinate but by his coarse red hair, his gaunt ungainly body, his still movements as of a Dutch clock, his badly rolled, shabby umbrella, he could repel. And yet with women he was gentle, deferential almost diffident (*Autobiographies*, 213-15). He died in the same year as Jemmet Stopford.

The second man who influenced Alice Green profoundly was Eoin MacNeill. From him she assimilated ideas about what has been called 'the immemorial identity of Old Ireland' (Tierney, 68), and received from him what Beatrice Webb had discovered she lacked, a cause to believe in. MacNeill had first encountered this Ireland himself when, as a boy in the Glens of Antrim, his nurse called him by the Irish language form of his name and when he was introduced to a kinsman who was fluent in both Irish and Scotch Gaelic. He was infatuated by this language and had an early realisation of its national and cultural significance. He spent his holidays in the cottage on Inis Mean in the Aran Islands where J. M. Synge lived much later, and his language discoveries became a background to his wide-ranging scholarship. He was the first scholar of the first rank to be interested primarily in Irish history, a pioneer who hacked his way through a primeval forest. He might not have said the last word on a topic but it was his particular glory that it was he so often who had said the first. He had some excellent personal qualities also. He was a man of moderate political views, an able negotiator, and as Vice President of the Gaelic League he was acknowledged by Hyde to have been the longest-headed and most clear-sighted of men. (Hyde Memoir, and F. J. Byrne in *The Scholar Revolutionary*, 35). No wonder that he impressed Mrs Green. Her preoccupation, henceforth, was with Ireland rather than England, with Irish rather than English politics, with Irish rather than English history. She produced a volume on *The Making of Ireland and Its Undoing* in 1908, another on the topic of *Irish Nationality* in 1911, a third on *The Old Irish World* in 1912, and in 1925, a fourth on *The History of the Irish State to 1014* the year of the death of Brian Boru the High King.

These works had a great success in Ireland: they sustained the nationalist movement, and MacNeill wrote of them as inspiring 'the people of Ireland with the spirit and hope of a sound future development'. Other contemporary scholars, however, referring to the *Making of Ireland* volume in particular, wondered whether Mrs Green had not begged the question as to whether Ireland was ever 'made' at all, and suggested that the people of the Gaelic society she wrote about appeared to live in a perpetual state of exaltation. She tended, they believed, to treat the poetic descriptions she encountered in her reading as hard evidence, and, for example, seriously exaggerated the degree to which law and order prevailed in Gaelic Ireland.

Robert Dunlop, who reviewed *The Making of Ireland and Its Undoing* in the *Quarterly Review*, questioned Mrs Green's adequacy and trustworthiness as a historian. To this hurtful indictment she replied spiritedly in the *Nineteenth Century and After* and included the reply subsequently in *The Old Irish World*. The difference between Mr Dunlop and herself, she said, lay deeper than any question of her merits and demerits. It was the old conflict between tradition and enquiry, and by tradition she meant how writers had hitherto tended to deal with the story of Ireland's past. Dunlop had dogmatically summed up the permitted belief about Ireland in his contribution to the *Dictionary of National Biography*, the *Cambridge Modern History* and elsewhere, and she gave a number of examples, beginning with his allegation that two-thirds at least of the inhabitants of Ireland had led a wild and half-nomadic existence, that outside the Pale there was nothing worthy of being called a Church, that while it was perhaps going too far to say that the Irish had relapsed into a state of heathenism, the tradition of a Christian belief had become a lifeless, useless thing. He had asserted that she had no judgment, less candour, and that in the use of documents she had produced a mass of mischievous fiction; but these words, she said, came oddly from a man who himself had shown a fairly easy attitude in these matters. In his own writings he gave no references at all.

The theme and tone of *The Making of Ireland* offended Unionist opinion in Ireland, with the result that the book was banned by the Royal Dublin Society. This provoked a response from Nationalist quarters; and Alice was given a dinner at the Irish Club in London's Charing Cross Road presided over by Tom Kettle, the leading young Irish parliamentarian of the day. Proposing her health Kettle described *The Making of Ireland and Its Undoing* in words similar to those which Eoin MacNeill had used. It had introduced a new spirit into the writing of history. It had been written impartially from original sources. It was important in itself, and gave promise of greater things. Kettle later raised in the House of Commons the banning of the book by the RDS and asked Birrell, the Chief Secretary, to alter the Society's charter so as to limit its activities to the importance of agriculture.

The Gaelic League and its interest in folklore, folk dialects, and national feeling, had an extraordinary effect, at first at any rate, on some of those who were writing wholly in English. C. P. Curran remembered seeing Yeats at a Gaelic League *sgoruiocht* in the Gresham Hotel about 1901, velvet-coated, with black flowing tie and a black lock of hair falling over his forehead, leaning forward from his great height as he told his audience that a time comes to every Irish writer when he has to make up his mind either to express Ireland or exploit it. He looked forward to the day when his own books would be unread in an Ireland that had become Irish-speaking (*James Joyce Remembered*, 18) which was a most extraordinary thing to say, for he had obviously no intention of ever becoming so proficient in Irish that he could compose in that language. George Moore was behaving equally oddly when he experimented with the translation of a short story into Irish, and back again, so as to capture the flavour of the Irish speech but he, too, did not intend to become proficient in Irish. He excused himself from being expected to learn it. He was too old at 48, he said, but he would see to it that his brother Maurice's children should have a nurse right away from Aran. For, he declared, it profits a man nothing if he knows all the languages of the world and knows not his own.

Yeats, under the influence of the language movement, did a very practical thing, however, when he advised the young Anglo-Irishman John Millington Synge to get away from Paris, to go to the Aran Islands and find a life there that had never been expressed in literature. He had not divined that Synge had any particular genius: he just felt that Synge needed to be diverted from the morbid and melancholy verse he had been writing, and would have given the same advice to any young Irish writer who knew some Irish as Synge did. Yeats had been that summer in Aran and was full of the subject. He reckoned anyway that Synge could not be worse off in Inishman than he was in Paris, where, 'a poor Irishman', he lived in an attic at the top of a high building. (*Autobiographies*, 439-40). When the *Playboy* was in rehearsal in 1904 Yeats began to realise Synge's greatness: he told Horace Plunkett that here was perhaps the beginning of a European figure. 'He had in him' W. R. Rodgers said, 'that Irish split, that dichotomy which produced so many fork-tongued writers — Congreve, Farquharson, Goldsmith, Sheridan, Shaw. He was Anglo-Irish; a Protestant in a Catholic country; a disbeliever reared in a devout environment; a Puritan and a playboy; a University prizeman in Hebrew on the one hand and in Gaelic on the other. Between the blades of these scissors he cut the cloth of drama, the many-coloured coat of comedy (*Irish Literary Portraits*, 97). Lennox Robinson, another Anglo-Irish playwright, and another parson's son, put it more simply when he spoke of 'the commanding force in his life, this strange Irish thing'.

Synge died in March 1909, and Yeats felt his death very much. He told Russell (AE) that Synge's executor, a Plymouth Brother, regarded his writing with disapproval and intended, if he got the chance, to expurgate objectionable passages. Russell told Lady Gregory to make sure that copies of the manuscripts should be made and retained so that when the Plymouth Brother departed this life and went to the Hell he deserved for his religion and tastes, they should then be printed. *The Playboy*, in AE's opinion, was a miraculous piece of writing. The row about it was really a newspaper row, rather than one emanating from the Gaelic League or the IRB. The night he saw it there was a great deal of applause and only a little hissing or booing at one or two of the phrases. If it had been acted more fantastically and less realistically there would have been no row of any kind.

Yeats, interestingly, in a comparison of Hyde's work with Synge's, admired the spontaneous joyous charm of the Irish Hyde wrote, and thought that if he had learned something about the construction of plays he might have grown into another and happier Synge. He had the folk mind as no modern writer had it, its qualities and defects. (*Autobiographies*, 439-40). George Moore was to make fun of these qualities. When Hyde spoke Irish, he said it frothed like porter through the droop of his moustache, and when he turned to English it was easy to understand why he desired to change the language of Ireland. Yeats, as far as we know, said nothing about Hyde as a speaker of Irish: as a writer of English he held him in high esteem. His translations from Irish were 'a mountain stream of sweet waters' and betokened the coming of a new power into literature. To praise Hyde thus was justified, we think, if we look at his rendering of *A Ógánaigh an Chúil Cheangailte.*

> Ringleted youth of my love,
> With thy locks bound loosely behind thee,
> You passed by the road above,
> But you never came in to find me.
> What was the harm for you,
> If you came for a little to see me;
> Your kiss is a wakening dew
> Were I ever so ill or so dreamy
>
> 'I thought, O my love, you were so
> As the moon is or sun on a fountain
> And I thought after that you were snow,
> the cold snow on top of the mountain;
> And I thought after that you were more
> Like God's lamp shining to find me,
> Or the bright star of knowledge before,
> And the star of knowledge behind me'.

Or this verse from *Mo bhron ar an bhfarraige*

> On a green bed of rushes all last night I lay
> And I flung it abroad with the heat of the day,
> And my love came behind me — he came from the south
> His breast to my bosom, his mouth to my mouth.

It was Hyde's achievements in translations from Irish that brought Yeats and Lady Augusta Gregory together also. She, a plainly dressed woman of forty-five, had no obvious good looks, but she exuded a charm that came from strength of character, intelligence and kindness. She was another Anglo, a Persse, descended from some Duke of Northumberland or other who had settled in Ireland in the seventeenth century. She was wealthy, lived on a great demesne in South Galway whose boundary wall was nine miles round, keeping four masons perpetually busy. Yeats stayed with her at Coole, went with her from cottage to cottage in Kiltartan gathering folklore material more or less as Hyde had done, but in translation, and talked over with her his project of an Irish Theatre which he was being forced to abandon for want of the few pounds necessary for a start in a little hall somewhere. She came to the rescue, promising to collect for him or give him, herself, what was necessary. Yeats did not forsee that, like himself, she might have plays of her own to be produced. He certainly did not forsee her genius, any more than he had forseen that of John Synge. 'Our Theatre had been established before she wrote', he recorded, 'and yet her little comedies have merriment and beauty, and her volumes of heroic tales, translated in an English so simple and so noble, may do more than other books to deepen Irish imagination' (*Autobiographies*, 386).

By this time, and certainly by 1904, the Gaelic League was ten years old, and had become one of the largest and most influential organisations in the country. It had some 600 branches, many of which had been set up by the League's own organisers. These men kept Hyde and the League supplied with detailed accounts of the support the revival campaign was getting, and of the obstacles that were being encountered, the most common one the belief among ordinary people that the revival of Irish would no nothing for them. 'What use is it?' In the schools they encountered the opposition of individual inspectors of the Education Boards, some of whom corrected teachers when they taught Irish history. That was not what was wanted, but the history of the Empire! Hyde and his colleagues had their own opposition to deal with, particularly from Mahaffy and Atkinson of Trinity College who tried to have Irish excluded from the secondary schools. And, of course, practical difficulties arose in the production of text books. Father Eugene O'Growney of Maynooth, who became a vice-president of the League, set about filling the gap by writing a series of simple lessons in Irish. He did this, encouraged by Archbishop Walsh of Dublin, and these ultimately filled a series of booklets which Eoin MacNeill completed on Father O'Growney's death. Help of an ecumenical character was also given. A Catholic priest wrote a prayer book in Irish that was paid for by a Protestant minister, the Reverend Eusetius Cleaver, out of his own pocket.

Progress was steady and uniform, and Hyde ably steered the League out of dangers that threatened from political quarters — first, from the Irish Parliamentary Party. Redmond offered Hyde a seat in the House of Commons, but Hyde refused it. He also made an excuse for not attending the Party's St Patrick's Day banquet in London, lest it should get him into trouble with extreme nationalists. One day, when travelling with the League's senior organiser Tomás Bán O Coinceanainn, the conversation turned to this subject. Tomás said: 'In these talks we are giving throughout the country we are making shots to fire against the enemy, [meaning no doubt the government]. Isn't it surprising we are not stopped?' 'Tomás', said Hyde, 'don't you see that that is the precise virtue of this movement that they can't stop us?' 'I saw clearly', Hyde commented later, 'from what happened to the Young Irelanders, that it was easy to enforce the law on anyone who gave the government the slightest cause. When the English Government wanted to suppress the people behind *The Nation* their excuse was that they had been marching in orderly formation through the streets and that was enough to put them away. But there was no law which empowered them to imprison a person for criticising the kind of education his son was being given, or the attitude of Trinity College, or for choosing people to replace a cricket bat with a hurley'.

What the Gaelic League meant to intellectuals at that time can be seen in a book of essays Lady Gregory edited in 1900 and entitled *Ideals in Ireland*. Her contributors were AE, D. P. Moran of *The Leader*, George Moore, Douglas Hyde, Standish O'Grady and W. B. Yeats. In a brief editorial note she said that 'Douglas Hyde, our *Craoibhin Aoibheann*, had stooped down to make an earthenware candlestick for his work, but when he lifted his head he knew it was not a candle he had lighted, but a star he had discovered, and it is now lighting up all the western sky.' In his article, Yeats spoke of the sudden change that had followed the fall of Parnell, and the wreck of his party, and of the organisations that supported it. The change was evident in the establishment of the Irish Literary Society in London, the National Literary Society in Dublin, the Irish Literary Theatre and Feis Ceoil, but more than all, in the Gaelic League. A new kind of romance, a new element in thought, was being moulded out of Irish life and traditions. The first, on the subject of education, accused the existing set-up of having succeeded in making bad Irishmen by the million: the cure for this mischief was to change the teaching, to teach Irish-wise and not English-wise, to make the Irishman respected again. The second, an extension of the same theme, spoke of the English mind and the Englishing of Ireland. 'The sky is smothered by it and the sun is chilled by it, the light is driven away by it, and it is it that has cast the fog and frost on the hearts of the poor people who live to-day on the grass-green sod of Ireland.' There was a change coming, and Hyde put it in a poem that began as if with economic overtones though he had something entirely different in mind:

> There is a change coming, a big change!
> And riches and store will be worth nothing:
> He will rise up that was small enough,
> And he that was big will fall down!

Moran of the *Leader* had seen the possibility of change, too, the outcome of 'the battle of two civilisations', if Ireland set to work to create what did not then exist, what mere political independence — a parliament in College Green — or the humiliation of British arms would not necessarily bestow: a nation. 'And unless we are a nation', he insisted, 'we are nothing.'

While this excellent company were doing what they could for the nation through language and literary renaissance, Sir Horace Plunkett was attempting something similar in the sphere of agricultural economics. Unlike the others he was born and educated in England but of indisputable Anglo-Irish stock and was able to claim a longer Irish affiliation. Sir Christopher Plunkett of Dunsany was deputy Governor of Ireland at the beginning of the fifteenth century and one of his sons was created first Baron Dunsany by Henry VI in 1439. Sir Horace, our man, was a child of the sixteenth baron. It fell to his lot in the late eighteen-eighties to manage the Dunsany estate, which is near Tara in the County Meath, and there, with the intention of doing good for his fellow country-men, he experimented with a Dunsany Co-operative Society, explaining in an article for the *Nineteenth Century* what he was about. There existed in Ireland 'a strangely unrecognised evil' for which there was 'a simple, effective and wholly inexpensive cure'. The Irish people were extremely poor, were badly supplied with the necessaries of life, and paid unheard-of prices for them, one reason for this being the inefficient sales system. Most of the country shops or stores were public houses as well, credit was universal, and the man who took credit 'for the love of God', had to take what was given and ask no questions. To make things worse, the rich did not deal at home; they supplied themselves more cheaply and with better goods from London or the larger Irish towns. To cope with this problem by supplying proper business guidance, Plunkett recommended the formation of a co-operative organisation society (Digby, 48-9 and *passim*).

Support for Plunkett's ideas was slow in coming, but in 1893, the same year as the Gaelic League began, an Irish Agricultural Organisation Society was launched in Dublin at a meeting attended by Catholics and Protestants, Unionists and nationalists, farmers and business men, laymen and clerics.

Plunkett in an address suggested the possibilities that lay in better transport, better relations between producers and consumers, and new developments in agricultural finance. The Society was to be non-political, Plunkett's maxim being that 'the more business you introduce into politics, and the less politics you introduce into business, the better for both. The Society would also be democratic, and based on a belief in the latent capabilities of the people. Plunkett was himself a politician of course: in 1892, as a rather unorthodox Unionist, he had won a seat in Westminster, accepting a general opinion that, with the fall of Parnell and the split in the Nationalist camp, Home Rule was dead for a generation. The Irish had shown themselves unfit for self-government. They might do better in business if they allowed the IAOS to show the way. With Redmond's support he made a good start by having a parliamentary committee formed during a Recess period, whose report led to the establishment in 1899 of a Department of Agriculture and Technical Instruction in Ireland. Plunkett became its Vice-President and guided its policy until 1907, striving all the time for an agricultural revolution through co-operation.

He wrote a famous book on *Ireland in the New Century* in which he introduced an epigram that went into general circulation, that Anglo-Irish history was for Englishmen to remember, and for Irishmen to forget. In the book he pleaded for a reconsideration of the Irish Question, not in political but in economic and moral terms. Economic grievances called to be dealt with by the acquisition of more skills, more technical knowledge, more organisation, more business experience. The era of the practical had dawned. When he spoke of moral terms, he argued that Ireland needed to be reformed from within. When Irishmen realised this, the splendid human power of their country, so much of which at the moment was running idly and disastrously to waste, would be utilised. He spoke of the weakness of the Irish character. Lack of moral courage might make leadership easy but it was 'the quicksand of Irish life'. There was a lack of serious thought on public questions, a listlessness and apathy in regard to economic improvement which amounted to fatalism'. The agencies which moulded Irish character were the political parties, the Catholic

Church, the educational system and the Gaelic movement and all of these he surveyed critically.

He was drawn to the Irish literary movement and sought to link it to his own. He sponsored a dinner one night in 1899 with the object of further promoting co-operation between what he called 'the practical men and the dreamers'. These included Yeats, Lady Gregory and George Moore. He appreciated, indeed enjoyed, their contribution to the national life, especially when it gratified his love of the theatre. He entered in his diary what he thought of their plays. He was attracted to AE's *Deirdre* which was splendidly acted by clerks and artisans. Synge's *Playboy* was very clever but he thought it rather foolish to have put it on; the Irish-Irelanders would be infuriated. Lady Gregory's *Kincora* was very powerful but oh! what a ghastly story any old history was. Two plays of Yeats he saw were too literary and undramatic. That was what Lady Gregory thought, too. Of an Abbey occasion she wrote in her diary: 'Yeats to-night; that means empty seats.'

Mrs Green was another acquaintance on the fringe of this group whom Plunkett met in the company of Roger Casement at Mount Trenchard and enjoyed an argument with, although he did not wholly admire her. He had spoken at an American banquet of Ireland as 'an English-speaking community' and she, in a passion, took him to task, 'No sooner do I begin to hope that your movement may have some gleam of Irish feeling in it', she told him, 'than you deal me a knock-out blow.' Was the natural, the permanent thought of his mind that Ireland was a detachment of England? She was so anti-English, Plunkett thought. He met Bernard Shaw also, and found him delightful. 'I never knew a more brilliant conversationalist. He is hopeless about Ireland, of course, but I think I could make him a little hopeful if I saw more of him.'

The person who out-dreamed them all was George Russell, better known as AE. Plunkett had taken him into the employment of the IAOS in 1897 from Pim's emporium in George's Street, and had trained him as an organiser, before making him editor of the organisation's paper, the *Irish Homestead*. Plunkett introduced this 'poet organiser' with some pride. His poetry might be trash, he said, but his character fascinated him, his business acumen shrewd, and his sense of humour delightful. Russell, a native of Lurgan and a Protestant, had been a student of painting in Dublin's Metropolitan School of Art, and there struck up a lasting friendship with W. B. Yeats on whom he exerted a masterful influence. Yeats for his part could see Russell becoming the dominant influence in the IAOS. He had taken up the question of agricultural banks, and within six months had founded more than others had done in ten years. And yet Yeats wondered how this could be, seeing that the visionary Russell had never read a book that was not in verse.

Russell, concerned with the preservation of what he called the National Being, answered critics of the Gaelic League idea who saw expressions of patriotism and nationality as only other names for race hatred. He personally did not love England, he said, but he had no hatred for the English, nor did he think his countrymen had either, however they might phrase the feeling in their hearts. The struggle the new Ireland was waging was not against flesh and blood but was a portion of the everlasting battle against principalities and powers and spiritual wickedness in high places. He did not say that every act by which England would make the Irish people other than they would be themselves, was stupid and invariably and inevitably wrong, but it was a terrible thing to hinder the soul in its freedom as the wild upheavals and the madness of protest bore witness. The national spirit, like a beautiful woman, could or would not reveal itself wholly while a coarse presence was near, an unwelcome stranger in possession of the home. If the Irish were debarred from the freedom they would have, how narrow would be the range for human effort. The Irish would keep in mind their language, would teach their children their history, the story of their heroes, and the long traditions of their race which stretched back to God; but everywhere they were thwarted. A blockhead of a professor, drawn from the intellectual obscurity of Trinity College, appointed as commissioner to train the national mind according to British ideas, met them with an ultimatum: "'I will always discourage the speaking of Gaelic wherever I can." We feel poignantly it is not merely Gaelic which is being suppressed, but the spiritual life of our race. A few ignoramuses have it in their power, and are trying their utmost to obliterate the mark of God upon a nation.' ('Nationality and Imperialism' in *Ideals in Ireland*, ed. Lady Gregory).

Outstanding in his extremism among the Anglo-Irish who turned to nationalism was Bulmer Hobson, who is rightly introduced in a current *Dictionary of Irish Biography* as a revolutionary. He was all that. Indeed at one time he was regarded by British Intelligence as the most dangerous man in Ireland. He was born of Cromwellian planter stock in Hollywood, Co. Down in 1883, was a Gladstonian Liberal in politics and a member of the Society of Friends until 1914. He then resigned, considering that the physical force possibilities of the work on which he was becoming engaged were inconsistent with being a Quaker. He was educated in the Friends school at Lisburn, and was there at the centenary of the insurrection of 1798. He was inspired by what he then learned of Wolfe Tone and Thomas Russell and of the activities of the Society of United Irishmen in Belfast. Tone's statement of his objects won his instant assent: to break the connection with England, the never-failing source of all our political evils, to assert the independence of Ireland, to unite all the people to substitute the common name of Irishman for Protestant, Catholic and Dissenter. Earlier, through his reading of the works of Standish O'Grady, his mind, like Yeats's, was peopled with the heroic figures of Irish mythology, while later on, he was influenced by Alice Milligan and Ethna Carbery, the editors of the *Shan Van Vocht*, and by James Fintan Lalor and Arthur Griffith from whom he learned an alternative way to that of futile insurrection or of docile acceptance of the English occupation. It was the way of moral insurrection, a defensive way that aimed to disorganise the enemy, the way that, towards the end of his days, he could see had largely been achieved with the withdrawal of Irish representatives from Westminster and the institution of Dáil Éireann.

To the development of that policy Hobson's contribution was unique, beginning with the creation of a long series of propagandist societies. The first were an Ulster Debating Club for boys, and a Protestant National Association from which sprang the Ulster Literary Theatre to which he contributed one of the early plays. He joined the Gaelic Athletic Association and the Gaelic League and was simultaneously Secretary of the Antrim County Board of one and of the Coiste in Belfast of the other. In the Gaelic League he began a friendship with Roger Casement which lasted until his death. On the strictly political side, he became a member of Cuman na nGaedheal which was then an open propagandist cover for the Secret Irish Republican Brotherhood into which he was sworn by Denis McCullough in 1904 and the forerunner of another of Arthur Griffith's foundations, the National Council. Dissatisfied with the inactivity of these groups, Hobson, with Denis McCullough, started a Dungannon Club in Belfast in 1905, published a paper he called *The Republic*, and collected money to put an organiser on the road. This was Sean McDermott, who had started life as a pupil teacher, was then a bar-tender in Glasgow, and when Hobson met him he was working on the Belfast trams. He was at that time an enthusiastic member of the Ancient Order of Hibernians and, according to Hobson, had acquired their habit of intrigue and wire-pulling behind the scenes. He established a number of these Dungannon Clubs in various parts of Ulster. In London P. S. O'Hegarty, a Post Office clerk who had begun to write for *The Republic* also formed one of these Clubs and drew into membership Robert Lynd, the essayist, Herbert Hughes the composer, and George, the lawyer son of the old Young Irelander, Charles Gavan Duffy. Such men, with Hobson, became able promoters of the policy of abstention from the British Parliament and defended their theories against the criticisms of Kettle and other parliamentarians.

The fact that they had common objectives brought Hobson and Griffith together in 1907 in an amalgamation of the Dungannon Clubs and Cumann na nGaedheal which they called the Sinn Féin League and, subsequently, just Sinn Féin. Again dissatisfied with the progress that was being made, and not hitting it off too well with Griffith, Hobson in 1911 decided to drop out quietly from Sinn Féin with McCullough and O'Hegarty and to concentrate on promoting the Irish Republican Brotherhood, of which he had been an active reforming member since 1904, and Fianna Eireann, which was his youth organisation, and on the production, with IRB backing, of a new paper he called *Irish Freedom*. *The Republic* had collapsed through lack of funds. From his position on the Supreme Council of the IRB he was able to get drilling encouraged among the rank and file, so that when the Irish Volunteer movement came into being many IRB men were ready to accept officer rank.

Years before on the Falls Road in Belfast, when he started the Fianna, he gave it a Constitution that provided for inter-club hurling competitions and classes in Irish language and history. 'We started off with great success for a while', he wrote, 'but then we ran into difficulties. It takes money to do these things. I had none, and the boys had none. I was running into debt. I was having considerable difficulty in making a living in Belfast. One firm dismissed me because I was Secretary to the Gaelic League, another because I was holding public meetings in support of the Sinn Féin move-ment. As other work piled up I was able to give less time to the Fianna, and it became rather neglected. . . . Seven years after that I was in Dublin and I told Constance Countess Markievicz, then a very new recruit into the Sinn Féin move-ment, about my venture in Belfast. She suggested we should start again in Dublin, and on my pointing out that I had no money, she said she would pay for a small hall to serve as headquarters for a new Fianna.' She, and Roger Casement, continued to support the movement financially, and it grew into an effective militant body many of whose senior mem-bers Hobson recruited subsequently into the IRB. Among these were men who played most important roles in later major events. A couple of them were executed as leaders in the Easter Rising.

Constance or Connie Markievicz, the wife of a Polish aris-tocrat, was the elder Gore-Booth girl of Lissadell we encoun-tered with Yeats earlier. Both the Gores and the Booths were of Planter stock, the original Gores being rewarded with grants of land by Queen Elizabeth and James I, the Booths similarly in Cromwellian times. Constance had been presented to court, had studied painting at the Slade, and was still so occupied when she met Count Markievicz in Paris and married him within a year of the death of his wife from whom he had been separated. They settled in Dublin in 1903 and were

attracted to the society that circled round the Lord Lieutenant. They were among the founders of the United Arts Club
and made some minor stage appearances. In a cottage
Constance rented in the Dublin hills, and in which Padraic
Colum had lived, she came across back numbers of W. P.
Ryan's *The Peasant* and Arthur Griffith's *Sinn Féin*, and was
aroused by what they told of Ireland's struggle for freedom.
When chance threw her across Griffith's path soon afterwards
she told him how his writing had affected her political thinking, but her confidences were received rather coolly, Griffith
suspecting that she might be an *agent provocateur*. Hobson
took a more favourable view of her, when he met her, and
soon involved her, not merely in the Fianna but in his con-
cept of 'the simple life'. His idea was to live outside the city
on a small farm, in an agricultural colony perhaps, which
would enable him to give half of his time to farming and the
other half to reading and writing. He had not the means to
do this, but she had, and soon it became known that they
had formed a co-operative society, taken Belcamp Park, a
large house and farm on the north side of Dublin, and had
engaged an experienced man to teach market gardening to
the members. It was all very innocent no doubt, but rumours
began to spread; one was that Count Markievicz wanted to
fight a duel with Hobson; another, that Hobson's Belfast
friend, McCullough, feared that this married aristocratic lady
would destroy Hobson as another woman not long before
had destroyed Charles Stewart Parnell.

The Colony in any event had a short life. Casimir had been
away in Poland when Constance with Bulmer had set up their
co-operative market gardening enterprise, but when he
returned and heard the story, he set off immediately in
search of Belcamp. He found it, not without some difficulty,
but found entrance more difficult still. He went all around
the outside of the house, knocking and knocking, calling on
Constance, without reply. Finally 'some dirty little raga-
muffins' — from Hobson's Fianna, no doubt — 'put their
heads out of a window and shouted "Who's there?" The Count
replied "I want to see Countess Markievicz."' After much
scuffling and running about, a door opened at last and in the
dark he could see Constance. 'We have only one lamp', she

said, 'and the gardener is reading with it.' They went into the drawing-room and there was the gardener with his legs on the mantelpiece, smoking 'a dirty filthy shag tobacco'. The Count asked for food and, again after some scuffling and whispering, they brought him cold meat and bread and butter. And, that, said Casimir, was 'how I returned to my home'. With AE's help he helped to kill the co-operative scheme, and went back to Poland, leaving Constance to pursue with Hobson their common interest in the Fianna.

A difficulty arose. The boys objected to her becoming a member of the organisation entitling her to go out on marches with them. She was an embarrassment and they did not at all like a comparison with a hen and brood of chickens. The senior boys recognised the importance of her money, however, and saw to it that a resolution was not passed which would have prevented the Countess from appearing in public with them. Instead a rule was introduced providing that no one was to participate in a public occasion with the Fianna except in a Fianna uniform. The intended prohibition did not work. She got a tailor to make a feminine form of the uniform, with a skirt instead of trousers, and in this garb she marched with the Fianna whenever she wanted to, leaving her critics swearing under their breaths. (Blythe in *Inniu*, 4/9/70). Because of these and other antics Anglo-Irish mouths were saying that she was a traitor to her class.

Among people 'who were Protestants in their religion and Catholics in their politics' was a small number who congregated in the Five Provinces Branch of the Gaelic League near George Moore's house on Ely Place in Dublin. The branch was nicknamed the Branch of the Five Protestants. There were more than that number of Protestants in the branch; I can personally recall five viz. Nellie O'Brien of the Inchquin family and a cousin of Mary Spring Rice who founded the branch, Dora French, Lily Duncan, Nora Cunningham and George Ruth. Other Protestant Gaelic Leaguers from that period — James Stephens, George Nicholls, George Irvine and Ernest Joynt — found their way there occasionally. Time was to prove that the most important Protestant of all from the point of view of the Irish language was a Central Branch man. This was Ernest Blythe, who, six years younger than Hobson, was cast in a similar mould. He was a native of Magheragall near Lisburn, and in that strongly Protestant area memories survived of the Protestant-led revolt of the United Irishmen a century earlier.

Blythe's Presbyterian mother — his father was an Anglican — claimed she was a distant relative of William Orr, the first United man to be executed for administering a treasonable oath to soldiers; and the aged mother of a friend of hers used to say that her father, Jemmy Long, had been a colonel of the United Irish at the battle of Ballynahinch in 1798. There were other things to stimulate Blythe's Irishness. A servant girl from Co. Down, hired by his father at Newry fair, had Irish, talked to young Ernest about it and gave him an elementary Irish book that belonged to her father.

Blythe went to the National school at Ballycarrickmaddy where the teacher, Jacob Begley, had a very special interest in preparing boys for the Civil Service. This was how he entered the Department of Agriculture in Dublin as a boy clerk in 1905. Not yet 16, and full of curiosity, he spent his first lunch-hour walking through O'Connell Street, noticed Father O Growney's books of Irish lessons in a shop window, and bought one.

He joined the Central Branch of the Galeic League and, through its classes, outings and hurling clubs, he met John Casey, otherwise Sean O'Casey (the future playwright) and was drawn to him. They talked about the Irish language, Irish literature, and Irish politics, and before long O'Casey invited him to join the IRB. After some months routine observation of him, Blythe was sworn in (Earnan de Blaghd, *Treasna na Bóinne*, 109).

O'Casey was rather pious at this time and interested in High Anglicanism; he was a close friend of the local rector and a member of the Select Vestry. With Blythe, John Lester and Harry Nicholls, they formed a committee of Irish speakers to agitate for services to be conducted in Irish. They had some success. They were instrumental in bringing an Irish-speaking minister to officiate at the first Irish service ever in St Kevin's Church on the South Circular Road, and prepared for Communion Services to be held in Irish at Christ Church

Cathedral. They also spoke about Home Rule at YMCA lectures.

Up to 1906 or thereabouts, IRB circles, according to Blythe, merely met to have rounds of drinks and to talk of revolution. Things changed when Bulmer Hobson and Denis McCullough took over, and collections began to be made to buy arms. There was some loss of members because of religious scruples, and to overcome this difficulty, a general meeting of the membership — an utterly unheard of thing — was held in the Clontarf Town Hall to listen to a priest from America who told them that in Clan na Gael, the IRB's counterpart, the oath gave them no such worries. At the meeting Blythe discovered that his own superior in the Department of Agriculture, Thomas Condon, was an IRB man. In 1909 Blythe left the Civil Service, and returned to the North to work as a journalist. As such he reported all kinds of Unionist and Orange activities, and was an observer of how difficult the Unionists found it at first to stir up a serious state of alarm about Home Rule. Until the Liberals introduced the 1912 Bill, few believed it was a serious menace at all. Then feelings rapidly hardened and Blythe became convinced that the kind of Ulster he believed had existed since the days of Grattan and Tone was well and truly dead.

While his reporting work kept him busy, Blythe was simultaneously 'centre' of an IRB Circle in Belfast, and writing for Griffith's *United Irishman*, Ryan's *Irish Peasant*, and Sean MacDermott's *Irish Freedom*. He met James Connolly and was impressed by his oratory and his capacity to harmonise nationalist and socialist convictions.

In 1914 Blythe determined to make a success of his efforts to learn Irish. He set off for Dingle in the Kerry Gaeltacht, and tried to get a job as a farm labourer, doing perhaps the sort of work he had learned on his father's farm. In an area of small farms, however, it was impossible to get any paid work whatever until Sean MacDermott found an opening for him at 15/- a week with the father of the IRB man Thomas Ashe who was to die on hunger strike three years later. Blythe, while thus employed, and with a few pounds he got now and again from Sean Lester, managed to continue the kind of work he had been doing in the North, organising the IRB, and the Irish Volunteers when they came into existence.

He had imposed a sort of vow upon himself never to read or speak a word that was not Irish on his working days but he used to spend a few hours at week-ends with Desmond and Maeve Fitzgerald who had a house in the locality. Conversation sometimes turned on Yeats for whom Desmond had a high regard. He confessed that it was Yeats who had made a nationalist of him, and what he had to say on that subject impressed Blythe who, like IRB men generally, had previously been prejudiced against the poet despite the strong effect on him of his one-act play *Cathleen Ni Houlihan*, and his recognition of the important national role of the Abbey Theatre.

Cathleen Ni Houlihan was the mystical figure of Ireland calling her sons to fight for her, and Maud Gonne who first played the part made 'Cathleen seem like a living being fallen into our mortal infirmity', or so said the infatuated author. The piece was 'a sort of sacrament' to P. S. O'Hegarty; and Stephen Gwynn, after seeing it, wondered if such plays should be produced at all unless one was prepared to go out to shoot and be shot. Even the next-generation Myles Dillon, a son of the Irish leader, could speak of missing a heart-beat when he heard the question, 'Did you see an old woman going down the path?' and the answer, 'I did not, but I saw a young girl, and she had the walk of a queen.' The play worried the government. At the enquiry which preceded the granting of a patent to the Abbey Theatre Yeats was asked if he had written *Cathleen Ni Houlihan* to affect opinion. He denied this. 'I had a dream one night that gave me a story, and I had certain emotions about the country, and I gave those emotions expression for my own pleasure. If I had written to convince others ... all would be oratorical and insincere. If we understand our own minds, and the things that are striving to utter themselves through our minds, we move others ... because all life has the same root' (*Explorations*, 199).

Cathleen Ni Houlihan was not the only play in the Abbey repertoire that encouraged Irishmen to rebellious ways. Lady Gregory had a little piece she called *The Rising of the Moon*

about a Fenian on the run who is allowed by a police sergeant, torn by conflicting loyalties, to make his escape. As he
does so in response to a signal and a verse of a patriotic ballad,
the sergeant wonders whether he is really as big a fool as he
thinks he is. Dr McCartan thought that this play may sub-
consciously have forced the Irish detectives in Dublin Castle
to supply Michael Collins with the information that was so
essential to the success of his work during the War of Independence. ('Yeats the Fenian' by Patrick McCartan in *Dolman
Press Century Papers*, 1965)

The Lester we introduced among the agitators for Church services in Irish had a number of other things in common with
Blythe. He was about the same age, came from the same
county, Antrim, was a journalist and worked at first on
northern provincial papers. He was a Methodist, and was
educated until the age of fourteen at the Methodist College in
Belfast. A small shopkeeper's son, he discovered his nationalism when he heard Irish in a Gaelic League school in Belfast.
This, he felt, was where he belonged. He changed his name
from John Ernest to Sean, and began to sign his articles Mac
Leastair. He met Blythe in Bangor in 1909, when working
on the railway, and under his influence his conversion to
nationalism was confirmed. He became a member of the IRB,
sworn in by Blythe and introduced by him to a Circle that
met in Dinny McCullough's shop in Belfast. There were twelve
members of the Circle, among them Cathal O'Shannon and
Albert W. Cotton. When working in 1913 in Galway on the
Connacht Tribune, Lester's centre was George Nicholls, and
in Dublin between 1913 and 1916 it was Hobson. He continued the study of Irish and joined the Volunteers when
they were formed, adhering to those led by MacNeill after
the split. In doing so he followed the IRB, whose officers
and active members, he said, directed the affairs of those
Volunteers to the extent of 80 per cent. He naturally became
a police suspect, an article he wrote in Sean MacDermott's
'grossly seditious' *Irish Freedom* on 'the economic basis for
a revolutionary movement' particularly interesting them. He
was detained briefly in connection with the Rising. His views
on that event were those of his friend Bulmer Hobson and,

fearing for Hobson's life, he sought him out in Dublin during the fighting. Through a variety of jobs, thereafter, he rose to be the news editor of the *Freeman's Journal*, and ultimately he became a diplomat of distinction.

So far all the Anglo-Irish deviationists we have been describing moved in a more or less straight line from unionism to nationalism. An outstanding exception to the rule was Herbert Moore Pim, the most curious figure of all in our gallery of eccentrics. Born in 1883 in Belfast into a Quaker family with a Cromwellian background, he was the son of an insurance company director. He was educated at the Friends School in Lisburn, at schools in Chester and Bedford, and studied French literature for four years in Grenoble and Paris. Later he was prominent in the Belfast YMCA where he met and married the daughter of a Presbyterian elder. It was an unhappy marriage and ended in divorce. Meanwhile he had followed his father into insurance, but a greater interest of his from his youth was writing of all sorts. He wrote unceasingly.

His most prolific period was between 1910 and 1920 when, apart from innumerable articles, largely political, he produced several romantic novels, a study of Belfast characters he called *Unknown Immortals*, and books of verse, the best of which was his *Songs from an Ulster Valley*. *The Pessimist*, a novel he considered his masterpiece, appeared in 1914 over the name of 'A Newman', and he explained the pen-name by saying that he was in fact a new man since his conversion to Catholicism in which a Passionist, Father Hubert from Ardoyne, himself a convert, played a part. After his conversion and those of his sister and his cousin, an Anglican clergyman, he wrote a good deal for the *Irish Monthly*, the Jesuit periodical. The subject of one of his devotional poems was the child mystic 'Little Nellie of Holy God' or, as he put it, Helen of Holy God, 'the smallest of saints, most fit for heaven's light'.

Pim was always interested in politics. He was at first a member of a Junior Conservative Club, but by 1912 with Home Rule in the ascendant, and possibly through the Catholic company he was now keeping in Belfast, he had become one of the star lecturers for the Redmondite United Irish League and Joseph Devlin's Ancient Order of Hibernians. On public platforms and in the columns of the *Irish News* he hammered the Ulster Unionists, the suffragettes, and all opponents of the Irish Parliamentary Party and the Liberal Government. He was recognised as the brightest ornament in the Dawn of Freedom branch of the UIL, which was a northern replica of the famous Young Ireland Branch in Dublin in which Tom Kettle, Francis Sheehy-Skeffington, Francis Cruise O'Brien, Rory O'Connor and P. J. Little were members. He joined the Irish Volunteers on their formation in 1913, was enormously impressed by Eoin MacNeill, and sided with him when he broke from Redmond after his Woodenbridge speech. All Pim's nationalist activity compelled the insurance company for which he worked to dispense with his services. That did not appear to make any difference to him, and as a writer and orator he became an increasingly significant figure among advanced nationalists. In the company of Dr Patrick McCartan and Denis McCullough he went about the North organising Volunteers and Cumann na mBan, and may indeed have become a member of the IRB. His bearded figure, sitting between Sean MacDermott and Sean Ó Muirthile, in a photo of a group of Volunteer officers in Cork in late 1915 or early 1916, suggests this; and an 'A. Newman' appears in an IRB list in Pádraig O Snodaigh's *Comhghuailithe na Réabhlóide*.

In July 1915 a deportation order was served on him for spreading disloyalty. Disobeying the order, he was locked up in Crumlin Road Gaol with Ernest Blythe and, as he entered, 'a most extraordinary coincidence' occurred. His cousin Jonathan Pim, an ex-Attorney General, took up his position as Judge of Assize in the Court House which was connected with the gaol. Pim thoroughly disliked his experience of gaol life, but reading a copy of *The Imitation of Christ* that MacNeill had given him, and also the Breviary made solitude more bearable. Blythe was impressed when he read in a paper that was smuggled in to him a poem of Pim's describing his prison experiences but, later, he learned that Pim had written it beforehand and arranged to have it published when he was 'inside'. Blythe had had earlier doubts about Pim. At their

first meeting Pim, then clean-shaven, had shown him a picture of himself wearing a beard and asked did he not think he
was like Parnell! When released that September, Pim set
about the publication of a monthly he called *The Irishman*
which was to be strictly non-party. He saw the *Irish Volunteer*,
the journal of the Irish Volunteers, through the press in
Belfast when it was in difficulties with the authorities, and
when Griffith's paper *Sinn Féin* was suppressed in Dublin, he
got a newspaper started for him in Belfast called *Nationality*.
The Irishman was described as a characteristic Pim production. Nearly every number was enlivened by a controversy
which might be trivial enough (Cathal O'Shannon, *Irish
Times*, 15 May 1950). Among his contributors was Lord
Alfred Douglas whom Pim introduced to his friends like some
prize exhibit when he came to stay with him. Douglas was
an admirer of Pim's poetry, while Pim supported Douglas in
his controversies with George Moore and St John Ervine.
This won him a commendation from Cardinal Logue for
waging a crusade against unclean literature. (Cathal O'Shannon,
ibid.)

'When all the papers were suppressed except MacNeill's
Irish Volunteer', Pim said some years later, 'I launched a
series of carefully written booklets, under the title of *Tracts
for the Times*. The success of this series was simply pheno-
menal. Upwards of seventy-five thousand copies were sold in
a short time, at a penny each. Of these booklets Pearse wrote
four, MacNeill three, Griffith one, The O'Rahilly one, and I
myself provided five. In March 1916 Pearse sent the manu-
script of his last 'Tract', and asked me to have it published
without fail not later than 17th of April.' This was done, and
the significance of Pearse's request became evident on 23
April in circumstances we shall describe in the next chapter.
In this 'Tract', *The Sovereign People*, Pearse, who had as
much entitlement as anyone to be deemed Anglo-Irish, his
father being an Englishman, made the case for the physical
freedom without which a nation dies, and for the total control of national resources in order to secure the completeness
of that freedom.

But our interest at the moment is in Pim's involvement in
Irish politics, which excited great interest and speculation.

Gaelic Leaguers, Sinn Féiners, parliamentarians and Irish industrial revivalists alike were puzzled to know who he was, and what his real object was in apparently hogging the limelight. Was he a humbug? He certainly seemed to be in earnest. His son Turlough or Terence remembered visiting Dublin as a child of seven with his father in the autumn of 1915 and meeting MacNeill, Griffith, Pearse and The O'Rahilly. He also recalled that, prior to the Rising, the house they lived in on University Road in Belfast was *stacked* with arms and ammunition, which was probably an exaggeration, and that his father carried a revolver. Pim himself mentions two other men he had been happy to meet on that Dublin visit, Tom Clarke the IRB leader, and Joseph Plunkett who cheered his spirits considerably when he told him how much he liked his *Pessimist*, that it represented practically all that he himself thought.

The young Stopfords were unlikely to have known anything at all of these persons and their preoccupations. What Dorothy knew of her Aunt's interests, for instance, was gauged from looking at the people who came to the house overlooking the Thames when she was there. In her diary she mentions Edward Morel who was a strong ally in a society Aunt Alice had founded to stimulate greater concern in Britain for the problems of colonisation in Africa. Morel had introduced Alice to the work of the Congo Reform Association, an interest they both shared with Roger Casement, an Anglo-Irish Protestant like Mrs Green, who came to see her whenever he was in London. They became the closest of friends for, apart from the Congo and Putumayo where Casement had worked, they had a common interest in Ireland's historical past and in the need to obtain Irish independence. Casement was even more obsessed by Ireland than she was, and his interest in the survival of Irish led him, for example, to patronise language summer schools and to provide school meals for Gaeltacht children. He tried seriously to learn the language himself but failed. Irish was difficult. Hyde met him at a *feis* in Sligo, 'I did not know from Adam who this tall, good-looking noble figure of a man who was going around was', he said, 'and I made many enquiries about him till I found out that he came from the

Glens of Antrim in Ulster. He was asking for me at the same time; so we met, and talked, and were friends thereafter' (Hyde, 125).

Alice Green collaborated with Casement in many other nationalist activities, and with Bulmer Hobson they put together an anti-enlistment leaflet which was circulated by the Dungannon Clubs. This said that any man joining England's army, navy or police force, took his stand in the camp of the garrison; he was a traitor to his country, and an enemy of the people. England should fight her own battles — the Irish had done it long enough. But gradually Alice found that she could not keep up with the pace Casement set. She believed in the inescapability of a political link of some sort with England, he did not; and Edie Stopford remembered an occasion in 1913 when, after Casement had dined alone with Mrs Green and herself, and the hall door had at last closed on him after a particularly vehement Irish tirade, Aunt Alice exclaimed — "Sometimes when I listen to that man I feel I never want to hear the subject of Ireland mentioned again!" Another man who spoke wildly when he came to see Aunt Alice was Henry Nevinson the journalist. He was an admirer of Casement but presented himself to the young Stopfords as a violent anarchist.

Casement was an extremely handsome man, Edie thought, with the look of a Spanish hidalgo — black curling hair and beard, pale complexion, fine eyes, and a harassed, even a ravaged expression — but she never found him personally sympathetic. He had little interest in young girls, and was apt either to be silent, or to embark on those favourite tirades of his about Ireland which Edie, though she sympathised with their subject, found tedious in their length and extremeness. But if Edie and some other women found him unattractive for one reason or another, there were others who literally adored him. One of these was Ada MacNeill, 'a very tall, dark, rather handsome Irish girl' who had an estate in Cushendun in the Antrim Glens where she bestowed hospitality on anyone concerned with the language or other aspects of nationalism. It was there, for instance, that Hobson and Casement first met. Ada developed a passion for Casement which was not returned. He had a place not far

from hers, but he ceased going to Cushendun if he heard that
Ada was about. For the same reason he avoided the local *feis*
of which she was a principal promoter, and also the Irish
language summer school in Donegal in which they shared an
interest. 'I wish, poor old soul', he would say, 'she would
leave me alone. These repeated invitations to go to meet her
are a bit out of place. I have very strong feelings of friendship for her, and good will, and brotherly Irish affection,
but I wish she could leave other things out of the reckoning.'

Among other Irish visitors Dorothy met at Aunt Alice's was
the young Tom Kettle who was about to abandon Westminster for a chair of political economy in Birrell's new
University College in Dublin. He was being allowed, even
encouraged, by the Governing Body of the College to remain
in Parliament, but he told Mrs Green that he had never been
happy in politics, and of course was getting financially poorer
every month he was in them. In any event, he was none too
sure he would be selected as a Nationalist candidate for the
next election — 'I have a lot of irritable and noisy priests', he
told her, and, even if selected, he thought he might lose at
the poll. So, he thought she would hear no more of him in
party politics or sectional squabbles. The College appointment would give him a chance to settle down to quiet work;
and he told the lady who had been so kind to him that he
was looking out for the appearance in print again of 'the
unspeakable Dunlop' obviously with the intention of breaking a lance with him on her behalf. She wanted him to come
more often to the house because, like others, she never left
his company without carrying the recollection of a clever
epigram or *bon mot*. He had described Tim Healy as 'a
brilliant calamity'; in office the Liberals forgot their principles and the Tories remembered their friends. Life reminded him of a cheap *table d'hote* in a rather dirty restaurant, with Time changing the plates before one had enough of
anything (Horgan, 204). His capacity to entertain apart, she
wanted him to meet people whom she believed would be a
help to him, but he excused himself by pleading that 'when
I get done up as now, meeting new people is the more exquisite torture to me' and that 'people out of sorts are unmitigated

nuisances who ought to endow themselves on obscure corners until they get into sorts again'. He was already struggling with an alcoholic obsession which wining and dining with distinguished people did not help to control. He could pay a compliment. Congratulating Mrs Green on a speech she had made, he told her that she had an easy task in describing the function of cultured women in politics, which was her subject. She had only to describe herself. 'It was such a pleasure to see you looking so radiant', he added, 'and so full of the passion of ideas'.

Another whom Dorothy saw twice at her aunt's table was the poet Padraic Colum who promised to write odes for Edie and Dorothy when they came of age. George Noble, Count Plunkett came more than once, too, as did a Mr Hobhouse, a cousin of Ada MacNeill's who was at New College, Oxford, with whom Dorothy talked 'rowing, cricket, footer and other youthful subjects'. He told her he was a Shinfeiner [sic], which was an interesting declaration for a young man to make in 1909. Sinn Féin had just emerged from the amalgamation of minor separatist parties, among them the Dungannon Clubs, and had fought a by-election in support of an Irish MP who had left the Irish Parliamentary Party in disgust at its failure to commit its Liberal allies to Home Rule. Dorothy also saw Charlie Dickenson at Aunt Alice's. He, 'a nice cousin' she 'loved to jabber with', had come over from Dublin to give evidence to a House of Lords Committee on the 1909 Land Bill. A particularly important caller was the Under-Secretary Antony MacDonnell, otherwise known as 'the Bengal Tiger'. Aunt Alice, taking Dorothy with her, returned his visit at the Irish Office in Old Queen's Street. Their talk was about Ireland, of course, but it is doubtful if the subject interested Dorothy very much at that time. In the area of politics, she commented more about the suffragettes and the marching unemployed. She felt she understood how deeply 'the hearts and minds of citizens of the Empire were touched by the problem of women's rights', nevertheless women should have 'some realisation of their responsibilities'. Suffragettes were not acting responsibly when they interrupted the serious business of parliament with their shouting. That sort of thing was 'foolish and undignified'.

Aunt Alice was inclined to be temperamental. There are references in Dorothy's diary which suggest that the girls never quite knew what to expect when they called on her. Thus: 'Alice and Edie went over to Aunt Alice one afternoon but didn't stay long as something had apparently upset her equilibrium, and she was most insultingly rude to them'. Dorothy seems to have got on better with her than the others, and defended her strongly against her critics. She received presents from her, including a very pretty clasp for an evening cloak, and a frock which Dorothy said was 'a great excitement'. 'It was a grey *crêpe-de-chine* empire gown with a wonderful long train which fitted me well, with a little re-adjustment. . . . We put a tuft of bright red ribbon to brighten it up, with two long streamers trailing against the skirt, and Aunt Alice had bought me deep crimson carnations which looked lovely fastened in amongst the bow ribbons of the same colour. The combination of grey and crimson was very effective.' On those occasions Dorothy would help her Aunt with her coiffure, 'rubbing and massaging her hair so as to make it nice and curly'.

Aunt Alice gave a dance now and again for her nieces and their friends, and chaperoned the girls when they were invited out. At one of these parties Dorothy danced with a young man who had worked for the Charitable Organisation Society where she herself was employed; he was a son of Aunt Alice's publisher, Macmillan. Conversation at these functions was as varied as Dorothy's partners. Her interest in theology was whetted in a great discussion with a Mr Murphy about 'Adam and Eve and the apple'. From him she heard of a new book on the subject and how its author, H. G. Wells, had found one of the apples from the Tree of Knowledge but decided to throw it away. These were important opportunities for young women to show themselves off and Dorothy made the most of them. She was naturally highly pleased when someone told her how nice she looked and that her cheeks were as pink as her dress. She was very proud of that dress. The first time she had worn it was at 'the delightful Mr Simon's dance', and she described it elegantly in her diary. 'I wore a pink liberty silk dress which my cousin Violet Kennedy had sent me' she wrote. 'It was trimmed with cream coloured lace, with a large and soft fold of pink ribbons of the same shade drawn across the breast, and was gathered at the top under a pink rose, caught in the belt, and flowing from the side like a sash'. And her hair was as nice as she could make it: she had it 'rolled up on top with a cluster of curls'.

With their ecclesial background it was not surprising that Edie, when she came to write about the Stopfords, touched upon their attitude to religion. Her father Jemmett, she said, was a regular church-goer, but she doubted if he was a convinced churchman or even a religious man at all. It fell to her mother, Constance, to lead in the family prayers and to see to the children's religious instruction. They attended church regularly but that this was a formality in Edie's own case became evident when she went to Cambridge. She ceased going to church altogether because she found doing so 'a trial', 'a bore'; she nevertheless continued to maintain that she was a Christian. As for Aunt Alice there is no evidence that she consistently attended church after her husband's death; but that she had a religious problem was observed by her friend Beatrice Webb. To her she seemed to be a blend of puritan and worldly egoist. Her religious feeling was a longing to feel assured of a God who loved and pitied her. She pined for a faith for which she would willingly exchange all her worldly goods (McDowell 56).

Alice, Dorothy and Robert had no such problems apparently. Dorothy appeared to enjoy her religion and, just when Edie was finding it a burden, she experienced a religious renewal, what she called 'a complete change'. She wrote in her diary that 'religion seemed to weave itself more into my daily life and to become less of a sacred thing apart, to be assumed at set times and places'. She savoured the set occasions. She went to church services with unfailing regularity, usually with Alice and Robert, and made a point of mentioning them in her diary with a sometimes fairly elaborate summary of the sermon.

Another Aunt Alice — Alice Young — had a hand in arranging the marriage of Alice Stopford — the daughter at home — to Christopher Wordsworth, the son of the Rector of St

Peter's, Marlborough, and grandson of one of the poet's brothers. That emerges from Dorothy's diaries.

> I knew that Aunt Alice Young was glad Mr Wordsworth and Alice met, because he had met her one night at dinner in Green Street, and remembered her and wanted to see her again. So, Aunt Alice brought them together and let them see as much as possible of each other and from the first moment Christopher saw her he was completely swept off his feet and had no doubt but that she was the wife for him. On the following Monday Bobbie [Robert] and I came up to town from Cookham; and that day he proposed. Aunt Alice sent them up the river to Bisham Abbey with a note, and they took a lunch basket, and just after lunch he asked her. She had up till that moment been in blissful ignorance of his feelings towards her, and promptly and in a final manner she refused him. But she went up that night to Hurst to Mother, and the next day promised to wait a week. So they (Mother and Alice) came up to town, and he came up on Thursday, and spent the day here, and they went for long walks together and got to know one another very well for nearly a week. Then she accepted him . . . and all was happy and joyful. We are all ever so pleased because Christopher is so nice and good and she and he love one another so very much and they are going to be married in November and go out to Bombay (where he has an appointment), and be ever so happy together. We are very rushed getting things done, letters written, calls paid, and we shall have such a lot of clothes to buy.

Apart from the dresses, on which much time and money was spent, Dorothy records that with Alice one day they bought 25 pairs of gloves, 24 pairs of stockings, 2 pairs of boots and 2 pairs of shoes.

Christopher and a Geoffrey Sparrow took the two of them to dine in Soho at a fascinating little Bohemian restaurant called *Aux Petits Riches*. Dorothy wrote in her diary.

> We got a secluded little table in an alcove, and had a charming little dinner. Then Alice and Christopher left, while I waited for Geoffrey who delayed over the bill, and as

the weather had cleared up, we walked to the Queens which is only a step. It was H. B. Irvine in *The Bells*, a marvellous piece. He acted so well that it was terribly realistic, especially when Matthias was mesmerised in court, and lived the murder over again, giving, in his dream, full proof of his guilt. Geoffrey and I appeared glued to one another, and I think Alice and Christopher enjoyed themselves very much. They two and I came home in a hansom, and I felt very much *de trop*. But I asked Christopher to sit on the seat beside Alice, and then as there wasn't much room left, I sat on their knees. It was very nice, as I had plenty of air and could not see them, and they did not fail to make use of the opportunity. I like Christopher more and more every day, and we tease him very much. He slept with us last night, and so Bobbie had to roll up in his blanket on the floor once more.

The marriage was 'the first break in our family life', Dorothy said. It was followed by a long honeymoon during which the couple came over to Dublin for a week and, staying in the Shelbourne Hotel, visited all Alice's relations and friends. Then they returned to England, and went from there to Bombay where Christopher was to resume work with an uncle who had an interest in manganese mines. This was a promising prospect in which Dorothy seemed likely to share when, in September 1910, she received an invitation to go out to India with Christopher's sister, Susan Wordsworth, and spend some months there. The acquisition by them of a couple of husbands was no doubt a possibility. Anyhow the idea of marrying was never far from Dorothy's mind, and Alice's quick success in finding a nice husband would have been a spur to her thinking. Describing a chat she had had with her Mother and Alice, she wrote in her diary: 'We didn't go to bed till 12 o'clock; we talked over old times at Wyvern [the home in Dublin] . . . and we talked about marrying. I change so much. Sometimes I want to, and at other moments it seems too great a tie and sacrifice, and yet on the whole I would like it.' She held a strong conviction about its sacramental sacredness. 'A perfect, almost mysterious and holy love must exist between the persons united, otherwise, how could they be helpmates to each other?'

But would men be attracted enough to her to want to marry her? She had doubts about her appearance, which she expressed rather frankly in her diary:

> I think I look best some time at night, when my hair is hanging about and I am in my night gown. I don't really think that dressing up improves me much. I look best in simple clothes, with my hair simply done. My upper lip is the source of great annoyance to me. It starts from the tip of my nose, and goes in a rounded curve until it meets my lower one; but it does not meet it fairly. It protrudes and this gives me a small-chinned air. My nose is also very weak and rather cocked out. It is so small and, though straight, the nostrils are uninteresting and flat, joining my cheeks at the side in a flat insensitive way. My hair is wavy and pretty enough in its way, but the colour is not remarkable, and I don't do it very well, I know. My eyes are the only good feature I have, but I hide behind glasses.

She would not have noticed, as others did, that she bubbled with personality.

But whatever the future had in store for her, she was intent for the time being on squeezing every ounce of enjoyment out of the long journey to Bombay in the company of Susie Wordsworth. She entered every trifling incident in her diary which she illustrated later with some drawings of her own. There were some nice people among their fellow-passengers but others were just 'too awful', among them an Australian who sat at the opposite end of their table and whom Dorothy called 'the second fiddle in a fifth-rate orchestra'. Fortunately he was to join a party that was going ashore at Suez; and Dorothy, hoping he would not return, wrote in her diary 'The back of my hand to him.' Susie and she would move their table if necessary. Then they received two telegraphed messages from home in quick succession. The first filled them with great joy: Alice had given birth to a baby girl. The second announced that Christopher had died of enteric fever, within five days of the birth of his child. Indeed, while the child was being born in one room of the Bombay flat, he was dying in the next room. The sorrow of Dorothy and

Susie must have been intense, which probably explains the strange silence of Dorothy's diary on the subject, though there are a few lines that may hint at her feelings. 'I went up on the deck,' she wrote. 'Everyone else was dressing for dinner, so I made friends with a second officer over a kitten which seems half-starved. . . . After dinner I watched the moon sink into the water. . . . It was the last evening I enjoyed.'

Susie and Dorothy's arrival in Bombay, so full of painful foreboding, is likewise underplayed in the diary:

We got into a large launch from the spar deck of the liner and came into the Harbour, and landed on the Bollard Pier. . . . We saw Gordon [Christopher's brother] , a soldier who was stationed in Bombay. He took our handbags and we did not wait for the large luggage, but just got into the *gharri* and drove to the house without delay. It is a short drive so there was not time for much, but he told us that Alice was well. We came straight upstairs to the flat which was the top one . . . and into the drawing room, a large room with a verandah, off which are the two bedrooms. The Eurasian nurse came in and shook hands, and then I went into Alice's room and made the acquaintance of my niece. She is a jolly little thing, rather long and thin with an awfully nice face. She is very like Christopher. . . .

Ten days later Dorothy 'was privileged to bath the baby. She was quite good, no screams, and I did not drop her, or do anything seriously wrong. In fact I rather fancy myself handling babies.'

The diary entry for the last day of December 1910 states simply that 'this is the day we sail again, for England'. 'We' meant Alice, the infant who had been christened Mary, Dorothy, and Susie Woodsworth. Alice with her child stayed first with her mother in London for a while, as did Dorothy; she then took a furnished house in Salisbury near her in-laws. Christopher's father, Mary's paternal grandfather, was a remarkable man. So small as to be almost a dwarf, as a result of an accident as a baby, but with the torso of a normal man. But he had great presence and dignity, and commanded instant obedience without ever raising his voice. His wife had borne him nine children, including Christopher, and on each occasion she locked the midwife out of the room at the actual birth and only unlocked the door after the baby had arrived: as Mary grew up she fell very much under the influence of this gentle, quiet man, and dearly loved him.

Her maternal grandfather being dead, the dominant figure from that generation in Mary's life was Aunt Alice Green; and Mary was always very much in awe of her. She was a formidable forbidding person who liked to run things her own way and to boss the young people about her. An example of this was how she treated her brother Jemmett's son Robert. She saw him as perhaps a future diplomat, who would have to entertain and, with such a career in mind for him, she considered it her business to teach him how to comport himself. He had an unfortunate habit, she had noticed, of eating too fast. That would not do. He would have to learn some manners. 'As a host', she told him, 'you must always be the last to finish each course. You must watch the guests' plates and keep some on your own until the others are finished.' And to give him practical experience, she put him one evening at the head of the table. Robert struggled to remember all she had said and succeeded pretty well for the first two courses. Then he became so engrossed in the conversation that was going on around him that he forgot everything else and speedily disposed of whatever was laid before him. This was too much for Aunt Alice. From the other end of the table she raised her voice and, pointing an accusing finger at him cried out, 'Robert, what did I tell you?'.

Susan Wordsworth was one of those involved in the *Lusitania* sinking. She was returning from a tour of service as a missionary in Japan, and when the emergency arose she put on her lifebelt and went to her lifeboat station. She was there knocked unconscious by a falling lifeboat and when she recovered she found herself floating in the water close to an overturned boat. She swam to it and kept herself afloat until she was picked up.

Chapter Two

CONSPIRACY AND REBELLION

By 1910 the Liberals were four years in office and their Cabinet representative in Ireland, the Chief Secretary, during that
time had been Augustine Birrell, a serious and able politician.
He had come to the Irish post knowing little about the
country other than what he had read about it, or discovered
in House of Commons debates. In Ireland he trod warily,
therefore, if somewhat oddly as many people thought. He
rarely stayed in the lodge that was an attractive perquisite
of the Chief Secretary's job; he barely concealed his con-
tempt for the Viceregal Court and its hangers-on; he regarded
Dublin Castle, where his office was situated and where he
functioned through a permanent Civil Service Under Secretary,
as 'switched off from the current of Irish life' and had ideas
of transforming it; he took his meals in pubs and small
restaurants, and kept away from the Kildare Street Club; he
did not like coming to Ireland because of the unpleasantness
of the journeys by sea but when he did come, he availed of
every opportunity to get out to the countryside, travelling
usually with some civil servants he liked and whom he had
met through his official connection with the Local Government and Congested District Boards. Some of the prettiest
places in Ireland happened to be in congested districts and
he often said he would be quite willing to spend the residue
of his days in the congested West.

The many police reports that were laid before him seemed
to him to give an unreal picture of life in Ireland. He preferred to form his own opinions; and, being a writer, he
looked to Irish literary and artistic circles to tell him what
the renascent Ireland was thinking. He read Synge, Lady
Gregory, Yeats, AE, Shaw, and Moore, and expected much

from the Abbey Theatre. It made merciless fun of mad political enterprises and lashed with savage satire historical aspects
of the Irish Revolutionary. He was often amazed, he said, by
the literary detachment and courage of the playwrights, the
relentless audacity of the players, and the patience and com-
prehension of the audience. Of course he listened carefully,
as his chief, the Prime Minister, did, to what the Irish Party,
under Redmond and Dillon, had to say about the contemporary situation. They held the balance of power in parliament, and for that reason, a close relationship existed. It was
admitted, Asquith declared, that Ireland was the one failure
of British statemanship. Birrell's Irish Universities Bill of
1908 was a considerable achievement, disposing of a problem
that had been carried over from the previous century. It set
up a National University with constituent colleges in Dublin,
Cork and Galway, and it gratified many people that chairs of
Irish and Early Irish History in the Dublin institution had
been filled by Douglas Hyde and Mrs Green's mentor Eoin
MacNeill. Birrell knew Mrs Green, of course, since the days of
their shared friendship with the Webbs, and he remembered
especially an occasion when, with Arthur Balfour who had
been Irish Secretary in the late eighties, he had dined with
her and been impressed by how queenly, witty, courteous,
and encouraging she was. But she had a strongly developed
anti-English bias and strange friends, and for this reason he
liked to keep her at a distance.

There remained the problem of finding a policy which,
while explicitly safeguarding the supremacy and indefectible
authority of the Imperial Parliament, would set up in Ireland
a system of self-government in regard to purely Irish affairs.
There had been Home Rule Bills in 1886 and 1893, but
these had perished either as a result of dissension among the
Liberals in the House of Commons or by being rejected in
the Lords. This time what was proposed had a prospect of
becoming law because of the Liberal-Irish alliance and the
procedure of the Parliament Bill of 1911 that was now available to the government. But the apparent inevitability of
Home Rule increased the opposition of Protestant Ulster, and
years were to pass in fruitless negotiation and strife before a
settlement of sorts could be achieved on the basis of the partition of the country.

Apart from self-government there were other issues, social and political, affecting Ireland generally and these were fought out with mounting intensity against the background of the Home Rule debate. James Larkin, a Liverpool man of Irish parentage fired the Irish working class with a new spirit of discontent with their conditions, focusing the struggle on the industrialist William Martin Murphy and the Dublin United Tramways Company of which he was Chairman. The conflict developed into a general lock-out in 1913, so that by the end of September that year there were 25,000 men off work with grievous consequences for their families which were only partly relieved by gifts from unions across the Channel. With these unions Larkin quarrelled in time, their support fell off, and the strike fizzled out. It had two lasting results, however, for which James Connolly, rather than James Larkin, was responsible: the creation of an Irish Citizen Army and a political Irish Labour Party.

Arthur Griffith saw Larkin as a trouble-maker, with the strike organised from England; and so did Douglas Hyde. Hyde was desperately anxious to keep the Gaelic League out of every form of public contention and was upset when he found Larkin on a wagonette beside him at a public meeting in support of the language: 'If I had known he was to be among the speakers I would not have attended, but they kept it hidden from me.' Larkin he described as a tall, black-haired, powerfully built man, with a great resounding voice and much fluency and energy, seeming to say a lot with great emphasis but really speaking platitudes, the gist of his speech being that if Irishmen really wanted Irish taught to their children there was no power on earth could stop them! Patrick Pearse, who spoke also, pronounced a great eulogy on Larkin, *he* at least was *doing something*, he was making history. 'So he was', said Hyde, 'for he had closed the port of Dublin, and the workers of Dublin had not got over the effects of the general strike into which he plunged them, apparently without counting the cost. It was characteristic of Pearse that he never stopped to enquire if the something that Larkin was doing was good or bad.' And Hyde added that 'the Archbishop of Dublin, Dr Walsh, was so offended at Larkin being identified with the language movement that he kept away from the opening of the Leinster College of Irish. That was typical, Hyde would say, of the obstacles that were being placed in the way of the movement by unthinking people (Hyde *Memoir*).

Constance Markieviez saw Larkin in an entirely different light. Looking at him, she realised that she was in the presence of a great primeval force rather than just a man. She accepted his belief that in regard to everything in Ireland, trade union or anything else, England was the foe (Emmet Larkin, 74).

The Citizen Army, which arose during the 1913 lock-out, discovered at the outset a robust leader in Captain Jack White, a son of the defender of Ladysmith. He argued for the belief that drilled and disciplined men would not allow themselves to be batoned by the police like clubbed seals, as had been happening. So he equipped the little army with staves — some of them later acquired rifles — and when the lock-out was over and the battle apparently lost, Connolly, coming to live in Dublin from Belfast, set the army on course as a separatist body to which the oncoming war was to give a *raison d'être*. Writing in the *Irish Worker*, later to be renamed 'The Worker's Republic', he suggested that the European working class, rather than slaughter each other for the benefit of kings and financiers, should on the morrow proceed to erect barricades, break up bridges, and destroy the transport service. The remote aim would be to abolish war, and dethrone the vulture class that ruled and robbed the world.

The Liberals retained power with the support of the Irish Parliamentary Party, the price for which was paid in 1912. A Parliament Act had been passed the previous year, the effect of which was to remove the veto of the House of Lords over legislation, and this promised that the third Home Rule Bill, introduced in 1912, could become law. The Bills of 1886 and 1893 had perished as a result of dissension among Liberals in the House of Commons and rejection by the Lords. There remained the possibility of the latest measure being stopped by unconstitutional means, and this was what the Ulster Unionists resorted to. The Dublin lawyer, Sir Edward Carson, led the Ulster opposition in the House of

Commons, and in September 1911 he told 100,000 Ulster-men at Craigavon what his programme was. They were not only to defy what he called Dublin's Home Rule but to prepare an alternative. They were to be ready the morning Home Rule became law to become responsible for the govern-ment of the Protestant Province of Ulster. A commission then proceeded to draft a constitution for a provisional government, and a vast force of Ulster volunteers started to drill. What was tantamount to a mutiny within the British Army followed, fifty-eight cavalry officers at the Curragh and Dublin choosing dismissal rather than engaging in 'active operations in Ulster'. The resultant political storm caused the resignations of the Secretary of State for War, the Chief of the Imperial General Staff and the Adjutant General.

So, with *Ulster* Volunteers arming themselves to resist Home Rule, with guns surreptitiously imported from Germany, their example proved a headline to various people in the South who had been thinking along parallel lines. A young militant known as The O'Rahilly, who was the manager of the Gaelic League paper, urged Eoin MacNeill to write a comment on the subject for the paper, and this MacNeill did in an article entitled 'The North Began'. That MacNeill rather than anybody else should have been approached to do this was not surprising. Through his Gaelic League activ-ities and his occupancy of the Chair of Early Irish History in University College, Dublin, MacNeill was known all over Ireland, and was regarded as a man of moderate views. He was certainly no doctrinaire either on behalf of physical force or against it, which was in accord with the mood of the times. His interest in politics was simple. He was a natural separatist, which meant he knew that the less the Irish had to do with Britain the better. In his eyes politics were a sub-servient matter in the context of Irish nationality. He was personally prepared to accept any settlement with the British that would enable Irishmen to order their own affairs, and had no difficulty in accepting what Redmond and the Irish Party were doing to obtain an effective if limited amount of home rule. He was an original thinker. In 'The North Began' he described the Ulster Volunteer movement as essentially a home rule movement, as indeed it proved in time to be, securing autonomy for six of the Irish counties. He advanced the argument that as the British Army had not been used to prevent the Ulster Volunteers from coming into existence, neither could it be used to prevent the rest of the country having a Volunteer force which, like that of 1782, could become an instrument of self-government. He repudiated the idea of an Ulster partitioned from the rest of Ireland, and told Carson he hoped the day was not far distant when the Ulster Volunteers would march peacefully to Cork to be greeted by ten times their number of National Volunteers.

No article could have evoked so immediate and striking a response. It was seized upon, notably by Hobson who recognised its revolutionary possibilities. A provisional committee was formed representative of the IRB, the Irish Parliamentary Party, the Ancient Order of Hibernians and of individuals not formally affiliated to any party, and within a month a monster public meeting, over which MacNeill presided, established a Corps of Irish Volunteers. The quest for arms then began and Roger Casement, who had retired from the diplomatic service and had recently been active on the political scene, went over to London to discuss the problem with some English and Anglo-Irish Liberals who had become alarmed at the apparent inability of the Asquith government to withstand Carson's attack on the Constitution.

Casement's immediate contact was with Aunt Alice, who approved of MacNeill's widely publicised assertion that Irishmen in general had the right to follow the Ulster example and arm themselves. In her house in Grosvenor Road, Westminister, the details were worked out for the purchase of a consignment of Mauser rifles in Hamburg, and Aunt Alice and Captain George Fitzhardinge Berkeley, who was acting as a military instructor to the Irish Volunteers in Belfast, advanced most of the money. The rest of it was whipped up from relatives, Liberals and other Anglo-Irish including Lady Alice Young, Sir Alexander Lawrence and the kilted Irish-speaking Lord Ashbourne. Darrell Figgis went to Germany to purchase rifles and ammunition, accompanied by Erskine Childers, an ex-British army officer and House of Commons clerk who had become a convinced Home Ruler. There was a problem about how to get the arms over to

Ireland, but Mary Spring-Rice, the daughter of Lord Monteagle, who was a good friend of the Stopfords — she had been teaching Irish step-dancing to Edie and Dorothy — found three men who were willing to do the job as unobtrusively as possible. These were Childers who was a skilful yachtsman, Conor O'Brien a cousin of Mary's and Sir Thomas Myles, an elderly Dublin surgeon who was both a Home Ruler and a friend of Childers. Mrs Green would have liked her seventeen-year-old nephew Robert Stopford to have gone on the expedition but his mother Constance would not hear of it.

The Mausers were duly landed in Howth and Kilcoole, and Aunt Alice went over to Dublin to greet the gun-runners, staying with a niece Elsie Henry. In the success of the operation, there were three factors of importance, the source of the purchase money, that the consignment was very small by comparison with what the Ulster Volunteers had smuggled into Larne and hidden away, and that, while the Larne landing was unimpeded, that at Howth was followed by confrontation with the police and military, and an affair next day at Dublin's Bachelor's Walk in which civilians were killed and wounded. Casement was highly delighted at the success of the venture. Writing as 'the Fugitive Knight' he told Mrs Green, 'the Woman of the Ships' that John Devoy, the old Fenian, had called it the greatest deed done in Ireland for a hundred years. 'Oh Woman of the Stern Unbending Purpose, Autocrat of all Armadas', he cried, 'may your knee never be bowed, may it be strengthened, and may the God of Erin put rifles into the hands of Irishmen and teach them to shoot straight!.

All of that happened at the end of July 1914. Literally within weeks, the world was at war, and the Irish Parliamentary Party had to take a stand in regard to it. It had been decided that the Home Rule Bill was to go on the statute book with its operation suspended for the duration of the conflict, and on that basis Redmond made a declaration in support of the government and subsequently called on the Irish Volunteers to show thair mettle by joining the British army. Many thousands of them and other nationalists did so, but the declaration split the Volunteer movement, the great majority

adhering to Redmond — they became the National Volunteers — while the remainder, retaining the original name and
motivated to a degree by the underground Irish Republican
Brotherhood, sided with Eoin MacNeill who became their
President and Chief of Staff. MacNeill's attitude was that
Ireland could not, with honour or safety, take part in foreign
quarrels otherwise than through the free action of a national
government of her own; and that Redmond had to be repudiated in offering the lives of Irishmen while no such government
yet existed. By this time Roger Casement, anticipating the
war in which he hoped for a German intervention on behalf of
Ireland, had left for the United States and later made his way
to Germany. These developments, involving such important
friends of hers, filled Aunt Alice with anxiety. Her political
instincts guided her in this issue to side with Redmond whom
she ordinarily did not like very much, while Casement's
behaviour, particularly when it took the form of an effort to
form an Irish Brigade with prisoners of war, seduced from
their allegiance to Britain, was utterly obnoxious to her.

The division in the ranks of the Volunteers, and especially
the movement of so many active, thinking, individuals to
MacNeill, filled Hyde with apprehension. He declared to a
Gaelic League meeting in Cork that while it was perfectly
true that some of the supporters of the League were strong
politicians of an advanced type, all were not, and the great
bulk were moderate men such as would be elected to an Irish
parliament. It was upon them the Gaelic League relied to
create an Irish Ireland through the medium of Irish education.
He stressed, however, that if any one party got control of
the League and ran it on party lines, the language movement
would fail and the entire structure of the organisation would
fall to pieces. Within twelve months this prophecy began to
be verified (Horgan 264-5).

The terrible war, as we shall see, had an upsetting effect on
the Stopfords, as it had on many families. At first, everything
went on as before, Alice and her mother Constance looked
after the Wordsworth child. Edie, a rather uneasy being, moved
through various secretarial jobs, and Dorothy continued to
look after 'cases' for the Charitable Organisation Society. In
other words, they behaved as far as possible as if there was

no war. Robert's case was different. When the German invasion of Belgium occurred in 1914, he was nineteen years of age and was due to go up to Magdalene College in Cambridge to do an economics degree. He went overseas instead with an Ambulance Unit belonging to the Society of Friends which was under the immediate command of his cousin Geoffrey Young and, working with the nuns of the Sacred Heart Convent in the town of Ypres rescued sick and wounded civilians. He joined the army in 1916 and for the rest of the war served in Salonika and Egypt with the Army Service Corps. In the Officers' messes he was looked upon with horror for declaring he was a Home Ruler.

As for Aunt Alice, she, despite the distractions of the war, maintained her close interest in the Irish situation. She had witnessed the dismissals that took place following the gun-running and the affair at Bachelor's Walk, and derived pleasure from the appointment to the Under Secretaryship in Dublin Castle of Sir Matthew Nathan, a former Colonial governor she had met through the African Society. He was a bachelor, and she admired, as many women did, his physique, his finely-shaped head, and his pleasant personality. But she also knew of his administrative qualities, his unlimited initiative and drive, and his capacity for hard work. Politically a Liberal, though a discreet Civil Servant, Nathan had the good fortune to number the Prime Minister Asquith and other members of the government among his friends and, from his arrival in Dublin he worked in close partnership with his political chief, Augustine Birrell, and followed him in getting to know the Irish people and their motivation. He read any books about Ireland he could lay his hands on, went to the Abbey Theatre, and entertained thinkers like George Russell (AE) in his lodge in the Phoenix Park. Mrs Green was in that category too, of course, and he had her to stay with him occasionally when she came over from London. She had ideas, and information. He knew about her connection with the gun-running, and her friendship with MacNeill and Casement. He also knew that openly she admired the Irish Volunteers, and was critical of Redmond for allowing such good material to slip from his hands. He knew further that Birrell did not like her; indeed Birrell had warned him that deep buried in widow Green was a fatal disease she shared with Casement. She was involved in what he called the hierarchy of treason, but not very high up in it, he believed. She had collaborated with the German scholar Kuno Meyer in establishing a School of Irish Learning in Dublin and was a close friend of his. At the outbreak of the war Meyer, like Casement, had become 'a plotter', and that was enough to increase Birrell's suspicions of the lady.

That did not put Nathan off seeing her, however. He invited her to the Lodge as so often he had done before, and there opened his mind to her about his continuing worry, the possibility of some action in Ireland that would set back what had already been achieved in the matter of giving effect to the Liberals' pledge of 1909 'to govern Ireland according to Irish ideas'. He was aware, as she vaguely was, of the existence of an underground movement which threatened MacNeill's position and which the government's intelligence services, such as they were, had been unable to penetrate. So they talked, and talked, and Nathan restated the policy of steering Ireland peacefully through the war to self-government. Winning the war, however, was taking much longer than anyone had anticipated so that the need of Irish recruits for the armed forces increased with each passing day. In that regard a dispiriting factor was the decline of the National Volunteers who had joined up in large numbers at the beginning of the war. The organisation by the end of 1915 existed in little more than name and the real purpose of its existence was being questioned. On the other hand, their rivals, the Irish Volunteers, if not yet very strong numerically, were growing ever more abrasive.

Nathan's intelligence agents were seemingly unaware of an extremely significant meeting that was held at the Gaelic League Headquarters, 25 Parnell Square, Dublin on 9 September 1914. This was by no manner or means a Gaelic League function and Hyde had no idea that the building was being used for such improper purposes. The meeting was called by the IRB, and the venue was chosen no doubt by Sean T. O'Kelly, who had an office in the building, being the manager of the League journal. Presided over by Tom

Clarke, those who attended, in addition to the organisers, were Sean MacDermott, Patrick H. Pearse, Arthur Griffith, Major John MacBride, Thomas MacDonagh, Joseph Plunkett, James Connolly, William O'Brien, Sean McGarry and John Tobin. With three exceptions, all of those, it may be taken, were IRB men, they were committed to achieving Ireland's freedom in the form of a Republic, by physical force, and were involved currently in the direction of the Irish Volunteers. Arthur Griffith, James Connolly and William O'Brien were not IRB men. Griffith had at one time been a member, was the leader of Sinn Féin and editor of its papers. Connolly commanded the Irish Citizen Army; and he and O'Brien were leaders of organised labour. He was one of the earliest of Irish socialists, and the founder of the Irish Socialist Republican Party whose aim was to secure the national and economic freedom of the Irish people.

The genesis of the meeting was described differently by two of the participants when they wrote about it in later life. According to William O'Brien he had asked for the meeting so as to enable Connolly to meet 'the right people', by which was meant the people who shared the conviction he had held since the outbreak of the war that the opportunity should not be missed of organising an insurrection, with the object of establishing the independence of Ireland as a republic. But according to Sean T. O'Kelly, Tom Clarke was already planning such a meeting, and for the same purpose, namely that the war should not be allowed to pass without striking a blow for freedom.

The historian F. S. L. Lyons put the matter in a broader setting. In his opinion, the earliest initiative was taken in America when in August 1914 Clan na Gael, the IRB's counterpart, told the German ambassador of their intention to organise an armed revolt in Ireland and asked for military assistance. This news was communicated to Ireland, and the Supreme Council of the IRB decided, the following month September 1914, that there should indeed be a rebellion, and that it should take place even if no German aid was forthcoming. Hence the conference of 'advanced nationalists'.

Lyons thought the discussion did not produce any overt result other than the formation of a short-lived league to promote an anti-recruiting campaign. But O'Brien says that Connolly advocated making definite arrangements for organising an insurrection and that two sub-committees were appointed, one to continue the contact with Germany, and the other for propaganda purposes and to promote recruitment to 'the secret movement'. O'Kelly, in his authorised biography, set out the decisions, as far as he remembered them, under four heads. '(a) that each of us would do his best to strengthen the Irish Volunteers and the Citizen Army, to get recruits for those two organisations, as well as for Fianna Eireann and Cumann na mBan (the women's auxiliary); (b) if German forces came to Ireland, to assist them on condition that we had their help to secure the freedom of Ireland; (c) if the application of conscription to Ireland was attempted, or a move made to disarm the Volunteers, that we oppose it with all our strength; and (d) if the war was approaching its end, without an attempt having been made on our part to rise in revolt, that we would organise such an attempt and declare the freedom of Ireland to the world. We thought that a rising and a declaration of freedom in that fashion would give us the right to promote the nation's cause after the war. We had little hope that the rising would be successful.' After the meeting, O'Kelly says, Tom Clarke and Sean MacDermott had a short private conversation with Arthur Griffith. They apparently invited Arthur to join, or rejoin, the IRB, but he, preferring to retain his position as an independent commentator declined though he asked to be kept informed about any important developments that might be contemplated, and this they agreed to do.

Rather oddly, O'Brien and O'Kelly did not advert to the fact that contact with the Germans was already being made by Sir Roger Casement. He had happened to be in the United States when the war broke out and, being for years convinced that a war between England and Germany was inevitable, and would be to Ireland's advantage, he consulted with John Devoy, and then went to Germany, financed by Clan na Gael money. His terms of reference, if we can call them that, were to recruit an Irish brigade from among prisoners of war, to secure general German support by a declaration of Irish independence, and to arrange for arms to be shipped to

Ireland. One thing that was done six months after the Dublin conference of September 1914 was to send Joseph Plunkett to Germany to discover what progress was being made. He brought back a disappointing report. Casement in fact warned that to attempt a rising on the streets of Dublin in 1915, which was the time contemplated, would be criminal stupidity.

Aunt Alice introduced her niece Dorothy to Nathan. His diary for 10 September 1915 shows that on that day he drove Mrs Green from the boat at Kingstown to the Lodge, and dined alone with her. Four days later Mrs Green and Dorothy were with him in a dinner party, and their names recur in the diary until 24 September when 'our visitors, Green and Stopford, left'. They returned for a day or two the following February, but meanwhile Dorothy wrote from London to 'my dear Sir Matthew' to tell him that she had spent most of that day (13 October 1915) typing a eulogy of him for the *African Journal* and had finished it during an air raid. He already knew that, having tried other things, she had decided, now that she was all of 25 years of age, to do medicine, and would be coming to Trinity College, Dublin, for that purpose in January. When she passed the entrance examination – not too brilliantly, as she admitted – he invited her to lunch and she accepted on condition that he would come afterwards with her to see Boyle's *The Miracle Workers* and a piece of Lady Gregory's at the Abbey Theatre. 'I am sure it will be good for you to come', she told him, 'the Abbey is educative, not dissipative'. He asked her to the Lodge for a week-end, but the invitation created a problem for her. 'It's most awfully nice of you', she replied. 'I would give anything to go, and am horribly tempted, but I think I mustn't all the same. I can explain why not better when I see you; it isn't anything to do with me...'. She got an opportunity to explain why not when, twice in March, she lunched with him at Mitchell's and Fuller's in Grafton Street. The problem was probably that of being alone in a house with a man; if she was to go at all, it would have to be with a female companion; and that the problem was solved in that way Dorothy made clear in a Ballade she subsequently wrote:

> To an official dwelling
> 'Neath the eye of the police
> Where dwelt a fearful ogre
> Came a lady and her niece

and the poem ended:

> The Ogre's Den did thus become
> The favourite spot of every one.

One woman who loved to go there, with none of Dorothy's inhibitions, was Mrs Constance Heppel-Marr, the young wife of a mining manager serving in the Army, who in a second marriage achieved distinction as Constance Spry, the floral decorator. Between January and mid-April that year she dined *à deux* with Nathan in the Lodge nine times and sang for him afterwards. He even had dinner with her one night in her 'top-back' in Lower Baggot Street. He obviously found her very attractive, and she confessed to a loving admiration that seems to have led to something more than a platonic exercise.

On 12 April Dorothy wrote from England to tell Nathan that she was coming over and would reach the North Wall on the 15th at 7.30 a.m. She was obviously relying on him for transport. 'I am looking forward very much to getting back', she said. 'Your beloved London is unbearable just now. So please have on all your robes and uniforms and stars to greet me on Saturday at breakfast.' She was going to stay with her Uncle Edward Stopford, a retired tea merchant, and Nathan's diary shows that he dined with them on the 19th, another guest being Douglas Hyde. Edward, like his sister Alice, was nationally inclined and was a co-worker with Horace Plunkett in the Irish Agricultural Organisation Society, and had a reputation for methodical industry.

This could have been an informative meeting for Nathan had Hyde been able to speak freely about something that had happened to him less than a year before. Birrell knew of this but had seen it as 'a melancholy but inevitable Gaelic League split'. He sympathised with 'poor Dr Hyde'. There was more to it than a split, however, and Hyde was still feeling bitter when he wrote a long memoir on the subject in 1918. He had always striven to keep the Gaelic League non-political, he explained, and to avoid the attempts of politicians on the Executive to get the League into trouble with the government. He was well aware that P. H. Pearse, a former editor of the League's journal and a high-ranking officer in the Volunteers, was by no means alone when he declared that the Gaelic League, as the Gaelic League, was a spent force. They had never meant to be Gaelic Leaguers and nothing more, he said. The European war, he went on, had brought about a crisis which might contain within it the moment for which generations had been waiting but it remained to be seen whether that generation had men among it who dared to make the ultimate sacrifice. The Irish Revolution had begun with the foundation of the Gaelic League, which brought that Revolution a certain distance, but the Gaelic League could not accomplish the Revolution. A new phase was now with them. Ireland was once more learning the noble trade of arms. Irish nationhood could only be achieved by armed men.

The intention behind that speech had gained momentum by 1915 when the annual Ard-Fheis was held in Dundalk. A great number of the delegates were Volunteers, and politics were more or less everywhere in the air. Hyde was apprehensive of the outcome:

There were many signs that I would have a disagreeable year of it, several items on the agenda being apparently more or less directed against myself personally. I presided for two or three days effectively enough and prevented a split taking place between the League and some excellent priests from the North . . . who could not express themselves in Irish, and who were going to leave the League, and actually got up to walk out of the room when the Ard Fheis refused to hear them in English. I conjured them to remain as a split of that kind would be the beginning of the end of the Gaelic League and got leave with extreme difficulty for them to be heard in English.

Pádraic Ó Máille of Oughterard in the name of some Connemara branch had a resolution that the objects of the

League should be extended by adding a further object, to make Ireland free from foreign rule. Up to this the League had only two aims, one was to revive the language, the other to encourage native industries. This third now, if carried, would make the League into a political body, and I could not have stood over it. I had again and again said in public that the League was non-political and that I would never while I was president allow it to become a political body. By speaking thus I had won a great deal of support in the past even from Unionists, from Horace Plunkett and others. In fact I was pledged up to the neck before the country against a political Gaelic League, and I had often said to the Executive that if the League became political I would be the first person to leave it. Pádraic Ó Máille's motion as it stood was a plain challenge, and I had to make up my mind irrevocably that if it was passed I should gather up any papers, vacate the chair, and walk out of the Ard-Fheis.

Unfortunately Colonel Maurice Moore who knew nothing of all this, he not having come near the Gaelic League for years, proposed that instead of the words 'free from foreign rule' the single word 'free' should be substituted. Over and over again I pressed him and the others to say what kind of freedom they meant, for if it was freedom from English rule they meant, I said the resolution was political. But Colonel Moore insisted on saying that Asquith had said we were a free people when he talked in Dublin about 'a free gift from a free people'. Nobody would define the word free, and I said I would interpret it during the ensuing year in a non-political sense, O'Máille's resolution was then passed by a large majority, and after that the election to the Executive took place. Now I was told by several people that Sean O Muirthuile had got 50 proxies which, instead of distributing to various Irish speakers as he was meant to do, he had handed over to 50 Sinn Féiners who did not know Irish, did not care for the language, had never even joined a branch of the League, but who now had their orders to walk in as delegates with these passes in their hands and vote on a pre-arranged ticket for all the Sinn Féiners and politicians and followers of Arthur Griffith

who were candidates for membership of th Executive.
These men walked in, voted, and were never seen again at
the proceedings, but they assured the election of a political
Executive or one preponderantly political, though indeed
I think that even without their help things would not have
been much different.

That night I did some furious thinking. About 12 o'clock
I ascertained from Pádraig Ó Dalaigh, the League's Secretary,
how the voting was going, and it was far enough advanced
at that time to show me that there would not be more
than a dozen men on the new Executive (out of a total of
some 50 or 60) who would support my consistently non-
political attitude, and that men who had been tried and
convicted for treason felony were being put high up in the
voting. That decided me finally. I wrote out a letter addressed to Ó Dalaigh to be read by him when the time
for electing the president came up next day, in which, on
grounds of health induced by over-work, I declined the
honour of re-election if any one should propose me. It
was quite clear to me that all the Volunteers and the advanced political section were sure that Germany was winning, and they would in the course of the coming year be
perfectly certain to throw the League into their fight
against the Government. . . . They soon showed how non-
political they were, for the very day I left the Ard-Fheis
they passed a resolution against conscription, as though
the Irish language had anything to say to that any more
than to 'felonious landlordism' or a dozen other causes. . . .
(Hyde *Memoir*)

Eoin MacNeill was chosen as Hyde's successor, and Sean
T. O'Kelly replaced Pádraig Ó Dalaigh when he resigned also.
O Dalaigh had been the Secretary of the League for about a
dozen years and always saw eye to eye with Hyde. In Hyde's
opinion, Fionán MacColuim was the League's best organiser
and should have got the secretaryship but his parliamentary
leanings were suspect. Hyde described O'Kelly as a very nice
little gentlemanly fellow. His politics were those of Sinn Féin
and he had actually been a couple of years in New York with
Clan na Gael as a deputy for their sympathisers in Ireland.

Ó Muirthile had thought that he, as a good IRB man, should have been made Secretary; indeed, his Irish was superior to O'Kelly's; but Tom Clarke, who had no Irish at all, preferred O'Kelly, and that was that. From this time onwards the League was handed over root and branch to Sinn Féin. The General Secretaries in succession were all IRB or IRA men, O'Kelly, Ó Muirthile, Fahy. Though it prospered for a while in the revolutionary Sinn Féin euphoria, it went to pieces, not surprisingly, when Sinn Féin itself disintegrated in the wake of the Anglo-Irish treaty of 1921.

John Dillon, the Irish Party deputy leader, had twice discussed the 1915 crisis within the League with Nathan, and had suggested that it was time perhaps that a new non-political language body was born. Hyde, he thought, could form such a body, but he feared he would be too timid to do so. Nathan had retained a certain uneasiness about the situation, and earlier had mentioned to Dr Denis Coffey, the President of University College, Dublin, that something should be done about MacNeill, the leader of 'the present dangerous movement', and Thomas MacDonagh, a lecturer on the staff, who was regarded by the police as even more dangerous than MacNeill. Nothing was done.

With Easter just a week off Sir Matthew again invited Dorothy to stay with him for the holiday. She was glad to accept. There would be no problem this time, for Mrs Estelle Nathan, Sir Matthew's sister-in-law, and her two daughters, Maud and Pamela, would be joining them. This settled, Nathan bid good-bye to his host and to Dr Hyde and returned to the Lodge.

Early next morning the Chief Commissioner of the Dublin Metropolitan Police was in touch with Nathan. He had got information that there was to be a general mobilisation of the Irish Volunteers to be followed by an attack on Dublin Castle, apparently the previous night. 'Needless to say', he said, 'I did not believe the latter statement. However, as the Sinn Féiners began to assemble with arms at various points, and the Transport Workers people at Liberty Hall, I thought it wise to take no chance.'

'The Transport Workers people' were, of course, the Irish

Citizen Army which was, and remained, a tiny force number-
ing at most 200 men. When the war broke out Connolly
recognised a new purpose for the Army in association with
the Irish Volunteers which had been formed about the same
time in other circumstances. Connolly was critical of the
Volunteers, at first asserting that there were no real nationalists in Ireland outside the Labour movement. 'All others
merely reject one part or other of the British conquest, the
Labour movement alone rejects it in its entirety, and sets
the reconquest of Ireland as its aim.' On the outbreak of the
European war, Connolly had moved to effect a reconciliation
with the Irish Republican Brotherhood which was the principal purpose of the September 1914 meeting in the Gaelic
League library on Parnell Square at which agreement was
reached that an insurrection should be the objective with
German help. P. H. Pearse, with more senior IRB people,
had determined that at a given moment the cream of the
Volunteers would be rallied behind a *coup d'état*. This was
very much in line with Connolly's thinking and he ultimately joined the IRB group and with them coordinated
the details of a rising.

For a long time Tom Clarke and Sean MacDermott had
been running the IRB virtually by themselves. They constituted with the President of the Organisation an Executive
Council which was permitted to run the show in between
meetings of the Supreme Council. With the President
McCullough living in Belfast and quite willing to leave things
to the other officers, Clarke and MacDermott had a virtually
free hand and ignored any restriction on their action in the
IRB's constitution. They were helped by Bulmer Hobson's
decision to resign from the Supreme Council, while remaining
chairman of the Dublin Centres Board and retaining his
position on the Volunteer executive. He was opposed to a
rising, believing that it was not justified by the IRB constitution and, with Eoin MacNeill, seeing the Volunteers as
a guarantee that Britain would have to respect Ireland's claim
to self-government. It was necessary, they both held, to keep
the Volunteers in reserve and not commit them to military
action unless the British attempted to disarm them or sought
to impose conscription. Pearse acknowledged that he could

not answer Hobson's arguments but that they must have an insurrection all the same, while Connolly told Hobson that Ireland was a powder magazine, somebody should strike a match, and he was quite prepared to do that himself.

Clarke and MacDermott joined themselves to a Military Council which had evolved out of the IRB's military committee, and with Pearse, Joseph Mary Plunkett, and Eamon Ceannt, all of them members of the Supreme Council and high-ranking Volunteers, led the preparations for a Rising. The American Clan na Gael were informed and they, through John Devoy, ensured a continuing synchronisation of plans with the German authorities. Pearse, with his eye on a *coup d'état*, if MacNeill's agreement proved impossible to obtain, made full use of his position as Director of Organisation in the Volunteers to appoint IRB men to key positions throughout the country, and particularly to the battalions of the Dublin Brigade. As early as March 1915 he discussed with the Commandants of these four units the possibility of a rising the following September, and got an assurance from them that in such event they would follow the instructions of their superior officer who, Pearse saw to it, was Thomas McDonagh, a man on whom he felt he could rely.

Pearse who, in the Rising, was to become the supreme commander of the Irish Volunteers, and Connolly, who would command the Irish Citizen Army, shared a philosophical outlook on the idea of confronting the enemy, even with the slenderest of resources. They were prepared to die for the cause, and no doubt assumed that the men who followed their lead would do the same. But their willingness to sacrifice their lives came from a strange conviction. Connolly, since the outbreak of the war, had seen the workers of Ireland selling their bodies to the British recruiting sergeants, and, in an excess of disgust, told the readers of his paper, the *Worker's Republic*, that only the militant few — he had in mind the officer body of the Citizen Army — had not apostatised. The sense of degradation was so deep that 'no agency less powerful than the red tide of war on Irish soil' could remove it. A little earlier Pearse had gone much further, but the idea was the same when he said that 'the rich heart of the earth needed to be warmed with the red wine of the battlefield'. Much earlier still he had spoken of bloodshed for the nation as a cleansing and sanctifying thing; and said that the nation which regarded bloodshed as the final horror had lost its manhood. When civilian lives were lost on Bachelors Walk, Dublin, in an affray with the King's own Scottish Borderers, he told an American correspondent that the whole country had been rebaptised by blood shed for Ireland.

Dorothy Stopford arrived at the Under-Secretary's Lodge early on Holy Thursday evening. It was likely to be a pleasant four days, and she felt she would enjoy the company. But things were to turn out altogether differently to what she expected. Sir Matthew had had a warning earlier in the week of a contemplated landing of arms and ammunition on the south-west coast of Ireland as a preliminary to a rising that was fixed for Holy Saturday or Easter Eve, but he was doubtful, as was the Inspector General of the Royal Irish Constabulary, whether this rumour had any substance. They both thought it wise, however, to put the County Inspectors in the southern and south-western counties on their guard. Dublin, too, had been full of disquieting rumours and the police could not escape hearing some of them. John Dillon learned that Clan na Gael, the American counterpart of the IRB, were planning something devilish, and he sought a reassurance from Nathan. He was obviously not convinced by what Nathan said to him, for he wrote to his chief, John Redmond, to warn him not to be surprised if something very unpleasant and mischievous happened the following week.

A strange document was read to the Dublin Corporation during Holy Week, by the Sinn Féin Alderman, Tom Kelly. It purported to be a decipher of a paper on an official file, giving details of an army order for large-scale raids on buildings in the city, as part of a plan for disarming the Volunteers. But things passed off quietly on Holy Thursday and on most of Good Friday so that Nathan was able to pay some attention to his guests. On Good Friday night, however, the Constabulary Office sent him a message that had come in from the County Inspector of Tralee to the effect that that morning a patrol from Ardfert, some five miles from Tralee, had captured a boat, 1,000 rounds of ammunition, three mauser pistols, and maps and papers, all German. They had arrested a prisoner, who turned out to be 'that lunatic traitor Sir Roger Casement', a man who by going to Berlin had made it easier for the authorities to believe that he was the leader of the separatists. Nathan had spoken of a *Casement* movement. Two men who had come ashore with Casement had escaped.

It should be said immediately that Casement had not come at the head of a liberating force. True, he had been landed from a German submarine and was being followed by a German arms ship; but he had concealed from the Germans that it was no part of his desire, as once it had been, that this should facilitate a Rising. Things had gone badly for him in Germany. He had secured a declaration that Germany would recognise and support an independent Irish government, if such were set up; but that did not amount to much. His attempt to recruit an Irish brigade from prisoners of war had been an almost total failure, and, since he had seen Joseph Plunkett in March 1915, his pessimism had greatly increased. The more he saw of the German authorities, the less he liked them, and the more he doubted their willingness to help substantially. At an early stage there had appeared a possibility that the Germans would sent a contingent of officers and men. That idea had been dropped, and a contribution of 200,000 rifles had been cut to 20,000, all of them old things that had been captured on the Russian front. It was, therefore, a deeply dejected and disillusioned Casement that the RIC patrol had picked up on the Kerry coast without a hand being raised either to greet or protect him.

On Easter Saturday the guests in the Under-Secretary's Lodge saw little of their host during daylight hours. He was in the Castle from 10.15 in the morning till 7.15 at night, and half an hour after that he was with the Lord Lieutenant in the Viceregal Lodge. He had learned that morning that a vessel, the *Aud*, disguised as Norwegian, had been stopped off the coast of Kerry and was being brought into Queenstown when it hoisted German colours and sank having been scuttled by the crew. It had been carrying arms for the rising. Nineteen German sailors and three officers had been taken off this ship and imprisoned. Other telegrams from Tralee told how a motor-car had driven into the sea at Killorglin the previous night, drowning all its Sinn Féin occupants, and that two men, Civil Servants, had been arrested at Tralee on a charge of conspiring to land arms, and sent up to Dublin.

All of this Nathan relayed to Birrell in a long letter to which he added that the Irish Volunteers were to have a 'mobilisation' and march out from Dublin on the following day, Easter Sunday. He saw no indications of a rising, however. Nevertheless, he was very much inclined, he said, to 'go for' some places in Dublin where the Sinn Féiners were believed to be manufacturing and storing arms, but some further information in regard to them was necessary. The Lord Lieutenant, when Nathan saw him on that Easter Saturday night, was all for action against the Irish organisations; no time should be lost in arresting and interning their Dublin leaders. Nothing was done in that regard, however, and Nathan returned to the Lodge, had his dinner, and talked for a while with Estelle Nathan and Dorothy before going to bed.

At six o'clock next morning, Easter Sunday morning, a message was brought to him to the effect that one of the men who had landed with Casement had been captured. His name was Daniel Bailey; he belonged to the Royal Irish Rifles and to the German Irish Brigade, and he had come to Ireland in a submarine for the general rising that was planned for Easter Sunday. But it was drawn to Nathan's notice that there was an announcement that morning from Eoin MacNeill in the *Sunday Independent* countermanding the parades and manoeuvres arranged for that day, and obviously intended to provide cover for the Rising. That surely was confirmation that there would now be no such eventuality.

Nathan was in his office in Dublin Castle by nine-thirty and an hour later he called on the Viceroy, who was pressing for urgent action against the Sinn Féin leaders. Having countermanded their Easter Day parade they were now, he suggested, 'sitting in conclave conspiring against us', which turned out to be the exact truth. Nathan still hesitated over arrests, but finally gave a qualified consent and sent Birrell a cypher telegram which, however, did not reach him until the next day (Easter Monday). This told of Bailey's arrest and asked for authority to proceed to arrest and intern the leaders, subject to the concurrence of the law officers, the military authorities, and the Home Office.

Nathan and his sister-in-law had a lunch appointment that day with Sir Horace Plunkett in Kilteragh, his place in Foxrock, and the party, which included Lord and Lady Fingal, were excited, but reassured by Nathan's account of what had been going on. They could all now go to the races at Fairyhouse on Easter Monday as had been the practice for generations, and Lady Fingal would take Estelle Nathan to see the show at the Abbey. Back in the Lodge, Sir Matthew relaxed until six o'clock and then went over to the Viceregal to discuss with His Excellency and senior army officers arrangements for a raid on Liberty Hall, the headquarters of James Connolly's Citizen Army, which they feared would be opposed in arms. A further, enlarged, conference was fixed for ten o'clock that night; and Nathan in the meantime ate his dinner and watched a play the Nathan girls put on.

The Military Council had estimated that they controlled about 3,000 Volunteers in Dublin and 13,000 in the Provinces, in addition to the Citizen Army's 200 whose action would be confined to Dublin only. They also believed that they had a firm arrangement that the Germans would land a considerable quantity of arms in Kerry on a date which was also believed to have been agreed. They hoped to confront MacNeill with an irresistible situation.

In September 1915, when MacNeill's suspicions were first aroused that something serious was being planned within the Volunteer Executive, he had reacted in a fashion which discomfited the planners. He had it accepted that, apart from matters of routine, no order would be issued to the Volunteer body without his counter-signature, and within the Executive it was known, of course, that the only circumstances in which he was likely to call out the Volunteers was a move by the government to disarm them or to impose conscription.

During Holy Week 1916, the Dublin Brigade of Volunteers were given orders to mobilise on Easter Sunday for a march-out, and the Military Council of the IRB put into circulation an alleged Castle Document that purported to show that the government was about to disarm the Volunteers. MacNeill was at first convinced that the document was genuine, and issued a general instruction that any attempt to take arms from the Volunteers was to be resisted. Later, however, as news reached him of the frustrated landing of arms from Germany, of Casement's arrest, and that a mission to Limerick to make contact with the Germans was said to have his approval when it had not, he recognised that the so-called Castle Document was bogus, that its real purpose was to commit him to a Rising for which the mobilisation on Easter Sunday provided the cover. He naturally reacted angrily and decisively. He confronted Pearse, wrung from him an admission that a rising was intended, and then told him that he would do everything in his power, short of informing the government, to prevent it. He wrote out orders instructing Hobson and J. J. O'Connell to take complete charge of Dublin and Cork respectively, and to prevent the Volunteers being drawn into an offensive against the government, and he dispatched messengers to the country cancelling any previous orders they had received. He also had a notice to the same effect inserted in Easter Sunday's *Sunday Independent*. That would have disposed of the planned *coup d'état*, one would have thought, but the Military Council were still intent on going ahead. They, therefore, simply accepted MacNeill's countermand as applying to 'the manoeuvres' of Easter Sunday, and decided to rise the next day.

'When I arrived at Liberty Hall about 10 a.m. on Easter Monday', said William O'Brien, 'all was hustle and excitement. Large numbers of Volunteers and Citizen Army men were continually passing in and out. Quantities of ammunition boxes were being taken out of the premises and loaded into cars and trucks. Shortly before noon, Connolly came down the stairs and spoke to us on the landing. Putting his head close to mine, and dropping his voice he said, "We are going out to be slaughtered." "Is there no chance of success?" I said, and he replied "None whatever"' (*Labour in Easter Week* 21).

The change affected the mobilisation considerably, of course. In Dublin about a third or a fifth of the force that had been available on the Sunday responded to the call-out on the Monday, and apart from a couple of isolated places in the country there was no rising outside Dublin. On Easter Monday at noon a number of prominent buildings were occupied in the city, and one of these, the General Post Office in the city centre, became the headquarters of Patrick Pearse as President of a Provisional Government of an Irish Republic and Commander in Chief of the Republic's Army, and of James Connolly who was effectively in charge of the fight in his capacity as a Divisional Commandant General. In the mixed force under his command in the GPO itself, he had about one-half of the Citizen Army; the other half he had divided up to assail Dublin Castle, where Nathan got his first taste of an Irish rebellion, and to occupy Stephen's Green.

Half a century later, Liam Ó Briain told how, returning from issuing MacNeill's countermand in the country, he and Harry Nicholls, one of the trio who earlier had sponsored Church of Ireland services in Irish, were attracted to one of the barricaded gates in the Green, and found a Citizen Army Officer haranguing a group of inquisitive people who had become aware that, inside, men, some of them in uniform, were digging trenches at a furious rate. 'If yiz are any bloody good, come in here and fight for Ireland', he was saying. And when Ó Briain and Nicholls told him they were Volunteers, but did not known in the confusion over the countermand where their units were, he looked doubtfully at them, and then insisted they should join him. 'Won't this place do you to fight as well as any other?' he asked. The appeal was irresistible. They climbed over the railings and joined in. By the end of the week Ó Briain, a future University Professor of Romance Languages, had been promoted to the exalted rank of corporal in the Citizen Army (Ó Briain: *Cuimhní Cinn*). 'There I was among the Citizen Army crowd, whom I didn't know, except one of the women. She got me a shotgun and a pocketful of cartridges. I'd never fired a shotgun in my life before.' He found himself under the Countess Markievicz, the Second-in-Command in the Green. 'She was dressed in the Citizen Army green, which was a darker shade to the Volunteer green — a sort of South African style shirt with knee breeches and bootees all in green, and a slouch hat and a big revolver which used to be called the Peter the Painter. She could use it too — she was supposed to be a dead shot. She was not there as a woman, she was there as a combatant. The men all worshipped her. They all remembered what she'd done during the strike three years previously when she'd been washing and cooking and bringing swarms of children home to her house — so much so that her husband, poor old Count Markievicz, used to say, 'I can't get into my own house. She said to me "Go away, there's no room for you here to-night. Go somewhere else." Oh, the Countess was really a great one' (Rodgers, 222-3).

On Easter Monday morning Sir Matthew told his guests that he would have to go down and work at the Castle, and Mrs Nathan walked as far as the Vicregal Lodge with him. When he got to his office Nathan conferred at length with Major Ivon Price, the Military Intelligence Officer, about the action that was contemplated. He then asked A. H. Norway, the Secretary of the Post Office, to come to the Castle. Norway left the GPO immediately and reached the Castle shortly before 12, and Nathan was explaining to him that he wanted steps taken to refuse the use of the telephone and telegraph service over large areas of the south of Ireland for all but military and naval use, when a volley of musketry crashed out beneath the window. Price rushed over and shouted to somebody below, and then ran down into the Upper Yard. There he saw something he did not believe could happen without a hint of it at least being given to him beforehand by the Intelligence Service he headed. Men in green Citizen Army uniforms were dashing about the yard, and the policeman at the gate lay dead in a pool of blood. A sentry who had fired a warning shot was racing to safety while Citizen Army men, jumping over the dead policeman, entered the guard-room and tied up the soldiers inside with their own puttees. Major Price, expecting to see a couple of hundred soldiers coming instantly to deal with the situation, fired a few shots from his revolver, but no soldiers came, for the good reason that on duty that morning there was only a corporal's guard of ten men. The Castle was wholly at the mercy of the attackers. Twenty determined men, and there were more than that number of Citizen Army around, could have taken it, Under Secretary, and all. But the attack was not pressed home; the gates were somehow closed from within, and Price got to a telephone and alerted Military Headquarters. Nathan had the armoury broken open in the hope of arming the handful of constables that were inside the Castle perimeter, but, while some revolvers were found, there were no cartridges for them.

So Nathan was left isolated within the Castle walls, wondering what would happen next. It was apparently no part of the insurgents' plan to capture the Castle. Their surprisingly poor intelligence had assumed that this, the centre of government, was impregnable, and they contented themselves with an effort to restrict movement in and out of the Castle by rifle-fire from the City Hall and other high buildings in the vicinity. This was undoubtedly the biggest miss in the whole Rising. To have held the Castle even for a short while would have been the most prestigeous victory for the insurgents, and for the British a great disaster. Nathan could see this, but for the moment he concentrated on sending out as many messages as he could and hoped and prayed that help would not be unduly delayed.

Meanwhile, having left Sir Matthew at the Park gate, Mrs Nathan returned to the Lodge and, taking Dorothy and the children with her, walked over to the Furry Glen and spent the morning there in the delightful sun. They got back at 1.15 and were sitting at lunch when Captain Maitland, one of the ADCs, phoned from the Viceregal and said 'The Sinn Féiners are out. They have surrounded the Castle and tried to rush it, but the police managed to close the gates on them. Sir Matthew is quite safe, but telephone connections from the Castle are possibly cut off.' They were all to stay put.

A little earlier Douglas Hyde, bicycling back along the Green, heard, as he thought, a sequence of what sounded like motor tyre bursts, and said to himself that 'there must be great mortality among tyres to-day'. He cycled past the Shelbourne Hotel and saw, what he found curious, the large gate of the Green closed. Then he saw a man inside the gate running with his hat off and discharging shots, apparently into the ground, and two or three gardiners walking stolidly away with their tools. To find out what was wrong, Hyde went over to a young fellow who was carrying a rifle at the gate and asked him what was 'up'. He got a short angry answer. 'What's that got to do with you?' And a bold-looking girl of about six-teen, beside him, with a bandolier or water bottle slung across her shoulder, hissed out the same question and looked as if she would have liked to kill Hyde. At that moment someone called 'Stand back!' and the big gate was opened to admit a motor van driven by a single man, probably the first motor that ever entered the Green. Hyde could not see what it contained but he noticed a rifle or two in it. The young fellow to whom he had first spoken, lean and shabbily dress-ed, with a plain belt round his waist, grime on his face, and the look of having come from the city slums, drew back and slowly and significantly threw open the breach of his rifle which seemed much too big and heavy for him, inserted a cartridge, half brought the gun to the present, and pointed it in Hyde's direction, while the young girl in the most business-like way sprang to the gate, closed it behind her, and walked off through Leeson Street in the most nonchalant manner accompanied by a second young fellow about her own age who took her arm. 'I now perceived', Hyde said, 'a couple of men at each side of the gate hard at work in their shirt sleeves digging two holes. I wondered to myself, "Are those fools thinking to hide something?" I afterwards found out they had started in to make trenches, which trenches I was told three days later were so shallow that they must have been nearly useless for defence, three feet at the most. I cycled back from the gate on my way home to Earlsfort Terrace past University College. . .'.

'Next morning, Tuesday, I got up', said Hyde, 'before the rest of the household and walked down Earlsfort Terrace to the corner of Stephen's Green to see if it had been evacuated during the night as I felt perfectly certain it must have been, for it appeared to me to be a place impossible to defend for any length of time.' He explored the area as far as Nassau Street and Trinity College by a most circuitous route and was told by someone he met on the way, authoritatively, that this rising had taken place over the head of John MacNeill and against his express orders and wishes. The O'Rahilly had stood out with MacNeill and, he heard later, to his great surprise, Bulmer Hobson also. Then despite MacNeill's countermand the Volunteers had been ordered out for Easter Monday, this action on the part of Connolly, Pearse, Plunkett and others probably precipitated by the disclosure and publication of the secret order sanctioned by the Irish Office, foreshadowing wholesale arrests and something like martial law in Dublin. 'This secret order', said Hyde, 'had been sent to me Wednesday 19th April. It so happened that that very evening I was dining with Mr Stopford, brother of Mrs Green the historian, and met Sir Matthew Nathan there. I showed Mr Stopford the document but he did not believe in its genuineness and to tell the truth neither did I. Neither of us alluded to it when talking to Sir Matthew Nathan. In view of the subsequent events it is quite obvious that the document was a genuine one, and that the military officers were preparing to meet some such conspiracy as that which was carried out on Monday.... I imagine that what may have happened was this, that Connolly called out his own Citizen Army, that the Countess Markievicz threw in her boy scouts, that Pearse, Clarke, Sean MacDermott, Thomas MacDonagh, Eamon Kent and Plunkett brought in with them their own followers and all those they could persuade.... The account, if it is true, of John MacNeill's disassociating himself from the extremists would seem to be borne out by what my friend [R.A.S.] MacAlister told me a day or two later. This was that he had gone to MacNeill's house in Rathfarnham about 4 o'clock on Saturday afternoon with some proof sheets of the *Leabhar Gabhála* on which they were jointly working, that he had tea there, and that MacNeill chatted and smoked and talked literature in the freest and most natural manner possible. He told me that it would have been utterly impossible for MacNeill if he had any great decision on his mind to have acted and chatted so easily and interestingly. But as he was going away at about 6.15 three young men drove up in a motor car perhaps to inform him of the machinations that were going on behind his back. . .'.

When word reached GHQ of the attack on the Castle, and

another message from the small guard in the instrument room in the GPO that that building was being swamped by insurgents, steps were taken with great promptitude to reinforce the Castle guard, to safeguard the Viceregal Lodge, and to ensure possession of the Magazine Fort in the Phoenix Park which a party of senior Fianna boys had taken but failed to destroy. This was done out of the force of less than 2,500 troops, most of them Irish, available for action in Dublin. A picket of 100 men of the Royal Irish Regiment was ordered to the Castle from Richmond Barracks, and had proceeded as far as the South Dublin Union when they were fired on. The main body following up cleared the area, however. That night a contingent from Portobello Barracks drove a Citizen Army outpost from Portobello Bridge and, with some of those from Richmond Barracks, succeeded in putting about 300 men into the Castle. Trinity College, which was nearer to the GPO on the south side of the Liffey, was also secured, the small garrison there from the University Officers Training Corps being augmented by late arrivals. The Commander in Chief of the Home Forces, Lord French, and Birrell, the Chief Secretary, both of them in London, had meanwhile been informed, and by Monday night the transport of reinforcements from Liverpool was arranged to supplement those from within Ireland that were already on the way to Dublin. A column of 1,600 men from the Curragh was called up by telephone at 12.30 p.m. — that was within half an hour of the attack on the Castle — and the first of the trains sent to transport it was back in Kingsbridge terminus within two hours, having deposited the entire body in the city by 5.30. That evening 150 men arrived at Amiens Street railway terminus from Belfast; a battalion of the Royal Dublin Fusiliers arrived at Kingsbridge from Templemore, Co. Tipperary, and some artillery from Athlone. Thus by nightfall, the military position on the south side of the city, including the electricity generating station at the Pigeon House, the telephone exchange in Crown alley and the Customs House, and the port of Dun Laoghaire, had been considerably strengthened. On the north side, too, the area of the docks and Amiens Street Railway Station were secure.

Among people caught up in the Rising was a man whom Dorothy Stopford was in time to marry. This was William George Price — Willie Price to his family and close friends and, like Dorothy, Anglo-Irish, Protestant and pro-British, which he showed by working in Cork with the Army Pay Corps. His home was in Leeson Street, a few steps from Stephen's Green, and he was there at Easter when 'this extraordinary business', as he termed it, started. He had seen Volunteers in the streets on the Monday morning but that was so ordinary a sight that he thought nothing of it. He went walking with his sisters over the Dublin Hills and got back to the city suburbs in the evening to find to his annoyance that there were no trams. The Sinn Féiners, he was told, were 'out'. He had to walk home, and there he learned of an attack on the Veterans Corps, the GRs, popularly known as the Gorgeous Wrecks, on their way back to Beggars Bush Barracks from a route march, and that the Irish Citizen Army were digging trenches in the Green.

After dinner he went to see his friend Diarmuid Coffey, who, as secretary to Colonel Maurice Moore, the Inspector General of the National Volunteers, would know something, he thought. In fact he knew nothing, but he confirmed that the events of the day had left him astounded and very worried. Price himself was obviously worked up, especially on account of the killing and wounding of the unarmed GRs, and he told Coffey that he hoped troops would soon come along to 'cut down' the rebels. Coffey hoped that would not happen, and he didn't think it would; but his own situation, he felt, was going to be at risk, for the police would probably arrest him, not knowing the difference between National and Irish Volunteers. He had been down to the Green, and had witnessed an extraordinary sight. All kinds of people, among them well-dressed old ladies, were walking about, none of them turning a hair at the shots that came from within the Green. He had seen the Countess Markievicz in uniform, and also the pacifist Sheehy Skeffington who was trying to stop the fighting that seemed now unstoppable.

The problem for Price next morning was how to get back to his job in Cork. Would the trains be running? Nobody could tell him, so he had to go to Kingsbridge and find out for himself. He set off on foot, and, avoiding Stephen's Green and the area around Jacob's the biscuit factory which was also occupied by the Sinn Féin rebels, he got to the South Quays and passed the Four Courts, on the opposite side of the Liffey, which were also held, he was told, by the Sinn Féiners. When he reached Kingsbridge he found a contingent of Lancers outside the station, but no trains were running, and he could do nothing but face home again. This time, being both inquisitive and courageous, he chose a somewhat different route. In Meath Street he saw a Major B. he knew. He was with a Colonel Wingfield and, in mufti, they were making for Kingsbridge on their bikes. He told them what the situation was there, so the three of them decided to go to Dublin Castle 'to get orders'. From Thomas Street onwards they encountered soldiers, some of them laying telephone wires. They were stopped now and again but, on the strength of Colonel Wingfield's pass, they were able to proceed down Lord Edward Street and into the Palace Yard. There were men standing at the *Daily Express* building who denied that it had ever been in the hands of the Volunteers as had been said. Across the gate of the Castle, in Castle Street, iron sheets had been placed, and sentries stood behind the loopholes. The soldiers were very cautious about opening the gate, but Colonel Wingfield and Major B. were admitted as officers, and the Major vouched for Price. Inside, a number of officers were standing in doorways or moving cautiously about. An officer guided Price through the Lower Castle Yard to the Command Paymaster's Office outside which some 150 soldiers were lying about. There was a guard at the Ship Street gate, and sniping was going on all the time from surrounding buildings. Price discussed his position in the Paymaster's Office with an officer he knew, and was advised for the time being to do nothing except arm himself with a pass authorising him to travel to Cork whenever he could find transport. In the Garrison Adjutant's office to which he was directed he was given two passes, one for the journey to Cork, the other simply to take him out of the Castle precinct. As he waited for these, he overheard the Adjutant arranging for the immediate despatch somewhere of 250 troops with one machine gun, and he saw another officer poring over a map of Dublin.

He picked up Colonel Wingfield outside and made his way with him towards the Palace Yard Gate. The sniping was continuing, so crossing the yard they separated in case they should be fired at. They got out alright. In the street a newsboy was crying *Irish Times*. He bought a copy but there was nothing in it but a Proclamation from Baron Wimborne, the Lord Lieutenant-General and Governor General. It said that an attempt, instigated and designed by the foreign enemies of King and Country, to incite rebellion in Ireland and endanger the safety of the United Kingdom, had been made in the city by a small reckless body of men. The sternest measures were being taken to suppress them and restore order, and all law-abiding citizens were enjoined to refrain from any acts or conduct which might interfere with the actions of the Crown. They went down Dame Street together but parted company at Trinity College, Price turning up Grafton Street and into Nassau Street, where he met Charles Bewley, an Anglo-Irish convert to both nationalism and Catholicism, who spoke about what was happening more or less as Diarmuid Coffey had done. It was a bad day for the Irish cause; he had seen a copy of the Proclamation of the Irish Republic signed by T. J. Clarke, a small tobacconist and newsagent from Parnell Street 'who was very good for country papers' — he had often bought papers from him — Connolly, the Labour man, Sean MacDermott, the editor — Price thought of *Nationality* — and Joseph Plunkett, a son of Count Plunkett's.

Price being aware that Bewley knew a good many fairly extreme men, asked him if he had had any hint of what was going to occur. Bewley said that he had been going over in his mind all he had heard in the previous few days; the only hint came from a man who, at St Andrew's Church on Sunday after Mass, said that there was going to be a big thing on tomorrow (Monday), and that they were all going to make their wills. He had taken this as 'cod'. On Good Friday he had been out with MacDermott who talked a lot about what the Volunteers would do if conscription came, but gave no hint of what had now taken place; maybe he did not know then. Price continued the walk home and, finding a fruit shop open, bought some fruit. He avoided the Green where the rebels seemed to be in an absolute trap. The firing was intense, a lot of it coming from the military who were on the top of the Shelbourne Hotel overlooking the Green.

On Wednesday morning the first thing he learned was that the Green had been vacated, so with one of his sisters he went down and, finding a small gate near the Russell Hotel unlocked, went in. There in the trenches were rugs and cushions evidently taken from motor cars that formed part of a barricade the rebels had set up on the public roadway. He saw a rifle, a belt and a pouch on the ground and took away the belt and the pouch under his coat. He was looking at the rifle when 'a shot was fired just above us. We rushed over to the gate which would not open, but it was only stiff and had stuck, so we pulled it open and went out. Anyhow I couldn't have taken the rifle. I might have been shot carrying it. Besides if I had got it home, a Volunteer rifle would have been a bad thing to have in the house, as when this thing is finished with, the military will probably search houses for arms.'

Getting a loan of a bike, Price rode over to Kingsbridge and was taken by an armed sentry to the Railway Transport Officer who looked at the pass and said that he might join a train that was standing in a siding and which might go at any moment. But having no luggage, and thinking of the bike which was not his, Price explained that he had only come to make enquiries. Then crossing over the bridge to the North Quays and up Arbour Hill to Manor Street and the North Circular Road, he worked his way to the Mater Hospital and Dorset Street where he saw soldiers being concentrated in big numbers for a move in the direction of the city centre.

His Easter week notes end there. He had learned two things of importance. The rising was limited to isolated areas of the city, and it had not the support of the Catholic and nationalist population. The vacating of the Green had taken place on Tuesday morning. At a quarter past two that morning 100 British military and a machine gun unit that had come up from the Curragh left the Lower Castle Yard and, like Price, were able to make their way through Dame Street, Nassau Street, and Kildare Street to the Shelbourne Hotel. The hotel was occupied, as was the United Service Club, which was also on the north side of the Green. At dawn the Citizen Army men who had spent the night in the Green were surprised by machine gun fire from the hotel and the club, and by 7 o'clock they had been forced to retire into the College of Surgeons where for the duration of the Rising they were unable to influence the course of events in any effective way. The City Hall and buildings in Parliament Street that threatened the Upper Castle area were likewise cleared on Tuesday. Indeed the occupation of buildings without any control of the surrounding areas was the major defect of the insurgents' revolutionary plan.

Hyde mentioned on Wednesday that they had now been three days without the papers or news of any kind except for a miserable edition of the *Irish Times* that cost 2d. That evening he went over to the Coffeys in Harcourt Terrace and met 'the young chap', Willie Price, whom we have recently met. 'He had been all over the city', said Hyde, 'in his endeavours to get back to his Paymaster's job in Cork. He had passed the Post Office which was still in the hands of the Volunteers and apparently strongly fortified. He had gone through Henry Street where there were more people than on ordinary days; all of them seemed to be carrying off something they had looted. He had also been in the Castle. There was no danger to civilians, and he, himself, was in mufti.

On Thursday Hyde had another peep at the Stephen's Green area. A horse that had been killed on the Monday was still lying on the road. The front of the Shelbourne was deserted, but there were some officers in uniform and well-dressed ladies looking out of the side window in Kildare Street. Probably they had no mufti, he surmised, and were afraid to show themselves in khaki. He met two senior civil servants, Bonaparte Wyse of Education and Bailey of the Land Commission, who had motored back 160 miles on hearing of the Rising. He also met a dentist he knew in Harcourt Street who asked him very belligerently, 'How much are you responsible for this?' Hyde asked him, 'How much are you?'

He muttered something about putting a bayonet into me. I should have answered, 'Your forceps you mean', but didn't. He then said something about changing mighty quick the professors of the National University. His bitterness was easily accounted for when I heard that his own son was a student of that University, and I believe rather prominent in some of the College societies, and was taking part in the fighting on the side of the Volunteers. His father had turned him out of the house for his Sinn Féin proclivities, but had made his other son enlist in the Army. This other son was shot in Flanders along with one of Count Plunkett's sons, both of them officers. It is curious that Count Plunkett also is said to have three sons fighting among the Volunteers. I suppose on account of Duffy's son being in the National University, and John MacNeill a professor in it, and MacDonagh an assistant lecturer that he must have confounded the University teaching Sinn Féin propaganda. I felt very sorry for him in spite of his impudence when I remembered afterwards what must have been the cause. Two days after my encounter with him, he lost his father too, killed on the street by a stray bullet.

That some tempers were running high over the Rising was reflected that day when the archaeologist McAlister told Hyde he was never so pleased to see him before as when he saved him from a tremendous attack from a man he was talking to, because he had said with perfect truth that the whole business could be ultimately traced back to Carson who was the real cause of it, as he first 'ran' rifles and started volunteers and then threatened the government.

If Willie Price's thoughts on Tuesday morning were to get down to Cork to his job, Dorothy Stopford's, when she woke up that morning, were on her 9 o'clock lecture in Trinity or, if she could not make that, to be in the Biology Lab at 10 where she had something to do. There was still no post and no papers; but Sir Matthew was on the phone early to say things were a bit better. Three officers of the Royal Irish Rifles had been killed, however, and so far not one on the Sinn Féin side. The morning dragged on, for Mrs Nathan would not hear of Dorothy going into town, but after lunch she went for a walk in the opposite direction with Maude, and posted some letters at the Castleknock Gate. Surely the old reliable Post Office would see that they were collected and delivered; no Rising could prevent that. On their way back, to their horror they saw in the distance five men, drawn across the road, signalling with a white flag, but when they turned their glasses on them they saw they were not Sinn Féiners, but a group of road workers just talking to a lady in a white jersey. That night as the gas pressure was low they were almost in the dark and had to fall back on candles. Dorothy went up to her room at about eleven, and went asleep to the sound of guns. It was a rather jumpy night; with rumours of German landings.

Pamela Nathan roused Dorothy at 7.15 on Wednesday morning, coming into her bed with her twelve toy animals. Guns were sounding all the time. There was still no post or papers. After breakfast Mrs Nathan rang up Sir Matthew. He said very little and seemed much occupied. They might go into the Phoenix Park on the north side, he said, but on no account to go down to the town. Stephen's Green had been retaken. After lunch Dorothy walked alone into Castle-knock to find if there were any posts going out. She met a woman in the Park who was obviously very nervous. She had a business in a street just behind the Four Courts. On Monday the Volunteers had just walked in there, and asked the char the way to Judge Kenny's room. She told them they could find it themselves whereupon they gave her half an hour to clear out. She flew. They were well armed, and she doubted if they could be dislodged. Her husband thought it was the American note which had brought things to a head. All the Sinn Féiners from her part of the world were corner-boys and ne'er-do-wells. Most of them had joined after the Bachelor's Walk affair. She had heard that the military were behaving with great leniency.

As Dorothy came back the firing got louder and more incessant, and a terrific bang caused them all to jump. Something had blown up. They began to make plans about where to go if bullets reached the Lodge. They decided they could easily get away by the north gate in the car and go out in the direction of Lucan. At 5.45 there was another tremendous bang, and Mrs Nathan phoned Sir Matthew to find out what it was. They learned later from the aide-de-camp, Lord Basil

Blackwood, that a shrapnel shell which was badly aimed fell into the Viceregal garden, but did no harm. This was the result of raw troops who lost their heads: it was nothing serious, nothing to do with Sinn Féin. About 10, Sir Matthew himself rang up. Things were troublesome, perhaps that was hardly a strong enough word, he said. It was a kind of Sydney Street business. Each house would have to be emptied of its occupants; there would, therefore, be awful destruction. Fresh troops were arriving from England. It looked like a long business and a terrible one. Casualties were heavy for ordinary times, but not in comparison to what they were used to. He had got through to Mrs Nathan's husband at the War Office each day. He himself hoped to get to bed that night; he had only lain down for a short while the night before.

Dorothy found things quieter that night but there was still occasional firing. It was awful being mewed up there in the Park, but 'they have a fit if I suggest going to Dublin to do something'. A Mrs Bell Irving rang up from the Chief Secretary's Lodge. Because she was such a good cook, she said, she didn't mind living in isolation. If the rebels came she, being also such a good linguist, intended to go out to talk to them in their native language while her daughter and the children escaped by the back door. In case they came that night she was packing her little week-end case which would just hold her spare wig and false teeth and, *comme toujours*, she would be very ladylike and not forget her *robe de chambre*.

Maurice Headlam, who represented the Treasury in Dublin, managed to get past the sentry at the Lower Castle Yard without difficulty on the Wednesday and went to his office. 'It was bright sunlight and a lot of soldiers were sitting, smoking peacefully, with their rifles against the wall. Occasional bullets whizzed over their heads, but no one seemed to be replying to the fire. My office-keeper told me that the Under Secretary [Nathan] was in the stable block, the buildings against which the soldiers were sitting, under cover from the fire from Jacob's Biscuit Factory. I went to the door and asked for the Under Secretary whom I found busily writing, as usual, and quite calm. He gave me no information about the origin of the outbreak, said reinforcements were on the way, and it would soon be over, but that there would be no possibility of work for a day or two. I gave him letters for England and asked him to put them in the official bag, which he said was going as usual' (Headlam, 167).

Sir Horace Plunkett also succeeded in reaching Nathan that day. He had come over from England with the intention of spending a quiet week-end at Kilteragh, his house in Foxrock, and on Easter Sunday had entertained the Provost of Trinity to lunch. He had not been to church and told Mahaffy why. He no longer believed in the dogmas of the Church of Ireland and, perhaps to his surprise or perhaps not, heard Mahaffy say that he did not either, but that there were other reasons in his case for going through the formalities. Next day, Easter Monday, was for Plunkett 'a black day, a *dies irae*'. His view of the Irish situation at the beginning of April had been that Birrell was continuing to treat his most exacting office as a sinecure, with the result that the country was utterly out of hand. The forces labelled Sinn Féin were becoming formidable. Now, Birrell had a rebellion on his hands, and there was his Under Secretary Nathan in the Master of the Horse's house in the Castle, trying to carry on the government of Ireland, and surrounded by a queer lot of police and military officers. Plunkett recorded:

> I drove my little motor to the Castle via Nassau and Dame Street. Dame Street from South St George's Street was deserted, the military at the Castle and the City Hall, whence they have ejected the rebels, firing at the houses occupied by the enemy' on the other side. I went into the Castle, which I had some difficulty in getting the guard to let me enter. J. H. Campbell, now Attorney General [whom he apparently met], was for the 'thorough', and told me he was going to ask a lot of awkward questions about the management of the business by the authorities at the proper time. General Friend, GOC was in England when the trouble began on Monday. (His *locum tenens* was an ass and a Christian Scientist). I learned that there was no 'Rising' elsewhere than in Dublin, that the rebellion was organised and led by Sir Roger Casement, whom the Govern-

ment had captured. I had gone to the Castle to get a cypher telegram through to Arthur Balfour, the first Lord of the Admiralty, telling him I thought it important to let the American people know of the German origin of the Irish trouble. I changed my cable to definite advice to give the capture of Casement as a piece of "exclusive news" to the American press representatives so as to ensure their co-operation.

In his diary next day Plunkett wrote: 'I went to-day to the Castle, where I spent 5 or 6 hours at Nathan's office. He showed me the official file recording the landing of Sir Roger Casement from Germany on the Kerry coast, his capture and removal to the Tower where he confessed his identity, and deplored the way this poor dupe had been duped by the Germans.

All day the Irish Volunteers held their own, and demonstrated the enormous difficulty of dealing with an enemy in your own city. . .' On the Friday he wrote that 'a large military force has gradually been got together, and the city is gradually getting under control. There will be hard, very hard work before the desperate men (those who will be shot or imprisoned for life), surrender unconditionally, as they must. How much of Dublin may be destroyed Heaven knows' (Digby, 209-11).

As the end was coming in view, a group of National Volunteers sympathetic to the insurgents suggested on Thursday that an attempt should be made to ensure that terms of surrender would be offered them. Their first step towards this was to ask the Lord Mayor of Dublin, J. M. Gallagher, to lead a deputation of citizens to the Lord Lieutenant or General Friend. Those who came to the Mansion House with the request were two members of the National Committee, Captain the Honourable Fitzroy Hemphill and J. D. Nugent, with J. A. Ronayne, and Majors Cullen and Crean. The Lord Mayor told the deputation that he had no power to intervene, the civil law having been suspended; that if the deputation of citizens was received at all, they would be unsuccessful; that, in any case, he was not favourable to the whole idea. Nevertheless he would join the deputation if it was to be received.

By now some telephones at least were working, and a call was put through to Sir Matthew Nathan at the Castle, to ask if the deputation would be received by him, by the Lord Lieutenant, or by General Friend whom they assumed was still in command of the Army; and a second unsuccessful effort was made to get into communication with the house of the Catholic Archbishop. Before the party left the Mansion House, the Lady Mayoress joined the gathering and said that she hoped that no guarantee would be given to the Sinn Féiners, and that they would be wiped out to the last man. Contact was made by telephone with Mr Redmond's secretary, T. J. Hanna, but he was not at all in favour of what was contemplated. In his opinion, no sane man would object to the government taking the severest measure against the Sinn Féiners. Later, while waiting for a reply from Sir Matthew Nathan, the Lord Mayor, who had been into the Castle on other business, said that he now took upon himself the responsibility of refusing to accompany the delegation. Nathan's call back came through shortly afterwards. He had consulted Lord Wimborne, the Lord Lieutenant; he had decided not to interfere with the Military Authority. That effectively ended the matter. A subsequent effort to summon the National Committee of the National Volunteers to discuss the situation also failed (Memo. by Thomas J. Cullen, 29 April 1916).

Dorothy Stopford was still waiting for a post on Thursday (27 April), but there was none. Sir Matthew rang up and had a long talk with Mrs Nathan. Birrell had arrived the night before on a torpedo boat and was now in the Castle. Things seemed rather better. They had decided on their policy. They would try and spare life, and casualties so far had not been heavy. It was just a matter now of blowing the Sinn Féiners out of the buildings, so a great deal of firing would be heard. They should not worry about their friends in England: nothing special was happening there or in France: and they knew even more than was known here. Mrs Nathan told him about Dorothy's anxiety to get away to some of her relations in Dublin and to be doing something, but Sir Matthew insisted she should stay where she was; there was nothing she could do anyway. 'So', said Dorothy 'stay here I must and fiddle while Rome burns.'

Dorothy had a talk with the under-housemaid. She and one of the others had been as far as Islandbridge and brought back a crop of stories. One of the Sinn Féiners had been caught inside the Viceregal Lodge, working in the garden, and there were women Sinn Féiners about with guns. The fighting was said to be terrible in Baggot Street, Rathmines and Ballsbridge. In all cases the Sinn Féiners had ensconced themselves in houses and fired perpetually into the street.

Before she turned in Dorothy wrote:

10.30 p.m. The night is very still but there is a tremendous angry red sky, a great blaze somewhere. A wonderful and awful sight. I have never seen such a blaze. What can it be?

Friday, 28 April. Mrs Nathan started us all off writing a paper called *The Feinick Spark*. She is splendid at keeping the children occupied.

Sir Matthew rang up at about 10 o'c. He has got a very bad cold and asked for a suit-case which one of the ADC's is to call and take down to him. The fighting now is all sniping by the Sinn Féiners from windows, a very difficult warfare for the military. The Sherwood Foresters had lost very heavily, mostly just after they arrived. A Committee was being formed to organise provisions. The military had drawn a cordon round the city and no food was passing either out or in. There is very little in the house here. No milk or butter can be got, and no meat or eggs. Clements, a man on the staff, was to go down to Chapelizod or Lucan to see if he could get anything. Of course, no shops would supply us.

Dorothy was surprised they had lasted out so long, but apparently the servants had been getting things in in a very roundabout way. 'I don't mind about us, of course,' she wrote. 'We shall be all right; but I can't imagine what they are doing in Dublin. No shops open or if people dare not go out of doors, what then?'

The boredom was so appalling that in the afternoon she was reduced to playing with a snail for some hours, making it jump over a gap on a seat. At 6 p.m. Sir Matthew rang up and asked about their food supplies. He told Mrs Nathan that on Monday there had been a Zeppelin raid on England, and several were brought down. Simultaneously the German fleet got out and as far as Lowestoft but were driven back. Dorothy was then hailed to the phone and Sir Matthew apologised for treating them so badly, but 'unforeseen events over which he had no control prevented him from being with us'.

That night Lady Freddy Conyngham and her mother arrived suddenly, driven in from their place in Meath by Maxie Arnott. There had been trouble at their place — Sinn Féiners out and about and they had seen one policeman dead, and three with bandaged heads. There had been trouble too at Ashbourne, so they had got away as quickly as they could. This was the first symptom of trouble in the country, but they thought it was an isolated case. The two refugees would stay the night and try to get to England the next day. They had thrilling and horrid tales of their experiences, but Castle Slane was safe.

Dorothy had a very bad night as the guns were firing heavily until 3 a.m. The fire was still blazing and dying the sky crimson. The news from the Viceregal was that the cook had struck. He refused to cook 'them' food while his wife and children were starving in Dublin. He threw the saucepan at Captain Murray Prentice, the ADC, and went off. The Under Secretary's driver had become extremely nervous, being sure he was a marked man. He had not refused to drive, but would probably not be asked to for fear.

Next morning, Saturday, arrangements were in train for Lady Freddy and her mother to cross to England. Mrs Nathan was anxious that she and her children should go too, and Sir Matthew, when he came on the phone, said he would try and fix this up. He had got a wire from Dorothy through to her mother. His cold was much better and Dorothy, in an unfortunate phrase, told him that 'he would be able to have a week's holiday soon, his record would be mounting so'. By 10.30, word came that they were all to leave, the others for England, Dorothy to be dropped with her Dickinson relations at Alban Grange, Foxrock. General Friend, the GOC of the Army in Ireland, had gone and his successor, Sir John Maxwell, had arrived with a staff of twelve to take over.

At 4 o'clock as they were preparing to leave the Lodge, Sir Matthew rang up to say that the Sinn Féin leaders had surrenrendered unconditionally. All was over. Dorothy wouldn't have minded staying but couldn't if Mrs Nathan went — the old chaperoning problem. Anyhow it would be rather nice, she thought, to get away from all the elaborate plain-clothes police protection. When she had finished squeezing the necessities of life into a handbag — they could not really take any luggage — she sat down and wrote some letters. She told her mother that she had known for some days that there was trouble in the air, but 'we were kept frightfully in the dark' for 'when the fighting got under way Mrs Nathan was rather anxious to be discreet and I gave in, though I am dying to bike down to see what I could see. But I didn't feel quite my mistress in the Lodge and didn't want to give trouble.' She told 'my dear old boy', her brother Robert, that in the Lodge she was in the dullest, jumpiest, safest place in Dublin because they were CB (confined to barracks), jumpy and safe for the same reason, because they had lancers in the ditch, and myriads of plain clothes police bicycling round them. In a letter to her erstwhile absent host she said.

My dear Sir Matthew,
    We shall have all successfully left by the time you get this.
    I must tell you that Mrs Nathan has been simply *splendid*. I am very glad they have gone as it was rather jumpy for the children. Pam said — 'It's quite easy to be brave, but it is nice getting back in time for Granny's birthday.'
    Thank you for being so awfully nice and careful of us in the middle of all your overwhelming anxieties. Take care of yourself too.
    I am glad every moment I think of you in charge of Ireland now.
    With love from,
    Dorothy.

The car in which Dorothy travelled burst a tyre twice: on the second occasion 'we shed the tyre', she said, 'and went on at snail's pace on the rim, a jolty ride. As we went along, all seemed much as usual, except that no one was at work, every one was standing at their cottage doors and gossiping. . . . At the cross-roads at Dundrum we were challenged by a policeman armed with a rifle. We showed our pass . . . He told us that news of the surrender had just been telephoned through to the barracks, and that the Countess Markievicz had been taken. [Someone had seen her on St Stephen's Green, a cigarette in her mouth, and a pistol in each hand (Pim, 206).] At Monkstown the car sat down finally in the cobbles . . . but I got the ADC's car on the way back from the boat to take me over to Foxrock . . . At Alton Grange I found that Charlie Dickinson had been in Beggars Bush Barracks since Monday after the attack on the Veteran Corps of which he was a member. I heard a lot of news that we had not heard out at the Lodge. The first decent night I've had for a week, out of the sound of guns.'

She went to church next morning (Sunday 30 April) and heard that her Church, the Church of Ireland, had made a formal protest again at this infamous rebellion which caused the people of Ireland to blush with shame . . . 'After lunch Lady Fingall and cousin-in-law Lady Hettie came over, and gave us all the latest, which turned out to be all false reports later.' There had been, allegedly, huge battles in the North Sea in which twenty ships had been sunk, fourteen of them German; and three German vessels were said to have landed in Wicklow. Dorothy was wondering what Lady Fingall now thought of her friend Sir Matthew who was being blamed for the rebellion, but on that subject the talkative Lady Fingall did not say a word. Would she stick to him? Dorothy wondered. An English paper she saw carried a scathing indictment of Birrell, but otherwise little about Ireland, treating the recent disorder as a small thing.

She joined in the search for foodstuffs, and chatted as she went about people's experiences. Her cousin Elsie Henry, who had been in the thick of things, supplying 'bandages etc.', told her that the Sinn Féiners had behaved like gentlemen; they never fired on nurses, nor on women of any sort. Dorothy heard that lectures in Trinity would resume the next week, so she put out of her mind the idea of going over to London to see the family. Trinity had come through the trouble all right. A garrison had been formed with Cyril Dickinson, a brother of Charlie's, among them, and it did splendid work. Some junior sophisters, including four young women, had turned up for a French exam on the Tuesday, but no examiner arrived, and Mahaffy the old Provost went across from his house and took it himself, and then asked the women candidates to lunch.

Dorothy made an effort on Tuesday (2 May) to join a party in Cabinteely that were making bandages, but that work seemed to have come to an end, so she returned to the house in Foxrock and again met Lady Fingall there. 'She told me that Sir Matthew was back at the Lodge. She says she kept on telling him that this would happen. . . . I said I expected a great many people would discover that he had been very blind, *now*; that, personally I had always felt there had been, if anything, too much strictness, and that his policy, even if it had proved a mistake in the light of after-events, was a clear policy, no drift about it, and not weak. It was the policy that did so splendidly in Natal, when it was touch and go. Really I thought she was not half bad about it; she's afraid he'll have to bear much of Birrell's blame; only it may be realised that he was doing what he thought right.

At about 6 o'clock that evening Sir Horace Plunkett's car drove up, and out of it got the conquering hero, Charles Dickinson. He was full of his adventures and the action he had seen. He had got into Beggars Bush Barracks and found it manned by forty decrepit old men of a garrison battalion of the Royal Irish Regiment, all wounded and unfit in some way, and with practically no arms. How he got from there in his GR uniform to Portobello Barracks was amazing. Near Portobello, a lady rushed out of a house saying 'Mr Dickinson, you'll get shot if you go across there in uniform.' She made him put on a voluminous and most unclerical waterproof of hers, and a curate's hat which was hanging up in the hall, and then he started out. Bullets were flying in all directions, and many rifles were levelled at him, but were lowered in time. He arrived somehow at the Barracks but there even his curate's garb could not protect him, and while he stood waiting admission, bullets were rattling around him. Inside, as soon as he was recognised, he was greeted with a cheer. Next day they were reinforced by some Sherwood Foresters, mere lads in training. The Regulars did any sortie work that had to be done while the GRs covered them with rifle fire. Charlie shot a man with his first bullet, and brought home the cartridge as a souvenir. A few days later he went out to the spot, and got the man's cartridge pouch; it was nearly full but the body was gone

Plunkett had got together a Food Committee whose purpose was to deal with the precarious position of areas of Dublin which were cut off from the supplies which normally came in from the country. Driving to his office in Plunkett House on Merrion Square one day — recklessly as usual, and being deaf, unaware of warnings — he was fired on. The glass screen was shattered and a man travelling with him hit through the arm. They held up their hands but the firing continued. One of Plunkett's officials in a following car got out and lay down on the road. 'This was our undoing,' said Plunkett. 'The stupid young soldiers thought he was a rebel going to fire on them from behind the cars, and several of them fired at him while others kept up a fusillade at us. The poor fellow was hit three times, twice in the back. . .'.

By nightfall Dorothy assumed that all resistance was over; she understood that a house-to-house search was to begin on the morrow for fugitives, arms and ammunition. Conversation had turned to the position of Eoin MacNeill. Everyone had a different story. Lady Fingall thought him despicable not having the courage to go forward and leaving his friends at the last to carry on alone, for it was evident he had taken no part in the affair. Some said that he was at his country house at Rathfarnham, the Volunteers having gone beyond his control. Then there was a rumour that, having cancelled all parades on Easter Monday by an order issued on Saturday, he went to the Castle and told them to expect trouble and went to all the priests in Dublin and besought them to preach resistance, and use their influence.

So Dorothy reached Wednesday morning to hear from Charlie Dickinson at breakfast that a man had come over to him at Beggars Bush from Portobello Barracks several days before, and told him that he had been in charge of a firing party, that Sheehy-Skeffington had been courtmartialled and shot. This was an odd business, as she was to learn later, for Skeffington being a pacifist, disapproved of the Rising, and when arrested had been doing something that, as a socialist, he disapproved: protecting private property against being looted. 'He was', said James Stephens, 'the most absurdly courageous man I had ever heard of' (Rodgers, 228). That evening — it had been a blazing day — she bought the Final Buff, the late night evening paper, and read in it that three men who had been involved in the Proclamation of the Republic had been sentenced to death by courtmartial and the sentence carried out that morning. They were Patrick Pearse, Thomas MacDonagh and Edward Daly. She actually got the number of executions incomplete and the order in which they had taken place wrong.

On Thursday there was the first delivery of letters, and she saw a baker's cart for the first time since the Rising. The food supply was nearly normal. That night's paper told of four more executions — Joseph Plunkett, Michael O'Hanrahan, T. J. Clarke and William Pearse — and many penal servitudes, some ten, some five years. The Countess Plunkett, Joseph's mother, was going about Dublin like a demented creature. MacNeill was said to be in his home on parole. The burning question was: how was Sackville Street to be repaired? The people were all saying. 'Ah, our beautiful city, look how the military have it destroyed. The English will have to pay for this.'

On Friday (5 May) she noted the execution of John MacBride and the resignation of Sir Matthew. MacBride had somehow joined the Rising on Easter Monday and, doubtless because of his experience in the Boer War, was appointed second in command to Thomas MacDonagh in Jacob's biscuit factory. It was an easily defended position but, apart from sending long-distance fusillades over the roofs into Dublin Castle, it was useless as a position to attack from. Indeed, the garrison was bottled up for the whole of Easter Week, unaware of what was happening even in Dublin. That MacBride was executed in such circumstances was extraordinary, unless it was an act of revenge for his past record (Hayes in *U.C.D. and 1916*, 44).

On Saturday Dorothy got a tram to Leeson Street Bridge and walked through Merrion Square to the back gate of Trinity. There were barricades still up in some of the streets, and sand bags; and sentries at every corner who took no notice of women while men were frequently asked to produce their passes. She heard a lot about the defence of the College by a complex force under Mr Luce, a parson who was home on leave. Having no hope of holding the park area, they concentrated on the front buildings and Botany Bay. Snipers were posted on the roof. Every day more members of the OTC poured in to sustain the garrison, while a regiment arrived to fire big guns at the Bank in Westland Row. Three of the Regulars were killed and were buried in the grounds. The best officer was Captain Ernest Henry Alton, a quiet little middle-aged man who had conducted Dorothy's last Latin examination: he took command splendidly.

After lunch Dorothy determined to go out to the Under Secretary's Lodge to fetch away her luggage. She got a cab and drove out. She saw on the way two of the 'armoured motors' which had been rigged up in eight hours at the Inchicore works; wonderful things of gigantic proportions with loopholes for rifles. At the Lodge she found the maids all nearly in tears at Sir Matthew's departure. He had left for England the night before. He didn't care a rap about losing office, but was very much cut up at the Rebellion. He would be back soon to wind up his affairs. On Monday night he had walked back alone through the Park and down again on Tuesday morning to the Castle just as usual.

Everything looked very desolate, Dorothy said. On the Quays bullet holes everywhere. The Four Courts were standing, but all the windows and sashes smashed. One house opposite was completely burnt down and still smoking, and several others half-burnt, but the wreckage was not quite as bad as she had imagined. In all Camden Street and the area around Jacobs the shops were shuttered, some after being looted, but most as a precautionary measure. All so desolate. And when next she wrote to her brother Robert she told him that 'they have already shot twelve rebels and sentenced heaps to penal servitude. It looked as if they were going to do more than was necessary, and to enjoy revenge. It was a ghastly business, because the physical force minority was very small, and heaven only knew how they might have wrecked Home Rule.' She hoped not. And added that she would miss Sir Matthew most awfully. A day or two later she told Edie in a letter that life in Dublin was getting horribly normal outwardly again, though feeling grew day by day. 'It is curious', she said, 'how little effect on the eye an earth-quake makes.'

Hyde's judgment on the Rising was understandably coloured by his own experiences. He told a friend that his work since the foundation of the Gaelic League had been aimed at restoring to Ireland her intellectual independence, and he would have completed it had he been let. The IRB had queered the pitch on him, mixing the physical and intellectual together, interpreting his teaching in terms of bullets and swords before the time, and this reduced him to impotence. He had been asked to return to the Gaelic League, but why, he asked, should he allow himself to be browbeaten and out-witted on every question of politics, and be held responsible by the public for acts of flaming indiscretion of the kind he had striven against in vain in the past? He could see what a nice figurehead he would make, to be thrown over like Eoin MacNeill when it suited the IRB men. Like Yeats, he had accepted the view of the great majority of Irishmen that Irish Nationalists should cooperate with England in the European conflagration. They had both for long recognised the need for orthodoxy in Irish politics, and John Redmond, who was after all still the national leader, had called upon the country to supply recruits for foreign service.

Over three years later Hyde was still writing in that strain. He admitted however, that he had not forseen the utter and swift debacle of the Irish Parliamentary Party and the apotheosis of Sinn Féin. He appeared to be hinting that another way had been possible, the way of unity within the Gaelic League as he had known it. 'By keeping strictly and sternly non-political we earned the good-will and kind words of such different people as Forde of the *Irish World*, Devoy of the *Gaelic American*, Cardinal Logue and the best of the Unionists, Horace Plunkett. Plunkett's words of appreciation were worth any money to the League, for with his support and the unanimity of everyone else it became impossible for the government to behave as it would have done in face of the least tendency towards anti-English politics. There was never any trouble about keeping 'national' politics as expressed by the MPs out of the League; the trouble was to keep out politics of the Wolfe Tone or Fenian type. These, growing stronger by degrees, came on with a rush in 1914 and 1915 and ended by capturing the League, its officers, its machinery and its money. It was then that Hyde had committed hari-kari with as good a grace as possible, and settled down to the work of the College. This he enjoyed very much especially the opportunities it gave for quiet scholarship rather than the teaching he had to do. He had no real interest in teaching, although he was rather good at it, providing the class with entertainment rather than instruction. (Dillon, 60).

Yeats had had difficulties in maintaining a neutral position. Keeping the Abbey out of trouble was not always easy. It had been difficult to avoid an official visit by the Lord Lieutenant, for example; and what was to be done about a production of Bernard Shaw's awkward skit *O'Flaherty V.C.*? The government would have liked to give him a knighthood but this he refused; nevertheless, on the other hand, though it was embarrassing, he kept an engagement to speak at a Thomas Davis Commemoration. This had been moved out of Trinity College when the Provost closed the gates against Patrick Pearse who had been billed to give the oration.

He happened to be staying with friends in England when the Rising broke out, and the news took him by surprise. He thought he should have been consulted. He knew a number of the men who were executed, MacDonagh, Pearse and Plunkett and, of course, Connolly, with whom Maud Gonne and he worked closely at the time of the 1798 celebrations. To Pearse he felt under an obligation for, unlike most of his Gaelic League and Sinn Féin associates, Pearse had spoken up for *The Playboy*. Interestingly Pearse had a profound admiration for Yeats. He would not tolerate any attack on him; and believed that, in days to come, people would say that this had been the age of Yeats (Rodgers, 210). Yeats spoke to his English hosts of innocent and patriotic theorists being carried away by the belief that they must sacrifice themselves to an abstraction, and, writing to Lady Gregory, he spoke of the 'heroic, tragic lunacy of Sinn Féin'. He turned to make poetry of the event, as was his wont, and noted that John MacBride, whom he had 'dreamed a drunken vainglorious lout', who had done most bitter wrong to some who were near his heart, had been touched by the heroic, so that he, too, had been transformed utterly 'in the casual comedy'.

This, and more, he said in a poem on the Rising, while in another he said:

> I lie awake night after night
> And never get the answers right,
> Did that play of mine send out
> Certain men the English shot?
> Did words of mine put too great strain
> On that woman's reeling brain?
> Could my spoken words have checked
> That whereby a house lay wrecked?
> And all seems evil until I
> Sleepless would lie down and die.

And, in October 1927, when Constance Markievicz died, he recalled the great windows of Lissadell and the two Gore-Booth girls,

> The older is condemned to death
> Pardoned, drags out lonely years
> Conspiring among the ignorant.
> I know not what the younger dreams —
> Some vague Utopia — and she seems,
> When withered old and skeleton-gaunt,
> An image of such politics . . .

> Dear shadows, now you know it all,
> All the folly of a fight
> With a common wrong or right.
> The innocent and the beautiful
> Have no enemy but time.

On 11 May the last of the executions — those of MacDermott and Connolly — took place. There had been some doubt about shooting Connolly, because of a wound he had received during the fighting, but Maxwell told Asquith that he had been found fit to be tried and that the fracture of the bone above the ankle would have cleared up in time. He was shot sitting on a chair; and was mourned as Ireland's first socialist martyr. Robert Lynd, who gave him this appelation, said that Connolly died as a witness to his faith in the brotherhood of man as he wished to see it brought into being and shape to Ireland.

Birrell resigned, the first major British casualty. Nobody, he told the Prime Minister, could govern Ireland from England save in a state of siege. He regretted that Henry II had not had the good sense of the Romans and stayed on the other side of the Irish Sea. He was personally smashed to pieces, he confessed, as the result of a surprise act of criminal folly. He knew the general verdict would be adverse; which, in fact, was the case. There were no tears shed after him. 'He will have a great political funeral,' wrote Horace Plunkett, 'as he has done the bidding of the Irish MPs for nine years. More than any other living man he fomented this rebellion.' In his diary Plunkett commented on the execution of the leaders of the Rising. By then eight had been shot and 'Con Gore-Booth of long ago, and the Countess Markievicz for the last 18 years, had been condemned to death. She is deeply dyed in blood, but her motives were as noble as her methods were foul. I met [Lord] Powerscourt, the Provost Marshall, and he was, he told me, begging the authorities to shoot her. She is to have her sentence postponed till Sir John Maxwell returns. I shall urge her reprieve.'

Plunkett had a long talk later with Maxwell. 'My object in calling upon him was to get the necessary help in collecting all the available evidence of German initiative and direction of the connection. This would very likely smash the German/ Irish alliance in America, as the Irish would be furious at having been dragged into a mad revolt by promises of naval and military assistance. I have three other aims in wishing to make the latest Irish folly part of the big war. The reconciliation of the moderates and extremists in Nationalist Ireland would be made much more hopeful, the destruction in Dublin and the other costs of the rebellion would be pooled with the costs of the war and not fall upon Ireland, and the soldiers who had died and been wounded in this business would not go down to history as the victims of street riots.

Maxwell agreed with all but the last point.'

Plunkett had written to Carson urging him to propose to disarm the whole of Ireland, beginning with his own Ulster Volunteers whom everybody else would follow, and he discussed this proposal also with Maxwell. Carson, however, replied that he could not do this. The women (especially) of Ulster wanted the arms kept while 50,000 of their men were fighting abroad to defend themselves against enemies at home.

Plunkett urged clemency. 'It there have to be further military executions, they should be restricted to cases where high treason was combined with murder.'

Maxwell, in his opinion, was a good type of commonsense Englishman with little imagination, but with a sound judgment where the situation was fairly clear. He had done well thus far, but Plunkett hoped he would not blunder when he had to deal with the aftermath of the crisis. He was soon to feel that Maxwell had blundered and he lamented the further executions. They would form a black chapter in Irish history. 'I do not think it was politically possible to avoid shooting a few of the ringleaders who were not directly responsible for the killing of unarmed policemen, soldiers and military. Anyone "who in the midst of a war" conspires with the enemy to overthrow a government of a country stakes his life on the venture, and no government would be safe if the penalty were not paid. But three wrong things were done: too many were shot; the executions were too long delayed; and the disproportion between punishment and the crime was given the worst possible appearance by minimising the gravity of the rebellion in order to save the faces of the civil government, who ought to have foreseen it, and to create the impression throughout the country that it had failed much more rapidly and completely than was the case, so as to dissuade others from joining in. I really cannot blame the military authorities when the whole matter was handed to them, but it was criminal neglect of Asquith to allow them a free hand' (Digby 213-14).

Asquith, confessing that 'you can never get to the bottom of this most perplexing and damnable country', had come over to Dublin on 11 May in something of a panic to see what could be done to prevent the wreck of the Liberal plan for Irish self-government. Plunkett had had a long private talk with him. Though fundamentally a Unionist, Plunkett had been moving towards a Home Rule solution, and now he unfolded his proposition. It was to put a provisional government wholly Irish — a sort of executive council — into power for the duration of the war. On this council North and South should both be represented. The experience in working together would be valuable. After the war the Home Rule Act would have to be *tried*.

Nathan resigned after Birrell, and Asquith put Sir Robert Chalmers, the Permanent Secretary of the Treasury, into the Castle to replace him; and when he could not think offhand of a successor to Birrell as Chief Secretary, he virtually took over the job himself for a while and spent a few days with Chalmers and other officials going over the files and discussing the problems. He then invited Lloyd George to explore individually with the Nationalist Redmond and the Unionist Carson the possibility of a political settlement which would enable the Irish Parliamentary Party to regain the prestige it was obviously in danger of losing. The general idea was that the Home Rule Bill that was in suspension would become operative immediately, subject to a decision about the exclusion of Ulster. A compromise did at first appear possible, but Asquith soon had to express regret that owing to the complete revulsion of public opinion he was no longer sanguine. The old absurd anomalous system of government was to be given another few years of life.

This was towards the end of July. By the end of the year Lloyd George had displaced Asquith from the premiership to become head of a small War Cabinet. He blamed the Irish themselves for the failure to settle the Irish question. Ireland was a quagmire of distrust that made progress impossible, he said. For the sake of keeping his Cabinet together, he guaranteed Ulster against inclusion in any Home Rule scheme; at the same time he publicly offered Ireland a Parliament for 26 counties together with a Council composed half of Northern and half of Southern representatives, but with no power other than to suggest measures which might apply to the whole country. As an alternative he threw out the suggestion of a Convention of all parties in Ireland as had worked successfully in South Africa, to decide the future of the country themselves. This was generally accepted and, to sweeten the atmosphere, at Horace Plunkett's suggestion, he amnestied the rank and file Republican prisoners.

Two Trinity graduates who had forsaken Unionism to become Home Rulers exchanged letters as the Rising ended. Both were also keen Gaelic Leaguers, were learning Irish and indeed wrote portions of their letters to each other in Irish. They were engaged to be married, signed letters with their initials only, so that it was extremely difficult to discover their identity. However, we now know that the man was Gustavius Everard Hamilton, a barrister in his mid-thirties who wrote a history of the Kings Inns, the lady, Ann Beatrice Culverwell, who was eight years younger. That the Rising had been a piece of criminal folly and an awful waste of useful lives on both sides was Gus's judgment (I am sure he was never called Gustavius): they, the constitutional Home Rulers stood to lose most by it, he said, and he felt very bitter against Birrell and Carson. Ann wondered what good anyone could have hoped for out of such a proceeding as the Rising and Gus considered that the leaders deserved their fate. There would be no stability or security unless everyone realised that those who rise against the government *de facto* — be it bad or good — must, if beaten, suffer the extreme penalty. He was very sorry for the loss of Pearse, and of MacNeill who, he thought, had also died. They were useful men before they took up such a wicked folly. Some of the others were a good riddance. Ann protested that she had no sympathy for Gus's idea of retribution, apart from the fact that it would create martyrs and rebels; but Gus insisted that the first and paramount duty of government was to see that the law was obeyed; in an imperfect world the only motive that would produce obedience in a very large section of the country was fear of the consequences of flouting the law. Of course, fanatics were almost devoid of fear, but even in a rebellion there were more people than fanatics among those who instigated and sympathised. The talk of making rebels and martyrs showed confusion of mind. Would the executions make anyone a potential rebel who was not a potential rebel already?

Gus and Ann discussed how the Irish Question might be settled. It seemed to Ann that the exclusion of Ulster was the only worthwhile proposition. It was the only hope for an ultimately united Ireland. Ulster, if forced into an all-Ireland Home Rule, would be a very determined and consolidated opposition and a very long-lived one. Such an Ulster opposition would make a rallying point for the opposition of the Protestant Ascendancy in the rest of the country. On the other hand, if the 'four-fifths' could be brought under one Home Rule Government, all sections would very soon come in, and eventually form a united nation sufficiently virile to absorb some day the remaining fifth. Gus doubted, however, if he could agree with the idea of excluding Ulster. The complications and difficulties would be too onerous.

On the effect of rebellion, the two lovers appeared to agree that it had done the cultural movement no good. Gus was afraid that Irish Ireland had received a serious blow and that everything national would be even more suspect than before in many quarters. The Gaelic League, Ann thought, might well die. When it had actually departed they might hope for something to take its place. It would be advisable to wait for this till after some political settlement had arrived (*Irish Times* 23 April 1976).

We go back to the beginning of Easter week to look at MacNeill's position. Early on Easter Monday Desmond Fitzgerald brought him the news that, despite everything that had been done the day before, a mobilisation of Volunteers had been called for 10 a.m. that Monday morning. There was a reference in the call-out to 'active service'. MacNeill could not believe that anything more was contemplated than a route-march, some sort of a parade to show that the countermand had not cowed the dissidents. He went to the house in Rathgar where on Easter Sunday he had issued the countermand and was there when he was told that 'action' had already started. Soldiers from Portobello Barracks had been spotted running along the canal bank nearby and firing into a public house at Portobello Bridge which had been occupied as an outpost by the Citizen Army. He was moved to the depths of his being, and confused. He first considered putting on his uniform and joining the action; but he soon realised that to do so would be illogical and irresponsible, having regard to his earlier warning that such action would be false to the country and would involve participants in the guilt of murder. So, he returned to his brother's house at Woodtown Park, where he had been staying. He was visited there by Alderman Tom Kelly, the man who a few days before had given the 'Castle Document' to the public, and was now in 'a state of indescribable anxiety'. He and others, including Eoin's brother James MacNeill, advised Eoin to seek some place of safety. The Jesuit house in Rathfarnham was mentioned, but it was made known in response to an enquiry that he would not be welcome there. He cycled to the Augustinian house at Orlagh on the mountain above Rathfarnham and was invited to become a guest for an indefinite period. He stayed for one night and then returned to Woodtown, and in an emotional scene told his wife that everything was ruined, that all he had hoped and worked for had been destroyed by the recklessness and treachery of his friends. Hobson came to see him. He had been released on Easter Monday and, walking down into Sackville Street, had seen the GPO occupied, with an Irish flag flying over it, and on the other side of the street a mob of looters in full cry. On Wednesday Arthur Griffith, who had cycled out from Clontarf by way of Lucan and Templeogue, came to see MacNeill. The promise made to Griffith at the September 1914 meeting in the Gaelic League headquarters had not been kept. He was totally unaware of what had been planned, and anyway was opposed to offensive action. He had sent a message to the GPO the previous day and was told that he should stay out of the Rising. Having talked things over, he and MacNeill agreed that an attempt should be made to bring some measure of relief to the insurgents who were already obviously beleaguered, but they could think of nothing effective, and Griffith went away.

On the Friday when it was clear that the fighting was over, and realising that the British, if past behaviour was any guide, would proceed to teach the Irish a lesson, MacNeill decided that, so far as it lay within his power, he would make that impossible. He, therefore wrote to Maxwell asking for freedom of movement in order to prevent any further collision between the insurgents and the forces of the Crown, and sent a copy under cover for the Chief Secretary at the Castle. He gave the letter for Maxwell to one of his sons who took it with him by bicycle. The boy was turned back, but MacNeill directed him to return once more, to ask to be arrested and brought to army headquarters. In this way the letter reached its destination.

The same day an army officer came out to Woodtown and took MacNeill away with him to see the General, but when they reached General Headquarters, instead of seeing Maxwell, MacNeill was arrested 'for being a rebel' by Major Ivan Price and lodged in Arbour Hill prison. Early the following morning he could hear the executions in the prison grounds. When later he was brought before Price it was to hear a suggestion that writing materials that had been left with him in his cell were for the purpose of enabling him to make a statement to avoid being executed himself, a statement, of course, which could be used by the authorities to ruin his reputation in the eyes of the public.

From Arbour Hill MacNeill was removed to Richmond prison, where a number of prisoners were herded together in very uncomfortable quarters. They slept on the floors, many in one room, and they ate food, six or eight at a time picking up mouthfuls from a large tin plate. He saw Asquith one day, and surmised that the object of his visit was to end the executions, the last of which was of James Connolly and Sean MacDermott whose health was precarious. On the 12 May he was told that he would be brought to trial before a General Court Martial. Four days later he was served with a charge-sheet and a summary of the evidence which it was proposed to put forward against him. He was to be charged on twelve counts, under the Defence of the Realm Act. The first and most important of these was that he had assisted at the creation of an organisation which on 24 April had risen in open and armed rebellion; at the court martial, prosecuting counsel said that MacNeill was not charged with taking part in the rebellion, but that he had incited it. 'The man who made the Irish Volunteers is as guilty of that rebellion as the man who had the courage to take part in it.'

MacNeill, in an elaborate and able defence, refuted all the

allegations in the Crown case, and specifically denied that the Irish Volunteers as an organisation had adopted any decision to take part in the Rising. Only a very small part of their total strength had in fact taken part, and that without authority. 'As soon as a reasonable suspicion came to me that acts were likely to take place which could lead to an insurrection I took the strongest steps possible to prevent even those preliminary acts taking place. On Easter Sunday afternoon about 5 o'clock my efforts had succeeded. On Monday morning about 11 o'clock they had been undone.' He did not know what caused the men who had given him an undertaking on the Sunday to change their minds. They were 'men of honour, truthful and honourable men'.

Some of the witnesses who had volunteered to give evidence and who were called by MacNeill's lawyers did more harm to his case than good. Though well-intentioned, James Creed Meredith's confused and inaccurate evidence was seen to have provided the prosecution with ammunition. Colonel Maurice Moore, with the best of intentions, was anything but helpful to MacNeill when he said that through indolence he had left the door open for schemers to operate behind his back; and the testimony of Tom Kettle, who appeared in the uniform of an officer of the Royal Dublin Fusiliers, was turned against him by a hectoring prosecutor and manifestly antagonistic court president. Poor Kettle, who had just asked to be sent to France, his usefulness as a recruiter being exhausted, was soon to die in the mud and among corrupting carcases on the Somme. The Sinn Féin nightmare, as he called the Rising, had spoiled his dream of a free united Ireland in a free Europe. Bitterly he recognised that Home Rule was done for, and the Irish Party finished.

The court's verdict was that MacNeill was guilty of all charges. Indeed, the court added for good measure that he committed all the offences with the intention of assisting the German enemy. He was put back for sentence. For five days he was held in Kilmainham and was there shown a rough deal box upon which Connolly, being unable to stand, had been seated to be shot to death. Large blotches of his blood were still visible. On the fifth day MacNeill was told that he had been sentenced to penal servitude for life. The decision not to execute him disappointed the Lord Lieutenant. During Easter week, and between the gulps of the brandy he drank continously, he had been heard by his aide de camp to say that he would hang MacNeill, 'I shall let the officers off, but I shall hang MacNeill.'

Until June 1917 MacNeill was held prisoner in Dartmoor and Lewes. The regime was strict, even severe. It seemed reasonable to allow a prisoner to read something published under government auspices, yet Mrs Green was refused when she appealed on his behalf to be supplied with the published volumes of the Ancient Laws of Ireland. However, MacNeill more than survived. His physical health remained good, and because he applied himself diligently to the study of languages his moral and mental health did not suffer. But in another respect, he and his family suffered. His conviction as a felon had legally deprived him of his chair in University College, Dublin and of his right to reappointment for life. He was also deprived of all civil rights. His reputation also suffered by comparison with those of his executed colleagues. He had one solid defender, however, in Michael Collins who later became the most brilliant tactician of the Irish struggle. He had taken part in the Rising, saw that it had been 'bungled terribly', and, in 1922, told the first of his biographers that accepting MacNeill's theory that the leaders had resolved upon launching a forlorn hope in order to awaken the Irish people, it was not at all difficult for him to accept MacNeill's explanation for issuing the countermand. 'Far from Professor MacNeill being in a minority in this matter', Collins said, 'it was we who were in the minority. With the German arms at the bottom of Tralee Bay, it must have seemed an act of madness' (Hayden Talbot).

As for Hobson, he remained in Dublin for several months and then went to Belfast for a time. 'I took the necessary precautions to evade arrest', he said, 'but then, not having been in gaol, I had no political future' (*Ireland, Yesterday and To-morrow*, 78).

The IRB remained in existence until 1924, but individual members had earlier considered their positions. Sean O'Casey had resigned in 1913 because the organisation refused to support the 1913 strike; Desmond Fitzgerald left in mid-

1917, possibly because of the effects of the take-over in 1916 and the treatment of MacNeill; Ernest Blythe followed in 1919, feeling that with the establishment of Dáil Éireann a secret body was no longer justified (Blythe to author, 26 May 1974).

Chapter 3

THE AFTERMATH OF EASTER

Birrell, and no doubt Nathan and others of the Castle frater-
nity lamented that they had not been able to place a spy in
the heart of the IRB conspiracy; they would then have had
prior knowledge of what was afoot. 'I always thought', he
told the Royal Commission of Enquiry in London, 'that I
was very ignorant of what was actually going on in the minds,
and in the cellars if you like, of the Dublin population.' But,
actually, if the ordinary police intelligence had been better
and properly assessed, they would have had sufficient information on which to act promptly. For seemingly half of
Dublin knew that something was about to happen that
Easter. On the Thursday before the Rising, Sean Lester joined
a party of Volunteer officers including Sean MacDermott
who had pooled their meagre resources to have lunch at
Jammet's restaurant, and gauged from their conversation that
the baloon was about to go up. John Dillon heard the most
disquieting rumours and correctly assumed that the Clann na
Gael men were planning some devilish business; and an
informer, who was present at a Volunteer gathering, reported
hearing Thomas MacDonagh saying: 'We are not going out on
Friday (Good Friday), but we are going on Sunday, and some
of us may never come back' (Ó Bróin, *Dublin Castle and the
1916 Rising*, 80), de Valera inspected his battalion on Holy
Thursday night and it was obvious, said Michael Hayes who
was present, that something serious was going to happen on
Sunday: 'We were told to parade all the weapons we had, and
that meant two hundred and fifty assorted weapons for
about four hundred men. It seemed to me a very dismal outlook. On the Saturday night, I went to confession.' There
were a great many men going to confession, many more than

usual on a Saturday night (Rodgers, 216). That, too, should have told the police something. Considerable, and fairly open, debate was going on in Volunteer circles as to whether there should be a rising or not, but none of this appears to have reached the Castle.

Desmond Fitzgerald knew of Hobson's attitude; he had said to Fitzgerald 'They' — meaning most of the officers of the Volunteer Executive — 'are determined to go ahead and nothing will stop them. They will ruin the movement. Germany is going to win, and we should hold our hand. If we did that, everything would be certain. But they are mad.' And, at a concert held at 41 Parnell Square, on Palm Sunday, Fitzgerald heard Hobson declaring in a speech that, in making a decision to take such action as was being contemplated one was bound to see to it that the right moment was chosen, that it should not be hurried, for postponement might give greater prospect of a successful issue. 'One could feel', Fitzgerald said, 'that Hobson was treading on dangerous ground. There was a certain breathlessness in the Hall. One could see glances passing between those who were probably aware of what decisions had already been taken. When the concert was over there were groups talking earnestly together, some denouncing Hobson and others praising his speech. On the following day the speech was a general subject of conversation. Opinions differed from those who thought that it was a timely word of caution, to those who thought it was black treachery. It was quite clear that those who knew most about the plans regarded it as disastrous (Fitzgerald, *Memoirs*, 116). So, naturally, the Military Council pondered what to do with Hobson, and decided to kidnap him and put him out of harm's way. 'On the afternoon of Good Friday', Hobson wrote in his autobiography, 'I was asked to attend a meeting of the Leinster Executive of the IRB at Martin Conlon's house in Phibsboro. I was reluctant to go, and did not see any purpose to be served. At the same time I wondered if this was a ruse to get me out of the way. I yielded to the importunities to attend, and was not greatly surprised when, as I entered the house, a number of IRB men who were armed with revolvers told me that I was a prisoner and could not leave the house. I felt that I had done all I could to keep the Volunteers on the course which I believed essential for their success, and that there was nothing further I could do. My principal feeling was one of relief. I had been working under great pressure for a long time and was very tired. Now events were out of my hands'. (Hobson, 76-7).

Dublin Castle would clearly have been glad to have had more information from their own sources, and if not actually aware, were inadequately aware that precise information was available to them through another channel for almost a full month before the Rising. On 22 March, to be accurate, the Director of Military Intelligence on the Supreme General Staff, Major General G. M. W. MacDonagh, informed the Commander of the Home Forces, General Lord French, in London, that he had received information from 'an absolutely reliable source' that a Rising in Ireland was contemplated, and that the Irish extremists were in communication with Germany with a view to obtaining German assistance. The Rising was timed to take place on 22 April and Germany had been asked to supply arms and ammunitions to Limerick by that date. Admiral Sir Lewis Bayly at Queenstown had been advised and had issued a stringent order for patrolling the Irish coast.

In a letter of 21 April to French from P. H. Brade, the Secretary of the Army Council, whose intent was to probe what had gone wrong, it was said that 'a secret memo, on the state of Ireland was sent from the War Office to your Irish staff, and . . . communicated to [General L. B.] Friend, [the G.O.C. in Ireland]. There is further reason to believe that on 16 April Friend received information from Brigadier W. F. H. Stafford, who commanded the Queenstown defences, which comprised an area from North Clare to Arklow in Co. Wicklow, that two submarines and a vessel containing arms had left Germany for Ireland. In connexion with these two events . . . it is noted that Sir Roger Casement was arrested on 20 April and the vessel sunk on 21 April'. French was asked to report fully the circumstances under which, in view of the very serious warnings that had presumably been received by him, Friend was not present in his command [but on leave in London], and officers were allowed to absent themselves from their stations [to attend a race meeting at a distance from their stations] .

French incorporated his reply to Brade's questions in a general report for the Army Council on the inadequacy of the steps taken by Friend to forestall the rising, but did not deny the statement that the secret memorandum — otherwise MacDonagh, the Director of Military Intelligence's message to him of the 22 March — had been communicated to Friend, so we must assume that it was, and we know that Friend had received the letter of 16 April from Brigadier Stafford and had handed it to Nathan on the 17th. Looking at the phrasing of Brade's letter — 'a secret memo on the state of Ireland was sent from the War Office to your Irish staff and . . . was communicated to Friend' — it seems as if the memorandum was sent from the Director of Military Intelligence direct to Major Price, Friend's Intelligence Officer, and that Price showed it to Friend.

Friend 'did not apparently think there was likely to be an overt act of rebellion', but he saw to the disposition of his troops so that they would be ready to meet an emergency. And when Nathan got Brigadier Stafford's letter from Friend on 17 April, he showed it to Neville Chamberlain, the Inspector General of the Royal Irish Constabulary. Neither of them was impressed by it. They were 'doubtful whether there was any foundation for the *rumour*', but, to be on the safe side, they put the County Inspectors of the RIC on their guard. Nathan also told W. Edgeworth-Johnstone, the Chief Commissioner of the Dublin Metropolitan Police, so that a watch might be kept on 'the turbulent suspects' in the city. Stafford himself did not appear to be unduly worried. There had been alarms before and nothing came of them. As for Birrell and Nathan, if they ever saw the secret document with its month's warning of a rising with German aid, which is unlikely, they did nothing about it.

So we go back to the beginning and ask what was 'the absolutely reliable source' of the Director of Military Intelligence's information. It would appear to have been revealed in the White Paper containing documents relevant to the Sinn Féin movement that was published by the Government in 1922, particularly if the Paper is read with Admiral Sir

William James's book *Eyes of the Navy, 40 O. B.* and H. C. Hoy's *How the War was Won*. The source was almost certainly the radio messages that were intercepted by the British Navy as they passed between the German Embassy in Washington and the Foreign Office in Berlin and were deciphered in Room 40 of the Admiralty Old Building in London under the direction of Captain (later Sir Reginald) Hall, the Director of Naval Intelligence. This interception had been taking place practically from the outbreak of the war, and an early advantage it conferred on the British was to add to their knowledge of Casement's movements and sexual interests (Sawyer, 115). According to Hall's confidential secretary, H. C. Hoy, the listening stations on the east coast of England intercepted as many as 2,000 German fleet signals and wireless communications a day. These were all, of course, transmitted in codes which were frequently changed but not one of the messages ever completely defeated Hall's experts.

In the particular sequence of messages intercepted between 10 February and 21 March, 1916, the agreement for collaboration between the revolutionary groups in Ireland, working through the Clann na Gael leader, John Devoy, in New York, and the German Government, was uncovered. This radio correspondence continued right up to the Rising, but by 21 March the intention to rise, the date of the Rising, the nature of the German contribution and the intended place where arms were to be landed were known to the British, that is to say to Captain Hall and his code-breakers in Room 40, and to MacDonagh, the Director of Military Intelligence on the Supreme General Staff; these handled the information with extreme circumspection so as to protect what was probably correctly considered to be Britain's most valuable weapon against Germany. By comparison with the uncovering of that source, the outcome of an attempted rebellion in Ireland was a small matter.

This explains the reference to 'an absolutely reliable source', a phrase which failed to impress General Friend. It would have been a different matter altogether if he had any notion of what Room 40 of the Admiralty Old Building was turning out. The Admiralty of course saw to it that the forces under their immediate control were sufficiently advised and put in readiness for action. Sir Lewis Bayly at Queenstown was alerted, and he, a very discreet officer, on 16 April gave the merest hint that something was on foot to his opposite number in the Army, Brigadier Stafford, who communicated what he had learned to General Friend, who communicated with Nathan. This roundabout business left the Irish Executive with five days warning instead of a month's. But in the upshot that made no difference. A bald reference to 'an absolutely reliable source' made no impression on them. They had heard that sort of phrase before. The only thing that would have produced a different reaction would have been an indication to someone in authority on the civil or army fronts of what 'the absolutely reliable source' was, and that was not 'on'.

Bayly was to play a vital part in scotching the plans for the Rising. Believing in 'the wonderful correctness of the Admiralty intelligence' he organised a close look-out for a disguised German arms ship and when Loop Head signal station, at the mouth of the Shannon, reported the steamer *Aud* acting in a suspicious manner he had her intercepted and escorted into Queenstown. In the channel she blew herself up, and a diver later discovered some of the cargo of old Russian rifles. Bayly was congratulated by the First Lord for his success in preventing a much more serious outbreak. 'If,' the signal to him said, 'the other Government departments had taken our *hints* I daresay the whole thing would have been stopped in the bud, but even Casement's capture did not seem to move them' (Ó Bróin, *Dublin Castle and the 1916 Rising*, 135-40).

Birrell and Nathan were the important witnesses at the Royal Commission when it opened in the middle of May in London. Birrell was vague and imprecise; and doubtless found it impolitic to confess, as he did in private correspondence, how he had used the passing Irish unity on the war issue to help recruiting for the forces. 'How can I', he wrote, 'for the first time in our long Irish connexion secure that Ireland should be on our side, and provide willingly and under democratic conditions, hundreds of thousands of fighting Irishmen to man our regiments?' Nathan, on the other hand, was clear and precise. He gave the facts as he knew them, contributing a picture of events leading to the outbreak, but what he had to say was seriously awry because of the fact that he was unaware of what had taken place inside the IRB. The Commission, when it reported towards the end of June, found against both Birrell and Nathan. The main cause of the rebellion was declared to have been the unchecked growth of lawlessness in Ireland and the fact that for several years the country had been administered on the principle that it was safer and more expedient to leave the law in abeyance if collision with any faction could thereby be avoided. That was a fair enough judgment in the circumstances. It ended Birrell's political career. Nathan, the civil servant, suffered, too — for a while. Just before the Rising, Lloyd George had pressed to have him appointed to the headship of the Department of Munitions but he was considered indispensable in Ireland and retained there. Now he was sent as a staff officer to the Chief Engineer, London Defences, and for five months helped to prepare for an invasion of England, in which no one greatly believed, by supervising the erection of earthenworks by men who were deemed unfit for active military service. Concurrently, he served on a Home Office Committee that tried to find useful employment for conscientious objectors. One of these jobs, given to Nathan to mark his disgrace, was as pointless, in his estimation, as the other. However, his luck turned before the end of the year when he was appointed Secretary of a new War Pensions Department. He was put back once more in the senior ranks of the civil service hierarchy, but he was to have no further official contact with Ireland. As regards the past, he told Mrs Green, he had nothing to take back from what he had said in their conversations in Dublin; he wished he had. 'I remember in one or two of those pleasant walks to the Park Gate', he said, 'telling you that my great fear, to prevent which was the one aim of my work, was that some actions of the anti-British in Ireland during the war, would set back the growing English sympathy with your country. The fear was justified and the work a failure.'

An unimportant yet embarrassing witness at the Commission of Enquiry was Diarmuid Coffey's chief in the

National Volunteers, Colonel Maurice Moore. Indeed the sole purpose of his testimony appeared to be to pay a tribute to members of the original committee of the Volunteers with whom he had worked before they split. Most of these men, he said, and he mentioned specifically MacNeill, MacDonagh and Pearse, were moderate men, men of the highest character whose lives from childhood had been permeated with thoughts, not of their own selfish interests but of the interests of their country. They were men who would have been the finest and choicest blossoms of any nation of the world, scholars, professors and poets whose absorbing passion was to lay down their lives in order that their country might be advanced even one stage in prosperity and enlightment.

Moore had had sad reason, as many others had, to question the administration of martial law by General Sir John Maxwell. The Irish Party leaders were particularly irate, John Dillon said, that the executions for which Maxwell was responsible had converted the Sinn Féin leaders from fools and mischief-makers, almost universally condemned, into martyrs for Ireland. T. P. O'Connor added that Maxwell's martial law had ruined the Party. Before the executions ninety-nine per cent of Ireland was Redmondite; since the executions ninety-nine per cent had turned to Sinn Féin. Maxwell was a wooden-headed soldier full of stupid little airs. He was a bloody fool, Dillon thought, a sentiment with which Lloyd George agreed.

One action of his was to stifle whatever little life remained in the National Volunteers after the Rising. Reading in the papers that they intended to hold a convention, he told the civil administration that any recrudescence of National Volunteers was to be deprecated. The convention should, therefore, not be allowed. The National Volunteers were not a legal body, he said; they had only come into being as a counterpart to the Ulster Volunteers; and any withdrawal of the restriction affecting them in the matter of drill parades and rifle practice would be weak and unwise, and was bound to have an effect on recruiting for the army. This view coincided with John Redmond's. He had been seriously upset by the Rising, and was unhappy at the prospect of a revival of volunteering of any sort. He, therefore, made difficulties about attending a National Volunteer meeting to discuss future policy, and things were allowed to drift until August 1917 when Moore succeeded in holding a convention at which, on his proposal, it was agreed that the split of three years earlier should be ended and a reconciliation effected with the Irish Volunteers who were known to be re-forming. The government reacted to this decision by sending the police to the National Volunteers headquarters in Dublin and other meeting places throughout the country and seizing any arms they found in those places. They were unable, however, to prevent the formal unification of the two Volunteer bodies which was brought about through a joint committee which included Colonel Moore and two men who had taken part in the Rising, Joseph McGuinness and Michael Collins. But by then, there were probably not many National Volunteers to reunify with.

Dorothy Stopford kept in touch with Nathan, 'the famous charmer' as Prime Minister Asquith's daughter-in-law Cynthia called him. She told him in September 1916 about 'all sorts of rumours' that were going round Dublin about his possible successor as Under Secretary. Robert Chalmers, a Treasury man who had held the fort since the Rising, was gone back to London; and no T. P. Gill, Sir Henry Robinson and Sir Edward O'Farrell were being mentioned. 'The opinion seems to be that if only they put in someone who'll do nothing he'll stay'. She didn't think that H. E. Duke, the Unionist lawyer who had succeeded Birrell as Chief Secretary, was very popular. The *Freeman* newspaper had changed its editor and was trying new tactics, while 'everyone was agin the Party' — this an early sign of impending political change at the national level.

She expressed her own feelings with characteristic frankness. 'The more one sees what rotten people over here have power', she told him, 'and how little they exert themselves except for themselves, the more sad it is that you are not here and able to go on doing so much for Ireland. Very few people and particularly Irish officials seem to care at all about their responsibility. I wish you hadn't gone; and they were mad fools to let you go when good people are wanted, and there aren't many able men. It's such waste. I hope you don't mind dreadfully...'. She asked him to accept much love.

A few weeks later – in October – she described a party she had given for her sister Edie. Dorothy was now moving in a circle that Aunt Alice knew well and which Nathan had also cultivated. AE (George Russell) was there, and Susan Mitchell, and James Stephens and Douglas Hyde – all of them Anglo-Irish. 'But all these', she added, 'don't make up for our ex-Under Secretary.' He could easily be depressed, she feared, by the commonplace jobs he was now doing. 'Some people, however', she thought, 'do more good by being alive than others do by any amount of work.' She had been to the Abbey to see *John Bull's Other Island*. It was excellently done, and she expected that Sir Matthew saw the humour of it.

She sent him Stephens's book, *The Insurrection in Dublin*, which had impressed her. 'The picture of the week day by day seems to be very good, and his conclusions, too, seem very fair. The sad part is that all the recommendations for a hopeful future that he suggests have *not* been carried out, just the reverse; and that the opportunity is gone for ever. And you can't fairly put *all* the blame on the Irish for their lack of cohesion, as people like to do.' What no doubt left a mark upon her was Stephen's avowal that there was no future for Ireland until the question of her freedom had by some means been settled, for that ideal had captured the imagination of the race. Stephens dismissed criticism of the leaders of the insurrection. Three of these whom he knew personally were more scholars than thinkers, and more thinkers than men of action, but they were good men who willed no evil. Their nominal President and Chief of Staff, MacNeill, was a good man, too. He had been accused of treachery to his comrades for his countermanding order, but men of his type were not traitors. Didn't he agree, Dorothy asked Nathan. And German intrigue and German money counted for so little in the Rising as to be negligible.

Dorothy liked to tell Nathan how she was getting on in Trinity. One story, that today is utterly incredible, is of a co-op club within the College where for 2½d she could get a meal that took her half-an-hour to eat. 'I dreamt of you the

other night,' she told him. 'You turned up on a visit here
with two wives and six grown-up daughters. In a motor car!
I have been having a series of strange vivid dreams. They say
it's a peculiarity of medical students at first.'

His work on Pensions seemed to her to be a little bit more
worthy of him; she hoped he would find it 'more interesting
than the last job, and a little less volcanic than the one before
that'. She had composed a second part of her doggerel Ballade,
and gave it to him. From it we get an idea of a War Pensions
department largely run by women while its head, Nathan,
had gone to live in the Albany Club. There he would occasionally entertain Dorothy to a war-time breakfast.

> Gold hangings, leather sofas
> The single mind o'erwhelms
> For he is the Lord of Pensioners,
> The stricken of our realm.
>
> He dictates to his Sovereign,
> His slaves wince at his glance,
> Twenty-five hundred brainy Eves
> Work for his schemes' advance
>
> Yet here on any morning
> As the clock strikes half-past eight
> You'll find your same old ogre
> Heaping sardines on your plate
>
> He is the same dear ogre
> Yet he's been through scorching flame
> And, more good to him accruing
> He's nicer than the same.

Among Nathan's correspondents was the lady who, in Dublin,
had entertained him to dinner in her 'top back' in Lower
Baggot Street while her husband was at the war and a governess was looking after their two children. This was Constance
Heppell-Marr, the daughter of the Englishman George Fletcher
who shared the secretaryship of the Irish Department of Agriculture and Technical Instruction with T. P. Gill. She told
Nathan she was often tired, cross and irritable and turned to
the poets for consolation. She drew on Shelley to tell him

how much she needed a green isle in the deep wide sea of her
misery, otherwise she could never voyage on. She sent him a
collection of her own poems and what she called an unutter-
ably stupid story she had written specially for him. This he
was to burn when he had read it. Nathan did no such thing:
he kept the story and, as she was in London where he was,
he invited her to dinner. She came, professedly with some
reluctance, because she was a candidate for a job with some
ministry or other and she did not wish to embarrass him on
that account. But when the ministry asked her for references
she wondered if Nathan would stand over the statement that
she was honest, certainly sober and possibly respectable. By
that time, of course, the Rising was over and Nathan in disgrace, whereas she had emerged with distinction. She had
organised a hospital, attended the wounded in the streets
under fire, and brought supplies through the firing line regard-
less of danger.

Three weeks after being Nathan's guest, she, with 'a lack
of maiden modesty', insisted on his coming to dine with her
at Cranston's Kenilworth Hotel in Great Russell Street, 'that
home of saddle-bag atrocities and Presbyterian principles'.
She later sent him books and a bag of dry lavender and
sweet thyme with 'the loving admiration of the humblest of
friends who had been tremendously impressed by his evidence
before the Royal Commission'. And after their next London
meeting she asked him to honour her by calling her by her
name, Constance. 'You will begin, "Dear Mrs Marr,"' she
wrote, 'and I feel like a stranger. Do you mind very much?'.
She continued to write letters and to send books and flowers,
and invitations to dine whenever she was in London, and
increasingly she emphasised her affection for him, and her
concern about his health. 'I'd like you to know a little' she
told him, 'about the happiness you have made in the world.
You said I was a very small person – so I am in body, and in
brain and in wisdom and experience and till now in heart too,
but since that little flame I spoke of began to grow I think
I'm growing too.' She offers him her thanks. 'Would you
accept it as one tiny jewel in a crown that you hide away?
You know it was said of you – "he is a man of kingly qualities" – it's very small for the crown of a king. Tell me ...

Your companionship is very precious — I'm not sure I don't owe you my sanity just now to it ... and I do appreciate your coming when you are so tired ... I *love* you to come ... but I pray that you never let it be a burden or a bore to you, and if ever it is I want you to say so. It would be an unforgivable hurt if you just bore it out of kindness — and I would know by instinct! Beyond that I ask you — with my arms round your neck — never let anything stand in the way — for in the years to come when I have to solace my heart and brain with memories, every hour will be a thousand-fold more precious. Do I take it all too seriously, dear? Forgive me, and if you want to know why, ask me on Saturday; that is if I'm not too shy to come after this screed.'

Her most romantic letter was written one Sunday night at midnight. 'Yes', she began, 'it has just struck twelve and I've whispered good night to you once, in case you might go to sleep and think I've forgotten, but I shan't say it properly till the light is out and that won't be until I've talked a while to you.' And she remembers that Nathan has been very dear and loving to her. For this she is grateful. She knows she indulges in silly talk and appears to have no sense of proportion or perspective, but she does not mind; all her concern is for him. 'I had such an unhappy dream the other night', she continued. 'I had been away for long and came back to where I thought to find you, but I could not find you and spent hours wandering about. I kept on waking up but every time I fell asleep it came back. At last towards morning I felt reassured. ... Come as soon as you can on Saturday for I shall be early and alone. ...'. And as she puts out the light she bids him again 'good night'.

The Easter Rising horrified Aunt Alice Green when she heard of it. Her brother Edward had told her from Dublin of great calamities and distress, and was trying to find out the extent of German involvement. And old Surgeon Stokes had had brought to him a youth so wounded that nothing could be done for him. When told he had less than an hour to live, he said, 'Thank God that I died for my country.' Arthur Griffith, whom Edward knew and admired, was a prisoner; but Edward believed that though he had not been 'actually engaged, he would get off badly. Alice knew that the Rising had occurred, despite Eoin MacNeill's attempt to prevent it, and when she looked at the names of the proclamation of the Republic, the only ones she recognised at all were those of Pearse and Connolly, and she may have been surprised by their conjunction. She had helped the finances of Pearse's school somewhat, and would have known him personally, if only slightly. She may never have met Connolly, but she would have known of his labour connexions and his position at the head of the Citizen Army. She could have heard of the Irish Republican Brotherhood, but would certainly have known nothing of what had recently been going on inside its Military Council, nor would it have occurred to her that MacDermott and Clarke with the consumptive Plunkett, the son of her friend from the National Museum, were behind the whole thing.

As for Casement, his involvement with the Germans had from the moment she first heard about it made Aunt Alice terribly angry; his actions, she thought, were a sheer calamity inspired by an insane desire to imitate Wolfe Tone. Then, as her puzzlement increased, she wondered whether his infatuation for the German people was not behind what he had done. He was misguided, she felt, but not treacherous. And when she learned that he was kept in the Tower of London behind barbed wire, in a damp, gloomy and airless cell, with the window boarded up except for one pane for the sentry to look through, she put aside all her doubts about his motives, and wanted to help. His clothes were filthy, his trousers still covered with the slime from the sea he had waded through. His braces had been taken from him, so he had to hold them up. He had not been allowed to take any exercise. His cell was verminous, his body covered with bites for which he had been given no treatment. Her first reaction, therefore, was to write to the Prime Minister, whom she had known personally for many years, and hint that if he took no action she would pass her information to the American press. Asquith acted. Casement was given a change of clothes, was allowed to have books and newspapers, to see visitors, and write letters. She then set to work, desperately, to ensure that he would not be executed – she assumed he would be found guilty of treason — but all the influential people she consulted refused to sign a petition to Asquith that she had prepared. She visited him in Pentonville Gaol and was affected by his gentle dignity, his serenity, his confidence in his friends. She was, he told her 'his true-hearted, ever-faithful friend'. She sent him books, found a solicitor for him, and raised funds for his defence to which she personally contributed generously.

Edie Stopford, on the day of the preliminary police court hearing in Bow Street, had a job in an office nearby, and was aghast to find a seething and angry mob surging up and down the street demonstrating their hostility to the prisoner. She battled her way through the crowd into the Lyons shop where she had arranged to lunch with Aunt Alice, and found her with Robert Lynd the writer. Both of them were greatly distressed. They had managed to get into the Court and, though they could not speak to Casement, he had seen them and smiled at them. Horace Plunkett was in court that day, too. He had made up his mind that 'the fool was guilty of High Treason, without a doubt'. He was, he thought, mad. Years before he had met him at the Monteagles' place, Mount Trenchard, and had talked at length with him and Mrs Green, but they were so predominantly anti-English that he feared there was nothing constructive in them. Alice Green's brother-in-law, the distinguished medical man Sir Lauder Brunton, offered to give evidence in a plea of insanity, but this plea was not made. Casement, when anxious to retire from the diplomatic service, had consulted Brunton in the hope that he might be invalided out but Brunton had found nothing much wrong with him. He had noted, however, one slight sign which might indicate a lesion in the brain, and later this came to seem significant (Pim, 191).

Casement was inevitably found guilty and made a speech from the dock that recalled many in the Irish patriotic tradition, particularly that of the Anglo-Irish Robert Emmet. He made no specific comment on the Rising which he had helped to bring about and ultimately sought to prevent. But he addressed himself to the charge that he had foresworn his loyalty as a British subject and servant of the Crown by his association with the German enemy. He explained where, in the struggle between the Anglo and Irish elements in his make-up, the true core of his loyalty lay, and why at Easter other men now dead had acted as they did. He spoke of Home Rule:

> Home Rule when it comes, if come it does, will find an Ireland drained of all that is vital to its very existence — unless it be that unquenchable hope we build on the graves of the dead. We are told that if Irishmen go by the thousand to die, not for Ireland, but for Flanders, for Belgium, for a patch of sand on the deserts of Mesopotamia, or a rocky trench on the heights of Gallipoli, they are winning self-government for Ireland. But if they dare to lay down their lives on their native soil, if they dare to dream even that freedom can be won at home by men resolved to fight for it there, then they are traitors to their country. But history is not so recorded in other lands. In Ireland alone in this twentieth century is loyalty held to be a crime. If loyalty be something less than love and more than law, then we have had enough of such loyalty for Ireland and Irishmen. If we are to be indicted as criminals, to be shot as murderers, to be imprisoned as convicts because our offence is that we love Ireland more than we value our lives, then I know not what virtue resides in any offer of self-government held out to brave men on such terms. Self-government is our right, a thing born in us at birth; a thing no more to be doled out to us or withheld from us by another people than the right to life itself — than the right to feel the sun or smell flowers, or to love our kind. Freedom is not something given by the English as a gift, but something which is mine and Ireland's natural right.

After an unsuccessful appeal the sentence of death was carried out at Pentonville on 3 August. Alice Green, 'fine as she always was', said Henry W. Nevinson, 'rose to unimagined greatness when we sat together, with Gertrude Bannister, Casement's cousin, and a few others, on the night before the British Government hanged my friend. While he in his cell was watching for the dawn of his death, she continued to speak to us of life and death with a courage and wisdom beyond all that I have ever known. It was as though we were listening to the discourse of Socrates in the hours before his own execution'.

The first political development of note in Ireland after the Rising occurred in February 1917 when a parliamentary seat was won in a by-election in North Roscommon by the papal Count Plunkett, whose son Joseph had been executed by the British. That fact counted greatly in the Count's favour, though his political position was not at all clear. He had not said until after he was elected that he would not enter Parliament, and there was some doubt as to whether he would or not. Dorothy Stopford appears to have picked up some of the depression in Unionist circles that he had been elected at all, as well as some of the slighting remarks that were being made about his immediate intentions. This she relayed to Nathan in a letter in which she said *'Weren't* you pleased about Roscommon? It must be in a bad way to make a hero of that old donkey. They say he will not be able to resist the £400 a year in the end and is already dodging about the Parliamentary Oath.'

A second noteworthy development was the election in Longford in May of an outright Sinn Féiner, and a convicted prisoner to boot, Joseph McGuinness. This was the man, who as we noted earlier, was to work with Michael Collins and Maurice Moore to end the rift in the Volunteer movement. He was a prisoner at the time of the elections, and an effective slogan in his campaign was 'Put him in to get him out'. These victories were seen as 'a message to the dead of 1916'. Within a few months Eamon de Valera, Arthur Griffith and W. T. Cosgrave secured parliamentary seats in Clare, Cavan and Kilkenny. The man who brought this unusual name, de Valera, into Ireland, had been a commandant of one of the areas in which there had been fighting during the Easter Rising, and on that account, in accordance with the policy General Maxwell had pursued, he should have been executed. He was saved, however, by the fact that his parents were American. As a young man and teacher, he had come profoundly under the influence of the Gaelic League. He served on League committees, acted as a marshal at the annual procession in Dublin, and represented his branch, the Central Branch, at the annual

Ard-Fheis. He was in Dundalk in 1915 and may well have voted for the policy change that forced Hyde's resignation.

In a paper he wrote about that time, he expressed his conviction that Ireland should get back to the point from which it had wandered, that Irishmen should make their own the ideals embodied in the language so that, imbued with a true Celtic spirit, they might advance along the paths their forefathers would have followed. This 'true Celtic spirit', or 'the true spirit living on in the people', he had learned from one of Hyde's ballads; from MacNeill he had picked up the commendation of the genius of the language as 'the chief thread of the nation's life, the purest manifestation of the Irish mind'.

De Valera had met in the Central Branch a young lady, Sinead Ní Fhlannagáin, who shared these sentiments. She married him in preference to Ernest Blythe and Sean O'Casey who were among her students, and an early joint undertaking of Eamon and Sinead de Valera was to conduct the Irish Language summer school at Tawin in South Galway for Roger Casement in 1911.

Douglas Hyde, still brooding over the politicisation of the Gaelic League, noted that two of its organisers, Peadar Ó hAnnracháin and Sean Ó Muirthile, were employed or had employed themselves in canvassing for the Sinn Féin candidate in Longford, and that 'my old friend Sean T spoke out of the windows of de Valera's committee rooms — thus, as general secretary of the League, committing it still further politically. At a meeting about the Lane pictures I heard him myself speak to a crowded meeting in the Mansion House and saying that he spoke as a representative of Sinn Féin. Notwithstanding this a number of Sinn Féiners make it a point to set up a horrible hullabaloo if any one ventures to say that the Gaelic League is political.' This Hyde described as an obliquity of view amounting almost to a disease, a kink in the mind. They had left the League a body to which no Redmondite and no Unionist could any longer subscribe, for their money would be going to a paper whose politics was to abuse John Dillon and the Irish members of parliament, and to support organisers and a secretary openly working for Sinn Féin candidates in parliamentary elections. Even as he wrote (April 1918) the new editor of the League's paper,

Pierce Beasley, had just been sent to jail for a political speech, and a new organiser for Leinster, Mac Coitir, who was married to Brighid Ní Fhlannagáin, Mrs de Valera's sister, had been taken with his brother in a boat in the Irish Channel apparently trying to communicate with German submarines. Hyde feared very much Mac Coitir would be shot for this. That was of a pattern with what had been happening since Easter 1916. He was aware that in the Rising all the League's officials, with the exception of Barrett the Treasurer who was lame, had been implicated, and sixteen of them or officers of the Executive had been shot, wounded, taken prisoner, or had disappeared. At the Ard-Fheis that followed, a resolution had been proposed and passed unanimously to the effect that there was nothing in the chequered history of Ireland that they were so proud of as the heroes who died in the Rising. The Gaelic League had been well and truly taken over.

Dorothy Stopford, as her medical studies progressed, was making the acquaintance of doctors, among them women, who were to be important influences in her life. She told Nathan that the finest person in Dublin seemed to be Dr Ella Webb, a tall woman with a mop of grey hair, a charming smile, a deep voice and an authoritative manner (Mary Smith to author). 'She lets me go down and help her in her slum dispensary on Tuesday evenings and shows what simply wonderful things a person can do besides doctoring.' She had been getting very bad accounts of events especially from Kerry where a policeman had been killed in an attack on a barracks. The general view was that the country would now take nothing short of dominion government. Dorothy went on:

> You can see it everywhere that the Sinn Féiners are multi-plying like flies, and they are very open too. The Longford election was a nasty blow for the Party. Goodness knows what is going to happen. I am giving up politics as unpro-fessional, and have taken up sailing, which is nearly as dangerous, with submarines in the Irish sea and everywhere. They are said to have fired on (and missed) the Mail Boat last week. . . .

I went to an evening at Susan Mitchell's . . . and there met Dr. Kathleen Lynn, who was a week in Kilmainham [Gaol] and deported last year, though I don't think anything was proved against her more than doctoring and bandaging Sinn Féiners. She is a very charming lady of an old-fashioned type, if you can imagine the exact reverse of Dr. Webb, who, indeed, is much more the Sinn Féin sort, you'd think. Otherwise I have kept to the most respectable circles.

Kathleen Lynn, who was in her forties, might have looked old-fashioned, but she was actually one of the most advanced women in the Ireland of that time. She had been associated with the Labour movement since 1913; in 1916 had been the medical officer of the Irish Citizen Army and had clambered over the railings of the City Hall to reach the Army's casualties in the fighting that followed the attack on the Castle. She was another of the rebellious Anglo-Irish, a daughter of a Canon of the Church of Ireland, and had had an English education.

Nathan had sent Dorothy a book of Augustine Birrell's essays, possibly his *Obiter Dicta* which was widely read and admired. To Dorothy, just looking at the volume, it seemed splendid. 'I have pasted inside the cover', she told Sir Matthew, 'a picture out of a newspaper of you and him walking along together in top hats.' This had been taken at the Commission of Enquiry. 'You are not very recognisable', she added, 'which reminds me that you had better hurry up and go to a photographer before anyone dies. It always happens.' When she dug into 'Your Augustine's essays' she found them quite delightful. She said so from Somerset where, doing her bit in the war effort, she was 'digging potatoes'. She signed her letter 'with love, yours affectionately'.

She spent the month of August that year at Mount Trenchard near Foynes, in County Limerick, in the home of Thomas Spring-Rice, Baron Monteagle of Brandon, who was held in high esteem, and whose patronage had won many followers to Plunkett's co-operative movement. On his own estate besides sawmills there were an industry society, a poultry society, a credit society, a wheat-growing society, an

Irish Agricultural Wholesale Society depot, a workman's club, a branch of the Gaelic League and another of the United Irishwomen which Plunkett had brought into being to promote better housekeeping and cottage industries (Bolger, 104 and 286). Lord Monteagle's son, Sir Cecil Spring-Rice, was the British Ambassador in Washington. His daughter, and Dorothy's friend, Mary, as we saw earlier, had been most actively engaged in the 1913 gun-running. 'It is very peaceful here looking out over the Shannon', Dorothy told Nathan. 'I am down to do what I can about the place, not technically "on the land", but doing odd jobs such as cheese-making, bottling fruit and so on. We sailed over to Clare Castle for the East Clare election, and got lifts to Ennis for the declaration of the Poll . . . and took two days over it, sleeping on board. De Valera struck us as a very fine man, and I think ought to be able to lead with a clear head and not get carried away.'

She mentioned a Convention that had been appointed to submit proposals for the future government of Ireland and felt that, under Sir Horace Plunkett, it might do more than Nathan might think. But that view seemed over-optimistic, considering that the Convention was to be boycotted by the Sinn Féiners and that the Ulster Unionists were as much opposed to any form of United Ireland as ever they had been. A proposal was made by Sinn Féin that individuals, including Alice Stopford Green, James Douglas, James MacNeill, and Robert Barton, might be co-opted to represent their point of view, but to this manoeuvre the Unionists would not agree.

Dorothy commiserated with Nathan whose nephew had been killed in the war: 'He seemed so full of life and cleverness and promise of good things, and it must be a grief to you. Terrible things seem to be happening every day.' In the last week of September Tom Ashe, one of a number of hunger-striking prisoners, died in Mountjoy of forcible feeding, Dorothy told Nathan how she regretted he was not in Ireland. If he had been, 'the Ashe Fiasco', as she called it, might not have happened. The peace of the country during the Convention was much more important than holding out against one or two men who had made seditious speeches but whom no sane person could call criminals.

I wonder what class such offenders are put [into] in England
— I am sure Second. The folly of giving the Sinn Féiners —
only too eager for any handle — a grievance and the opportunity over this funeral for them to turn out by the thous-
and and parade themselves! I really don't know what's
going to happen. Sinn Féin is so much on the increase. It's
awful.

I was told the other day by a friend that three different
Nationalists had told her that they wished you were here
now, that you were the only man we'd had who really
got things done. But you would hate it now — even I do
sometimes, when you hear of officers being followed home
from theatres, and shadowed. It is all a ghastly misunder-
standing surely? Aren't all these situations — the French
Revolution and all patriotic movements — a mutual mis-
understanding of governing (mostly) and governed. I loathe
politics and fly to solider things — hospitals and concrete
facts. I begin in a hospital here to-morrow with intense
expectation. . . .

I've met a few interesting people lately, John Ervine,
the author, and Dr. Barry (a lady) who is great on babies,
just after your own heart; and from a room full of people
I selected a man and asked him who he was, and heard it
was Stephen Gwynn. [The dramatist Ervine had turned
from nationalism to become a rabid Unionist and, joining
the army, went to France where he lost a leg in the fighting. Gwynn, a godson of William Smith O'Brien, the '48
leader, also a Nationalist and M.P., had likewise served in
France, but with the Connaught Rangers.]

Aunt Alice is here, and I don't think doing anything
dreadful. It is a great wakener-up having her in Dublin.
She keeps us all up to the mark, and is awfully nice.

In her next, a month later, Dorothy declared that the Sinn
Féiners were going too far, even for her. If they wrecked the
Convention, it would be very annoying; but if the Convention
died a natural death they might be very useful in having an
alternative scheme. De Valera and Eoin MacNeill were more
competent and level-headed than a great many people in
Ireland at present. There was talk of German influence being
at work but she did not believe this.

She had found the Meath where she was now working a very nice hospital. She had also been 'dipping into' the conditions of sick and invalid children in the city, and running round the baby clubs. She had great schemes if only they could get going, but she would have to wait. At week-ends she went camping with Doreen Synge, usually in a field in the mountains where Doreen's relative, Ned Stephens, had a cottage. In this atmosphere she heard much talk of the Irish Literary movement, and, of course, of the Synges' and Stephens' most distinguished relative, the author of the *Playboy of the Western World*.

The circumstances in which the Easter Rising occurred had a confusing effect on the Volunteers in the northern counties as elsewhere. Herbert Moore Pim was opposed to any action being taken in Belfast, and was in Tyrone with McCullough and Mac Cartan when they discussed with the limited number of poorly armed Volunteers who had mobilised what was to be done. Nothing was done, in fact, and in the wholesale arrests that followed, Pim was arrested and lodged in Reading Gaol with the second echelon of Irish leaders, those who had helped to foment the Rising but had not been involved in the fighting. There he met another colourful Anglo-Irishman, the bearded Darrell Figgis. Pim's beard was a full dark silken affair, giving an Assyrian effect to a large face of rather sallow complexion (O'Shannon, *Irish Times*). Figgis's was shorter, of a different hue, and more stylised. Figgis, a Dublin Protestant, had a similar career to Pim's. He had given up business as a tea broker to become a freelance journalist. He had been involved in the Howth gun-running, and subsequently went to gaol more than once for his political activities. He had a pen name too, wrote novels and biographical studies, as well as a volume of recollections of the war with England. Like Pim, also, he had a marital problem, and a mistress, which culminated in a triple suicide. Pim's marriage broke up less tragically but tempestuously after his return from Reading Gaol.

The outstanding prisoner in Reading when Pim was there was Arthur Griffith, and they no doubt discussed the future of Sinn Féin. It so happened that Pim was released before

Griffith into what he described as an Ireland of apathy and chaos. His first notion of action was to call a conference in Dublin, mainly apparently of representatives of a Repeal League and the Irish National League, which came to nothing. There were others at the conference, however, among them Paddy Gleeson, a friend of Griffith, who unexpectedly said 'Why not revive Sinn Féin? The headquarters is there and has not been interfered with by the Government.' Pim's summing up of Sinn Féin's position was that it had been practically dead for seven years, that John Redmond had called the Irish Volunteers Sinn Féiners as a nickname, so that to call a man a Sinn Féiner was to associate him with a failure. Nevertheless, no better idea than Paddy Gleeson's being forthcoming, Pim told the conference that the best they could do was to revive Sinn Féin, and that he intended to make the attempt in *The Irishman*. Out of thirty-five persons present at the conference, only three supported him. He secured a tattered copy of Griffith's *Sinn Féin Policy* and from this he designed a leaflet, *Sinn Féin in Tabloid Form*, and sold countless thousands of it. What it taught latched on to the immense movement of popular sympathy for the men shot after the Rising, so that Pim felt entitled to claim that it was through this leaflet that the public unconsciously adopted Sinn Féin. Griffith did not like some of Pim's work, however, and from Reading he made it known that 'his well-meaning friend seemed to be muddling up Sinn Féin a bit. They would have to trust to God to take Pim in hand and show him how to unmuddle it'. But on starting up *Nationality* again after his release, Griffith must have been impressed by Pim's publicity work when he found the readership of the paper had gone up from 7,500 to 60,000.

Pim exerted all his energy to getting Griffith into control of the movement, and he seemed to be making progress until the advent of de Valera. He came forth from prison, Pim said, endowed with accidental popularity, and the excitable nationalists called upon him to pit his brains against John Redmond, the British Empire, and incidentally the Ulster Unionists. He set about the task by declaring that Englishmen must clear out of Ireland, bag and baggage, and to effect this expulsion he invented the policy of 'ten-foot pikes'. He gave the Ulster Unionists six months to get out. But a change was on the way.

'My eyes were beginning to open', Pim said. Sinn Féin, from being a constitutional association for teaching self-help and self-reliance, was becoming an armed pro-German society whose followers amused themselves by raiding the houses of peaceable people in the dead of night, and by preventing people from having opinions of their own. The business of a cousin of Pim's had been destroyed because that cousin had dared to vote for conscription at a meeting of a local authority. Pim finally decided to resign from the National Council of Sinn Féin, and this he did in June 1918; it meant abandoning his position as editor of the *Irishman*. He foresaw that Sinn Féin would become as harmless as any constitutional movement which had gone before it, and that the men who would give it its death-blow would be those who preached physical force (*Nineteenth Century*, June 1919).

Thereafter he reverted violently to Unionism and produced a booklet he called *Unconquerable Ulster* with a few lines of a foreword by Lord Carson. Carson appreciated the spirit in which the booklet had been written, and no doubt relished a Ballad of Ulster, a Ballad of the Ulster Volunteer Force (UVF) and a Ballad of Derry Wall with which the booklet opened. One verse of the first of these ballads evoked Ulster's cry of No Surrender. It ran:

> We know what we mean, and we mean what we say;
> And we love our land and our liege the King;
> Let the future bring what the future may,
> Ulster is ready for anything.

The spirit of Ulster, Carson emphasised, was not a poetic or political invention. 'Many cannot learn, and some can forget this elementary fact.' But he steered clear of saying anything about Pim, who found his re-entry into official Unionism not as easy as he may have thought it would be. According to Ralph Bossence, who wrote a series of articles about Pim in the *Belfast News Letter* in November 1966, the offer of his services to the Party was declined.

Pim explained his object in writing *Unconquerable Ulster*. It was to expose the fraudulence of the nationalists' claims —

to show who the nationalists really were and the real nature of their work. 'As one who knows the inside of nationalist politics I can assure all and sundry that there is about as much unity among the nationalists of Ireland as there is among the now defunct cats of Kilkenny. You have "the Irish Party" which has its eyes on jobs, and which claims to be imperialist and nationalist at the same time. Then you have the old Sinn Féiners who recognise the King, and the new Sinn Féiners who cry for independence. . .'. Nationalists of all sorts should be kept at a distance, he said, and there was not a Unionist family in Ireland whose history had not some dramatic episode. His own family possessed two such episodes. 'Two and a half centuries ago one of my ancestors, a young handsome woman, was murdered. Her body could not be found; it was afterwards discovered that the murderers had boiled the body for the purpose of making candles. . . . My own grandmother at Anner Mills rang the alarm bell of the great house on the night of an attack. Her father's watchman's throat was cut that night, and my great grandfather escaped as by a miracle from being murdered. . .'.

He contrasted the physiognomy of Unionists and Nationalists to the advantage of the former. 'The loyalist type in Ireland is a well-set up individual, with clear, straight, honest eyes, and clean skin and well-formed features such as are found in human beings of the English type. Every loyalist knows the nationalist type — a person with thick, black hair, or hair of a pale mousy colour, with shifty or dreamy eyes, and features which proclaim it as belonging to a low order among civilised people. . . . These people are the ancient servant caste.'

In the light of this rubbish Pim's subsequent career was not surprising. His friend Lord Douglas took him over to London and made him assistant editor of his provocative paper *Plain English* and its successor *Plain Speech*; and was to say that it was Pim's knowledge of Ireland and Sinn Féin that enabled him in 1921 to conduct his campaign against the Anglo-Irish Treaty and the betrayal of the Irish loyalists. He remarried in France, played with Fascism in Italy in the 1930s, but died in England, a staunch British imperialist, in the arms of the Catholic Church.

Aunt Alice Green was so powerfully affected by everything that had happened since Easter 1916 that in 1918 when seventy years of age she uprooted herself from London, bought herself a handsome house on Dublin's Stephen's Green, and contemplated staying there till the end of her days. She made sure to have a good cook as well as an intelligent maid, and, to be her secretary, she engaged a young woman from Wexford, Mary Comerford, who was to become a real firebrand as the guns came out. Aunt Alice herself was none too happy with the employment of physical force, but her admiration for the Sinn Féin generation grew apace and, as we saw already, she regarded the breach between the young people of that generation and the leaders of the Irish Party as a disaster. To her, Home Rule now seemed an inadequate policy for Ireland; and in a pamphlet on *Ourselves Alone in Ulster* she attacked what Carson was doing.

A matter that gave her much pleasure was the improvement in Eoin MacNeill's position. Following his discharge from prison he had applied to University College, Dublin to be re-appointed to the chair of Early Irish History. A vacancy was advertised and, when the governing body met in April 1918 it noted that the only application was from MacNeill, and that he had been unanimously recommended by the academic council on the report of the faculties of Arts and Celtic studies. The report quoted the testimony of Osborn Bergin, the highly esteemed professor of Early Irish, to the effect that included among MacNeill's many publications was 'the finest example ever published of an exhaustive and critical study of one of the sources of Irish history', while Robin Flower of University College, London had written that MacNeill's researches provided the indispensable basis for all advance in the study of early Irish history. He was 'the most original and stimulating of living Irish scholars'. The matter ended happily with MacNeill returning to his old chair.

In Dublin Mrs Green may have seen more of some of her nieces than when she had had them around her in London. Dorothy was there, of course, all the time doing her studies and, since the autumn of 1916, her sister Alice Wordsworth had been keeping house for her, first at 32 Hollybank Avenue,

Ranelagh and then from early 1917 at 53 Leinster Road, Rathmines. Neither Dorothy nor Alice had much money but, by sharing such pittances as they had and taking in a few students as boarders, they managed to survive. Alice had her daughter Mary to look after, of course, and this she did devotedly. She sent her to school to the Wesleyan Nightingale Hall on Clyde Road and the Rathgar Junior High; and took her on Sundays to a service in St Ann's in Dawson Street. For a while she even managed somehow to give her a governess. Edie was not in Dublin. She had made her home with Aunt Alice in London during the war and was glad to do so, for she had been through a bad time as the result of the death in the war of a lover. His loss so affected her that whenever later a man began to show a serious interest in her, she turned him off abruptly. Her sojourn with Aunt Alice ended abruptly, too. She just walked out one evening and did not return. She explained her action subsequently in a letter but did not say what the cause of it was. Aunt Alice, we know, could be temperamental, but Edie refused to blame her for whatever had happened. She did not blame herself either, however, but insisted that, in leaving her aunt, she did not mean to cause her pain or distress, and that she had not acted through callousness. She had nothing for Aunt Alice, she told her, but affection and respect. The two years they had been together were more important than any other two in her life. Aunt Alice had taught her something of the real value of qualities she had never before realised had values. But when Aunt Alice decided to live in Ireland, Edie did not come over with her. And Robert was serving overseas.

Dorothy continued to write to Nathan, she told him in the early days of 1918 that the talk of Dublin town was *Blight*, a play of Dr Oliver Gogarty's concerned with the horrors of slumdom, which had just been presented at the Abbey. Gogarty was much disappointed that the play had not been censored, and yet, as produced, the play was not quite as he wrote it, for the actors had absolutely refused to speak some of the lines. Dorothy did not know Gogarty, but she mentioned an acquaintance she had struck up with her very nice neighbours, the painter Jack Yeats and his wife. 'When all the world is talking of conscription and political crises they go on gently with art and poetry and beautiful things and peaceful minds. They are not like the brother W. B., but very human and ordinary mortals.'

Dorothy personally was finding it very hard – in fact impossible, she told Nathan, to work at all, with crisis following crisis, and not knowing what was going to happen next. The Cabinet wanted 50,000 recruits for the forces from Ireland, and determined that without them they would have to impose conscription. With that in view they had nominated Field Marshal Lord French to be Lord Lieutenant with powers to deal with the expected resistance. His first move, with Cabinet approval, was to arrest almost the entire leadership of Sinn Féin and the Volunteers and to announce in a proclamation that Sinn Féin had been engaged in a treasonable conspiracy with the Germans. Dorothy was one of many people who refused to believe this. This scare of a German plot, she told Nathan, was alienating all reasonably-minded individuals who loved their country, and was creating patriots every day.

She began an apology: 'When I began to write [this letter] I meant to keep off politics.' But, changing her mind, she asked why she should pretend that she was thinking of anything else. She had in fact become a Sinn Féiner, reaching the same conclusions as James Stephens had propounded in his book on the Rising. Indeed she was one of a vast number who at that time were changing their allegiance because of the executions of the 1916 leaders, the murder of the pacifist Sheehy Skeffington and other murders, but more than anything perhaps because of the threat of conscription. It was in that mood that she told him that she could not see her way to taking up a holiday job in his department that he had offered her, though the pay would have been useful as she pursued her studies. 'My dear Sir Matthew', she wrote, 'you will be annoyed with me I'm sure when I tell you that I cannot go to work for you in the summer. I would do it for *you* personally as you know to any extent, but after the things I have been feeling and saying about the Government's treatment of some of my fellow countrymen, it would simply be not straight to go and take paid work under it. I am very sorry. I will try and find something else useful to do, perhaps land work. . . . When one comes here the biggest issues of the war are forgotten and, the crying-out all round for some sort of change of conditions rouses all one's feeling more strongly than one felt in London, so I suppose I must cast in my lot with Ireland, and try to keep a sane view of it. Anyhow the London intervals [her occasional visits to London] prevent one from believing all the rubbish that England hates Ireland intentionally and so forth. The miserable present state of affairs shows no way out but Home Rule; and let Ireland work out her own salvation, with no one else to blame for mistakes. She can't make more and may very easily make less.' And she ended by saying that 'this is a hateful letter to have to write, because I'd been looking forward to the work'.

The Irish Convention over which Horace Plunkett presided was a quite extraordinary body. It comprised 101 members, nearly half of them drawn from local government, the rest representing the political parties including Ulster and Southern Unionists, industry, labour and the Churches. It sat from July 1917 to May 1918, with intervals, one of them to enable members to attend the funeral of John Redmond. Unanimity, it need hardly be said, was not achieved. Plunkett gave the Prime Minister a report which had been adopted by 44 votes to 29, two minority reports and five 'notes', and these he covered with a letter in which he tried to give a clear idea of the significance of what had been achieved. 'We had', he wrote, 'to find a way out of the most complex and anomalous political situation to be found in history — I might almost say in fiction.' The difficulties that faced the Convention he summed up in two words — Ulster and customs. But the nationalists and the Southern Unionists, by mutually making concessions and by agreeing to postpone a decision upon the ultimate control of customs and excise, had managed to agree on a complete scheme of self-government for Ireland. 'Is it too much to hope', he asked, 'that the scheme embodying this agreement forthwith be brought to fruition by those to whose call the Irish Convention has now responded?' But on the day he brought his report to London, Plunkett heard Lloyd George introduce a Military Service Bill which conscripted men of the whole nation, including Ireland, for war services. To him, fresh from the atmosphere of Dublin, it seemed madness. He dined with Erskine Childers, who had worked so hard in the secretariat of the Convention and displayed great ability and moderation. Now he noted that he was 'more than ever doctrinaire, noble, and impracticable about Ireland'. ·

The Convention had had the support of the Catholic Church from the beginning, the ablest and most statesmanlike member on the nationalist side being perhaps Dr O'Donnell, future Cardinal Archbishop of Armagh, with whom Childers had collaborated closely in writing one of the reports. The predecessor in that See, Cardinal Logue, had warned that if the Convention failed, all would be chaos. And that indeed seemed to threaten when in April 1918 the House of Commons passed the Conscription Bill to create what Dorothy Stopford saw as 'the greatest moment in Irish history'. The Irish Party withdrew from Westminster, the trade unions linked up solidly against the measure, and the Catholic bishops not only denounced it from the altars, declaring that the people had the right to every means, consonant with the laws of God, to resist such an oppressive and inhuman law, but asked men and women to pledge themselves publicly to do whatever was in their power to make the bill inoperative. A church-door pledge campaign was organised and politicians of all parties united to support it. Dorothy feared a massacre if the government, despite all this, tried to enforce military service; and, to avoid seeing her sister Alice and her eight-year old child Mary caught up in the disorder, she thought they should return to England. She hoped, too, that Nathan somehow would influence the government in the matter and wrote to him to that effect. He made it clear to her, however, that he could not interfere. 'I must not forget', he told her, 'that after my year and a half in Ireland in which I advised against conscription — which advice was then taken — a rebellion came, with the inevitable "I told you so" from the reactionaries and not *one* word said *for* the policy by the Irish! For me to offer advice not asked for would be not only ineffectual, but might not unreasonably be held to be impudent.'

Despite all the political distractions, Dorothy made some progress with her studies and gained some unusual experience during the 1918 influenza epidemic. One of her professors, William Boxwell, 'was mad on post-mortems', she explained in a slice of autobiography, 'and I was acting as his clinical clerk. He tried to get a portion of lung from every victim of the 'black' influenza and pneumonia, and to help him every night at 10 p.m. I biked down to the mortuary and, with or without the aid of the night porter, carried in two or three corpses into the Post Mortem room, stripped them ready and put them back tidily afterwards. These were all surreptitious p.ms. and once or twice we got a fright when someone came to the door which was locked. I well remember nights when the rain came pelting down on the glass roof, and I alone inside trying to get a corpse into its habit and back to its bench. The Professor often helped but was run off his feet and frequently had to leave at midnight on a call. The results of microscopic examination of the lung were disappointing; engorgement in the blood obscured the picture.'

She was just *twenty-eight* that September. She told Nathan that 'it had been jokingly solemnised with a cake on which *thirty-eight* night lights in green, white and yellow, or red, white and blue shades, according to the political opinions of the company' had been placed. The green, white and yellow, the republican shades, would now accurately enough correspond with her personal position. The celebration was held in the Grand Hotel, Greystones — 'a horribly swell place', she told Nathan, 'where they give you four courses for breakfast, five for lunch and seven for dinner and, as it is pouring with rain, in between meals, you have to sit in the lounge and smoke. You feel like I don't know what but very bulky and brainless. Sir James Campbell (the Unionist Attorney-General) is here, and my joy is to appear at dinner and sit with my back to him clad in a bright green frock, white collar and gold scarf. So far, to my chagrin, I have not been asked to remove myself from this respectable establishment. But I am returning to the wilds on my bicycle to-morrow and know that life will be good again instead of an intolerable period of self-indulgence and consequent boredom'. The place might suit Nathan, however, she playfully suggested. 'They dance on Saturday nights. Last night there were six lovely damsels and one Highlander, and he was so tremendously in demand that I kindly refrained from adding to the number seeking his favours, and went to bed instead, nose in air.'

Sir Matthew, maintaining his interest in Ireland, asked Dorothy towards the end of the month for the latest news. She told him that there were 500 persons in gaol under the Defence of the Realm Regulations; and Lady French had been bribed by the government to postpone her divorce suit against the Field Marshal, so that he would remain in office for the time being. That was the gossip. She had invited Nathan to holiday with her at Lough Dan in the Wicklow hills, but this he felt he had to decline. If the place were a little nearer and not quite so windy he would be glad to accept — 'for at the minute', he said, 'I feel absolutely of no good here in London'.

She had been staying in Glendalough, another Wicklow beauty spot, with Robert Barton to whom, and to his cousin Erskine Childers, she had been introduced by Aunt Alice. Barton, a middle-aged bachelor who was with the British Army in Dublin during the Rising, had resigned his commission, because, it was said, of the ill-treatment he saw being meted out to some of the insurgents as they surrendered. He cast in his lot with Sinn Féin in 1917 as Childers did a little later, though his first reaction to Barton's decision was that it was a rash one. Childers had fought against the Boers, participated in the 1913 gun-running, had joined the British navy on the outbreak of the Great War and won the DSC. He had subsequently been released for service in the secretariat of the Irish Convention because, like Diarmuid Coffey, he was accepted as an authority on Home Rule and had written on aspects of it. This was the company Dorothy was keeping just as Barton was chosen as the Sinn Féin candidate for West Wicklow at an impending General Election. She told Nathan she was afraid she was not staying in a respectable house.

The Great War had ended that 1918 November and gave rise to wild deliberations. Dorothy quizzed Nathan as to whether he had wound a Union Jack round his hat and sat on the bonnet of a motor bus. 'I have kept out of the flag-waving here', she said, 'because it [the peace] doesn't take me that way.' About Ireland, she told him that 'things are not too depressing, in fact, quite gay, despite Lloyd George and Sir Edward Carson. Why, oh why, did the influenza bacillus, that had laid so many people low, miss that pair out?'

She worked hard for Barton in the Election, and gave Nathan an account of some of her experiences. 'I attended a forbidden political meeting not long ago and had ready my name concealed in Irish and, if they asked for an address (which they didn't) I thought of giving R2 the Albany [Nathan's London home] just for fun. Would you mind very much? Let me know for future reference. I had the day of my life on polling day just buzzing around a lively constituency. I never heard so much cheering and excitement. We did 160 miles between 8 a.m. and 11 p.m. and won hands down.'

All the successful Sinn Féin candidates who were not in jail came together on 14 January 1919 to constitute themselves the Parliament of Ireland, Dáil Éireann. A week later a public inaugural meeting of this Assembly was held in Dublin's Mansion House, and Dorothy was brought along to witness the proceedings, by Barton. She told Nathan of this engagement beforehand but 'I don't expect to understand much', she said, 'as I was brought up in such an anglicised manner'. Most of the business would be transacted in Irish, which the *Manchester Guardian* was to call Republican theatricalism. The name on the admission ticket which she kept as a souvenir was in Irish also, Deora Nic Ghiolla an Phairt. For a while, Barton addressed her in his letters as Deora and signed them Riobárd, but that appears to have been as far as either of them got in acquiring the language.

A little later in 1919 she was coming home one night with Barton from a meeting when they were halted by a patrol, separated and questioned. When the inquisition ended Barton came over to Dorothy and said, 'I'm afraid you will have to go the rest of the journey by yourself. I've been arrested.' He was sentenced to a term of imprisonment for making seditious speeches and lodged in Mountjoy Prison, but with help from Michael Collins he managed to escape and resumed working underground. While he was in Mountjoy Dorothy sent him in books and sweets. 'I have read all the Wordsworth', he told her, 'but I could not find one complete sonnet which satisfies me.' He indulged his sense of humour, leaving a letter of apology for the Governor the day he got away from the 'Joy'. He was sorry, he said, for any inconvenience he had caused, but he felt he could not stay any longer, as the service was not to his satisfaction. He also hoped that the wardens would not get into any trouble because of his departure. Barton was again arrested in February 1920.

Dorothy, and indeed Aunt Alice, may have gone sometimes to the Arts Club where Dermot Coffey was a member, and where a new kind of nationalism was being voiced. George O'Brien, who had succeeded Tom Kettle in the Chair of National Economics at University College, was surprised at what he heard. He had thought that the upper classes in Ireland were all Unionists and that nationalism was confined to the lower and middle classes (Meehan 75). Not all the members of the Club had succumbed to the new nationalism, however, not to its political manifestations at any rate. Sir Horace Plunkett, for example, had formed an Irish Dominion League, believing that, with remedial legislation, good relations, despite 1916 and Sinn Féin, could be established between Great Britain and Ireland. But neither the Dominion League nor another earlier idea of his, the Irish Reconstruction Association, ever really got off the ground, though he put a lot of effort and money into them. The Dominion League bequeathed a valuable legacy, however, in the *Irish Statesman* which, though intended by Plunkett as the organ of the Dominion League, effectively became a national forum of quality to which writers as diverse in their fundamental positions as AE, G. B. Shaw, James Stephens, P. S. O'Hegarty, Stephen Gwynn, Erskine Childers and Darrell Figgis could contribute. The *Statesman* lasted for just one year, until June 1920, by which time dominion status appeared to be a non-runner (Meenan, 81-5). The journal was revived, however, in 1923 and lasted until a libel action bankrupted it in 1930.

Another venture that evoked some interest was the Irish Book Shop in Dawson Street, Dublin, which was started by a group of twelve that included Mrs Green. They formed a co-operative society to which they each contributed £50 and raised a loan from the National Land Bank. On Mrs Green's recommendation P. S. O'Hegarty was made manager. He had given up his Post Office job because he could not conscientiously take an oath of allegiance being administered to Irish civil servants, and was unemployed. Apart from that he had three substantial qualifications for the appointment at that time; he had close links with the national movement – with the IRB, Sinn Féin and the Gaelic League – going back to the beginning of the century; he was a writer, editor, and amateur historian; and a distinguished bibliophile. During the couple of years that he was in charge, the Irish Book Shop became the centre of literary Dublin, and many of the customers would go down to the basement where in the delightful kitchen atmosphere of the *Sod of Turf* they could have tea and home-made scones served to them by an Irish-speaking red-petticoated Aran Islander. Aunt Alice Green went down there sometimes with her grand-niece Mary Wordsworth. It was recognised as a rebelly sort of place, and on that account was often visited by the forces of the Crown.

When, after an interval of months, Dorothy wrote to Nathan again, she assumed he had been busy as she had been, 'busy with her studies, leaving little time for politics and bomb-throwing' of which quite a lot was going on. Accordingly, she said, you will not see me lodged in jail immediately, though, if she could spare the time, she would hop in for a bit. Mrs Green had been laid up with sciatica but was better again more or less.

Despite the pressure on her time, Dorothy had kept abreast of what was happening in the political field. The latest Chief Secretary, Ian Macpherson – there had been two others since Birrell departed – was having a rest cure in England. Since an attempt to assassinate him in the last days of 1919, Lord French, the Lord Lieutenant, was a prisoner in the Viceregal Lodge and never seen. 'Black and Tans' had begun to appear in support of the Royal Irish Constabulary. A British Labour delegation that had been studying the Irish situation would be returning to London soon, and she hoped Nathan would be able to see some of them. 'They have been seeing things for themselves, and you should talk to them, as they came over so prejudiced that they refused even to meet Sinn Féin'. She had told him before that 'all sorts of upper class respectable people', with money, too, were joining Sinn Féin. . . '. 'We have some nice intellectuals, like the Erskine Childers, who have come over here for weal or woe . . . Mrs Childers is going to be a great help over social work, babies' clubs, hospitals etc, and they are a great addition.' Sinn Féin had done very well in the local elections under proportional representation, and now held the country and the Dublin Corporation. It was likely that Alderman Tom Kelly MP (whom Nathan would have remembered since 1916), would be the new Lord Mayor. He was at the moment in Wormwood Scrubs awaiting trial, or rather waiting for a charge to be preferred against him. Things were looking lively, but the people were being very patient and forbearing. But, having gone on for so long, she suddenly remembered that she had got on to the question of Ireland again. 'I had better switch off', she said, and she signed her letter, as she had done before, 'With love, yours affectionately, Dorothy'.

Inconsistently, in her next letter she apologised for not having had the time 'to write a long discourse on Ireland' as she would have liked to do. She had been doing the first part of her Final Medical exam, and she wanted to tell him that 'in spite of Martial Law and the Army of Occupation' she had managed to get through. It was a narrow shave though. She had been *last* on the list of successful candidates and to emphasise this she added three exclamation marks. 'A very proud mother' sent her 'heartiest, lovingist congratulations' by telegram from London. 'It's splendid', she added, 'so thankful'. She started in to practise right away, putting up her plate on the house in Fitzwilliam Square where she had a flat. She did her first ten-guinea operation and then went over to London for a week, to see her mother, and invited Sir Matthew to come and have tea with her at 24 Coulson Street, Chelsea. 'I must counteract the influence which your new Minister will malignly cast upon you with regard to Ireland.' Instead of his taking tea with her she had lunch with him at the Albany. That was in April 1920.

In June she was staying at Mount Trenchard when a number of Royal Irish Constabulary men at Listowel, which was not far away, mutinied, rejecting an instruction from their divisional commissioner to wipe out Sinn Féin by the employment of methods of which he gave an example. They were no longer to confine themselves to patrolling the main roads as they had been doing traditionally but to get into the heart of the country, to lie in ambush behind fences, and when they saw civilians approaching to call on them to put their hands up. If the order was not obeyed immediately, they were to shoot, and shoot with effect. If the persons approaching carried their hands in their pockets, or were in any way suspicious looking, they were to be shot down. 'You may make mistakes occasionally', he told them, 'and innocent persons may be shot, but this cannot be helped and you are bound to get the right persons sometimes. The more you shoot the better I will like you, and I assure you that no policeman will get into trouble for shooting any man.' There would be no coroners' inquests; they were to be made illegal.

The Mutineers, recognising that their own lives were now in danger, went on the run, and one of them, a John Donovan, who came from Foynes, made his way across country and hurried to consult Lord Monteagle whose sympathy with the nationalist movement was well known. Monteagle brought his daughter Mary and Dorothy into a discussion which ended with their all agreeing that Dublin would provide the best hiding place for Donovan and that he should make for there right away. Dorothy wrote her sister Alice's Leinster Road address for him on a piece of paper and Alice was understandably suspicious when a young man who looked every inch a policeman arrived on her doorstep one evening quite unheralded. But she brought him in, was convinced by his story and by the piece of paper, and later thanked Dorothy 'for the parcel which arrived quite safely'. She introduced Donovan to the Manager of the Court Laundry in Harcourt Street who gave him a job in which he stayed happily for forty years. Donovan used to visit Alice regularly: one day she was out when he called and he left a mystified maid with a message to 'tell Mrs Wordsworth that the parcel called'.

That would have been a story for Nathan, and Dorothy may well have told it to him. Her last letter to him that we know about is not dated, but was written some time in 1921 in reply to a farewell letter from him. He had been appointed Governor of Queensland and was about to leave England. She hoped he would be very successful in the post and enjoy his new life. She was very sorry not to see him before he went; she was not coming to London 'But I will write from time to time. Please don't forget me. I shan't you.' She wrote from North Wales where she was recuperating after having her appendix out. She explained:

> At least a month ago I was working hard at surgery and apparently 'caught' appendicitis from my patients! It was only mild, and I feared a return of it at some inopportune moment, so decided to have it out. Also the family was all away and I thought it a good chance to get it out on the quiet. My chief Billy Taylor (Sir William Taylor) did it. I was only 11 days in hospital. It wasn't bad and I was quite amused being in the Meath with all my friends round. . . . When you return from Queensland I hope you will come and visit our republic and perhaps by then I shall be able to enterain you in Merrion Square.
>
> Au revoir, and the best of all go with you.

Nathan was none too happy during the five years he spent in Queensland. Former colonies had acquired self-governing dominion status with the result that Nathan found that the Colonial Office in London, later the Dominions Office, preferred to listen to any source in Queensland rather than himself. His position became largely ornamental, his political influence minimal. He travelled widely through the territory, made gracious speeches and sent long despatches home. In 1925 he was allowed to take his pension and retire. He went to live in Somerset and there quietly put his papers in order and indulged his interest in local antiquities. He modestly refused a request from an American publisher for biographical material to be included in a proposed encyclopedia of 'the lives of 20th century statesmen'. 'I don't feel that I would be justified', he said, 'in giving the public details of what has been, after all, a very ordinary career of a servant of the Crown. It has been the sort of life that one hopes may be remembered by a few friends, but is otherwise scarcely worthy of record in this world.' He never returned to Ireland again, and it is not likely that he missed Dorothy very badly, for he was never short of female company. One particular lady in her early thirties who came into his sights just as Dorothy was leaving them, and who won his affection, as Constance Heppel-Marr had done in 1916, was Amber Pember Reeves, a Fabian Society lady who had figured in the plays of Shaw, was one of H. G. Well's mistresses, the heroine of his novel *'Ann Veronica'*, and whose civil service career Nathan helped to advance. She was beautiful, but not universally admired. Aunt Alice's friend, Beatrice Webb, saw her as 'an amazingly vital person, very clever, but a terrible little pagan, vain, egotistical, and careless of other people's happiness'; and Shaw told Wells — as if the latter had not discovered it himself — that Amber was, 'an ungovernable young devil'. Her letters to Nathan from 1919 until his departure for Queensland, and from 1926 when he returned till 1930, are addressed to a man who was almost twice her age and when she was the mother of three children. They have survived among Nathan's papers whereas his letters to her have not, for, at his request, she burnt them all, while he, rather dishonourably, kept hers. 'I could not have believed', she told him, 'that it would hurt so much [to burn your letters]. Little sullen glassy flames have eaten your words, and crumpled the paper on which your hands had rested. There were things in them that had made me hide my face for joy'. She referred to this matter later when, one thinks, with some deliberation she said, 'Darling, you complain that I don't write to you often enough. . . . You have this great advantage, that all your letters are burned, so that they can't be referred to and brought up against you.'

Her letters spoke of a liaison — her word; the need for a good comfortable shoulder to put her head on; her intention to write a novel for him as a proof of devotion; which she did — one entitled *Give and Take*; of an affair she wished should never have happened and that they had just been friends; of the receipt of the most wonderful letter she had ever had; and of being terrified of him sometimes when she realised he had a mastery over her of a sort she would not have thought possible. She sent him kisses. She professed she was his lover, his mistress. She *adored* him, 'an awkward word to use in this world where to be adorèd is embarrassing'. There was on earth no joy like his presence and no satisfaction like his companionship; to love him was what she was made for, and why she came to live.

Their relationship — which began with an invitation to him to go with her to the Russian ballet while her husband, the barrister Blanco White was taking his Phyllis dancing — petered out in time. When, as I have told elsewhere, I went to see Amber in her Hampstead home about thirty years after Nathan's death, she looked back, from her chaise longue, with cold detachment on their long association. She made no mention of her correspondence with Nathan, nor did I. Her husband was lying upstairs, seriously ill, and she was having trouble with her Irish maids, about whom she talked a good deal. But when she turned to the subject of Sir Matthew Nathan, which she had told me in advance she would be willing to discuss with me, she told me she had met him on some committee or other when she was in the Ministry of Labour and he in Pensions. He was a dear, charming, impressive-looking man, but a philanderer, a man who thought women existed to serve him; a bit of a humbug too, she thought, and not very sincere. He had talked to her about his past, about Ireland and 1916. From being 'the star of the Civil Service' he had been degraded on account of what happened that year, but the many friends he had taken pains to cultivate rallied round and put him back in the firmament. It seemed to me, as I listened to her, that she was describing something rather unimportant that had happened in a far distant past. In 1939, the year Nathan died and the Second World War started she had a book published on *The New Propaganda* and, ten years later, another, *Ethics for Unbelievers*.

The Stopfords knew nothing of all this. They would have been surprised by Nathan's liaisons. Dorothy would have been mortified. She was by now a member of Cumann na mBan, the IRA's auxiliary.

Chapter Four

INDEPENDENCE AND CIVIL WAR

It was in November 1919 that Hyde spoke of the apotheosis of Sinn Féin. It was an accurate judgment. For in the ten months that had passed since the emergence of Dáil Éireann not only had the Irish Parliamentary Party and its popular organisation literally disappeared, but British government in Ireland had effectively broken down. With de Valera, the President of the Dáil, campaigning in the United States for the recognition of Ireland as a republic, his cabinet under Arthur Griffith endeavoured to function independently if mostly clandestinely. Its propaganda, for home and overseas consumption, was of a high order and the political backing it enjoyed in the country won it considerable success in the sphere of local government and in the operation of local and land courts. A great deal depended on the capacity of individual ministers and their opportunities. It was most unlikely, for instance, that Eoin MacNeill could do anything worthwhile in the industrial bailiwick that was assigned to him, whereas Michael Collins was able to use his position as Minister for Finance to oversee many projects including the raising of public loans, and simultaneously to direct organisation and intelligence-gathering for the Volunteers, soon to become the Irish Republican Army. It was in this area, more perhaps than in any other, that what the government called Sinn Féin made its greatest challenge.

Asquith's government had foundered through lack of proper information; Lloyd George's had begun to fall for the same reason; and it was Collins who saw to it that in Dublin the Metropolitan Police's Division, and in the country the Royal Irish Constabulary, traditionally the eyes and ears of the government, were rendered incapable of functioning properly, while his own sources of intelligence were extra-ordinarily extensive. Collins undermined the British machine by recruiting policemen to work for him even inside Dublin Castle itself; and, by shooting a few of the most officious G-men, he left the remainder unhappy about doing the work they were paid to do. A campaign against the Royal Irish Constabulary had a somewhat similar effect. Attacks on some barracks caused others to be evacuated before being attacked at all. Hundreds of these buildings were then burned down for propaganda purposes as well as to prevent reoccupation. The morale of the force, which had suffered through boy-cotting and other practices, deteriorated rapidly, and there were many resignations. In a review of the situation early in 1920 General Sir Neville Macready, who had been appointed to command the British Army in Ireland, told the Cabinet that the RIC might collapse at any moment and that the DMP was absolutely useless. Already a decision had been taken to find recruits for the RIC in Britain. Recruiting offices had been opened, and a special recruiting office had begun to travel the country. By the end of January, 100 men had been appointed, and the foundations laid for the expansion that took place during the summer of 1920.

The Army had hitherto kept a low profile, and the Prime Minister, Lloyd George, desired that that should remain the position. It suited his book that the world should see that what was happening in Ireland was a police war, something the police on their own could handle. Hence he did not object to finding recruits in Britain for the RIC. But after an ambush attempt on the life of Lord French, the Viceroy, in December 1919, that position was no longer maintained, and the powers previously vested in the police were transferred to the Competent Military Authority who were usually brigade commanders. The Army at this time consisted largely of inex-perienced troops: they were certainly ill-fitted for the sort of work that now fell to their lot, raiding and searching private houses for wanted men and arms, and trying to build up an intelligence service on little more than captured written material. Macready hoped a reorganised police force would help, and he allowed himself to be overborne by his Police Advisor, Major General H. H. Tudor, into making extended

use from April 1920 of the new recruits from Britain, categor-
ised as 'Black and Tans' or as Auxiliaries. These men, more
efficiently armed than the old RIC had ever been, and equipped with 'cage cars and Crosley tenders', now roamed the
countryside, terrorising all before them, shooting on sight,
beating up prisoners and conducting reprisals. These were
either 'official' reprisals that involved the deliberate destruction of property near scenes of ambush, or 'unofficial' ones
including the shooting of prisoners allegedly when trying to
escape. The worst case of 'unofficial' reprisals was the bur-
ning down of practically the whole of the main street of
Cork city. The Government sought to minimise these outrages, but they could not suppress all knowledge of them. The
British Liberal newspapers were wholly condemnatory and
members of parliament harried ministers at Question Time
and in set debates. The Labour Party set up a Commission of
Enquiry. A former Liberal Home Secretary, Sir John Simon,
was a particularly conspicuous critic of government policy
and, employing Edie Stopford, who was a relative of his
deceased wife, for the purpose, he organised an anti-Black
and Tan campaign. Edie, with Sir John's second wife, 'an
ardent Irishwoman', travelled with Sir John to meetings all
over England, usually organised by local Liberals, at which he
was the principal speaker. These were most successful occasions; four thousand people, for example, packed the Free
Trade Hall in Manchester. Sir John had to contend at times
with Empire Loyalists but his formidable debating skill
overcame the opposition.

On a visit to England Dorothy spent a week-end at the
Simons' country house, with Edie, and joined Sir John at a
Birmingham Liberal Club dinner. He was anxious to show
Dorothy that there were some people in England who were
right-minded on the Irish question. A couple of hundred
people sat down to the meal, Dorothy being placed between
the Chairman and Sir John. When the dinner was finished but
before the speeches began, the loyal toast was proposed.
Everybody, including Edie, who admitted that she was
nothing if not conformist, rose in their places – everybody,
that is, except Dorothy, who remained rooted to her chair.
'Sir John took this adventure very well', Edie said, 'but Lady

Simon, who had remained at home, was shocked when she heard of it.' However, the Liberal Chairman, who came over to Sunday luncheon with his wife, was not a bit upset apparently. Indeed, he seemed to have admired Dorothy's courage and would talk to no one else. As for Sir John, Dorothy's conquest of him was complete when she beat him easily at billiards, at which he was rated to be good. He told Edie afterwards in confidence that Dorothy strode round the billiard table, a cigarette hanging out of one corner of her mouth, and curses streaming out of the other.

Some months later Sir John released Edie so that she might become Secretary to a group who, under the chairmanship of Lord Henry Bentinck, a philanthropic Conservative member of Parliament, had formed a Peace with Ireland Council, inspired by Captain George Fitz-hardinge Berkeley. The honorary secretary of the group was Oswald Mosley, the treasurer was the historian Basil Williams, and on the executive committe were such well-known figures as J. L. Hammond, H. W. Nevinson, and Leonard Woolf. This Council was essentially an organisation of British people who wished to see peace and self-government in Ireland. It had no official connection with any British or Irish parties, it subsisted on subscriptions and donations and, during the year and a quarter that Edie was employed by it, it organised meetings, sent representatives to Ireland to report on conditions there, established a rota of members of Parliament to ask questions in the Commons, arranged for pamphlets to be written by celebrities like G. K. Chesterton, Hilaire Belloc and Robert Lynd and did all it could to have the death sentences imposed by British military courts commuted.

The largest public meeting organised by the Council was one for women only which was held at the Central Hall, Westminster, where even the stewarding was done by women. One woman was designated to speak for each of the major political allegiances – Lady (Mark) Sykes for the Tories, Lady Violet Bonham Carter for the Liberals, Margaret Bondfield for Labour – and there was to be no other speaker. But Lady Aberdeen, the formidable wife of a former Lord Lieutenant of Ireland, insisted on getting up while her diminutive husband was smuggled into a place at the Reporters' table, which was still a men's preserve. A sure proof that the meeting had been a great success was the fact that the collection was the largest ever taken up in the Central Hall.

In the course of her duties Edie found herself in some unusual situations. She arrived at the office one morning to find a strange man awaiting her. This was Brigadier-General E. F. Crozier who wanted the support of the Council in the lurid report he was writing about the Black and Tans. He had resigned his post as their commanding officer because he could not continue to lead what he described as a drunken, insubordinate body. He left his draft report with Edie, somewhat to her alarm, for she feared that there might be a raid on the office, and that 'incriminating documents' might be said to have been found there. She determined not to keep the report at the office, therefore, and left it with the sympathetic wife of a civil servant until the officers of the Council could decide what to do with it. They came to the conclusion that the Council should not get mixed up in the affair, which was complicated; and they may have ascertained that Crozier had a reputation for unreliability among people who knew him well. He eventually published a couple of books on the subject which caused a stir, and embarrassed the government greatly.

Yeats raised his voice. He had a house in Oxford at this time, and was so stirred by an account from Lady Gregory of the shooting at Gort of an expectant mother that he wrote:

> Now days are dragon-ridden, the nightmare
> Rides upon sleep; a drunken soldiery
> Can leave the mother, murdered at her door,
> To crawl in her own blood, and go scot-free.

Speaking to a motion of no confidence in the government's Irish policy at the Oxford Union, he tore into the English position with extraordinary vehemence 'striding up and down between the Ayes and the Noes waving his arms and shaking his fists at the audience, and pouring out a sustained flow of language. At first the house was changed into a theatre audience, but as he went on it became more and more beaten and subdued. Eventually Yeats sat down amidst unexampled enthusiasm, and the motion was approved by an overwhelming majority. The occasion was considered unique in the history of the Union' (Hone, 330).

The murder of Mrs Quinn of Gort that inspired Yeat's poem gives us an important date in the Anglo-Irish war – November 1920. By then Dáil Éireann, which had been formally suppressed in September of the previous year and its staff arrested a couple of weeks later, had been very much 'on the run' and in 1920 only met three times. Everything had to be done in secret. The location of Dáil departments, organised usually on a tiny scale, had to be concealed, and the GHQ staff of the IRA were compelled to maintain separate peripatetic existences. The British naturally intensified their efforts to eliminate the extremist elements – notably Michael Collins's active service unit who had been responsible for an unending series of 'outrages' – and for that purpose introduced into Dublin a Secret Service group. The IRA dealt with this danger on 21 November 1920 by shooting the bulk of the Secret Service officers in their beds; while that afternoon, in retaliation, the Black and Tans in a swoop at a sports meeting, killed fourteen people and wounded sixty. That 'Bloody Sunday' has gone down in history. It was followed by a huge military and police operation. Internment on suspicion was restored, curfews were extended, and a massive programme of road blocks, searches and arrests was set on foot. The pressure was intense, and by July 1921 nearly 4,500 IRA men from Brigade Commandants downwards were in custody (Townshend, 130). Among those arrested were Arthur Griffith, Eoin MacNeill, and Eamon Duggan, a triumvirate that the British found useful to negotiate with, for it was their policy, while suppressing the IRA, to explore the possibility of a political settlement. With Griffith a prisoner, Collins acted as head of the Irish government, such as it was, until de Valera returned home in December 1920.

Of all the Dáil members, Mrs Green knew MacNeill best and admired him most. His arrest did not worry her unduly; she knew that he could spend his time profitably behind bars, as indeed he did. He was able to obtain the published volumes of the *Ancient Laws of Ireland* from the library of University

College, Dublin, and by the time he left Mountjoy Gaol he had prepared the bones of an important paper he was to read before the Royal Irish Academy on the law of status or franchise. Its quality was so good that MacNeill's friend Thurneysen said that any really patriotic government would keep MacNeill in gaol for nine months each year.

MacNeill and his colleagues, imprisoned as they were, had the comfort of feeling that the days of the British in Ireland were pretty much at an end. They gauged this from the unusually polite attitude of the warders to them, and from the stream of visitors that came to them at the instance of the government. First among these, under an assumed name, was Lord Derby whose principal object apparently was to ascertain for Lloyd George whether the morale of Sinn Féin was breaking down. The Catholic Archbishop of Perth, Dr Patrick Clune, came twice, first with the same object as Lord Derby, but then apparently to explore the ground further. Members of what was effectively a peace party among the civilian officials in Dublin Castle came also more than once: James MacMahon, an Under Secretary, who was known to MacNeill personally, and Alfred Cope, a former Customs detective who enjoyed a special relationship with the Prime Minister.

Alice Green's gracious house on Stephen's Green beside the Russell Hotel meanwhile was a salon in which every form of national activity was promoted and where foreign journalists could meet national leaders. She received there, as she had done in London, scholars and literary men like Douglas Hyde, George Russell (AE), James Stephens, R. I. Best, Osborn Bergin and Edmund Curtis; and political figures like Horace Plunkett, George Gavan Duffy, James Douglas, Erskine Childers, Mary Spring-Rice, Desmond Fitzgerald and Frank Gallagher, some of whom were 'on the run' from the British. Mary Comerford, who was with Mrs Green daily from 1919, used to recognise Michael Collins's tall bicycle if it was standing in the hall when she entered the house, and she would wait on the alert till she heard him leave. Mrs Green was an admirer of Collins and paid a tribute in print to the efficiency of his intelligence service. It was, she said, a wonder to both friends and enemies. Dublin Castle had never been able to grapple with it, and she ascribed its success partly to the fact that the whole Irish nation was involved in the conspiracy. But she recoiled from physical force, and pleaded for Ireland's case to be submitted to international arbitration. Nevertheless she was suspected by the British (Pim, 212). Her house was systematically raided by military and police, her papers and manuscripts seized and returned to her in chaotic confusion, her movements dogged by police. Through it all, she neither complained nor despaired, and in the darkest hours continued to plead for tolerance and patience. At the same time she refused to have her hall-door repainted lest the marks of the raiders' knuckle-dusters and rifle butts should be obliterated.

One night when the Auxiliaries came, Mary Comerford saw Mrs Green standing, in contemptuous silence, outside her bedroom door at the top of the stairs. She was wearing a stiff brocade gown which hung straight from her shoulders. Her head was high, her hands low about her figure. She had in fact a whole file of the banned *Irish Bulletin* inside her gown, and could not have moved without it slipping. Two days later, she with Mary, was at a meeting in the Childers' house at Bushy Park Road when the same party of Auxiliaries arrived. The leader asked all present to give their names. Mrs Childers, an American, smiled and said nothing; when he came to Mrs Green, he said, 'I know you.' Mrs Green smiled, too, we imagine, and, speaking across the room to Mary, she said, 'This time he knows us even when we are dressed.' The questioning went no further. 'She was an old woman writing history,' Mary said on another occasion, 'getting up to work in the morning long before I did. Whenever a bomb went off or she heard shooting in the street she'd send me out to see what was happening. Because she wanted to keep in touch with the history that was being made outside her door.'

On Wednesday, 30 March 1921, Dorothy Stopford travelled on the 9.30 mail from Kingsbridge to Limerick and went on by a 6 o'clock train from there with Lord Monteagle to Mount Trenchard. There had been what she called a shooting match, which was heard at Mount Trenchard, at Ballyhahill between the police and the IRA, one Volunteer being killed and another wounded. The next day the Black and Tans raided Mount Trenchard. 'Mary and I', Dorothy wrote 'were making first-aid outfits, and just had time to stuff everything down our front when an officer and twenty men walked in. They were very polite in the big house, but broke windows in a house nearby and beat up a Unionist boy on the avenue.' On 3 April Dorothy was taken by two of the Ballyhahill lads at night time to the wounded man who was lying in a remote farmhouse across the Kerry border. He had an ugly bullet wound in his jaw, 'luckily in and out', and it needed attention badly after days of amateur dressing. Dorothy fixed him up and while the lads slept on the kitchen table she dozed by the fire until dawn when she redressed the wound, and then showed the lads how to make a chair with their hands so as to carry the patient down to the roadway. She, herself, was given a bike to take her back to Mount Trenchard; and on the following day was able to see the fellow again and dress his wound.

She spent the night of 5 April in Limerick with a view to catching the Cork train next morning. 'I saw five prisoners and half a regiment of British at Patrickswell. Visited Miss [Madge] Daly [of Cumann na mBan]. There was a shoot-up somewhere at 10 p.m. curfew time, and forming fours under my bedroom window. Next day the curfew was put to 4 p.m.' On that day she went on from Cork to Bandon and was met at the railway station there by Maud O'Neill and Baby Lordan who was a qualified nurse. They had a trap and drove Dorothy out to the O'Neills of Maryboro' [in the Kilbrittain area] about 8 miles away, where she was to stay, sleeping with Baby in one bed while Maud slept with her mother in the other. Her sleep all that night was disturbed by the flashing on her eyes of the lights of the Old Head of Kinsale.

This was the starting point of an assignment that had been given to Dorothy by the Headquarters of Cumann na mBan, to lecture on first-aid to the Kilbrittain branch, which was closely caught up in the activities of the West Cork Brigade of the IRA and its Flying Column. The assignment caused Dorothy some anxiety for, having passed all her final examinations, she did not want to get into any trouble until Trinity had actually conferred her degrees. She was not sure whether, in the event of finding herself a prisoner in Mountjoy — which was not unlikely — they would confer *in absentia*. It was necessary, therefore, to be circumspect, though how this was to be achieved in a hotbed of Sinn Féin was problematical.

To call Kilbrittain a Sinn Féin hotbed was no exaggeration. As early as June 1919, only five months after Soloheadbeg, members of the Kilbrittain company of Volunteers, which Tom Barry was to claim was the best company in Ireland, intervened in a local land dispute to disarm a combined police and military patrol. No shot was fired; and the captured rifles formed the basis of such armaments as the West Cork Brigade ultimately possessed. That December the company shot 'a most aggressive policeman' and, in the first half of 1920 the Kilbrittain men participated in attacks on coast-guard stations to obtain further arms, and on the Black and Tans who had established a post locally. When that summer GHQ directed that a Flying Column should be started in each Brigade area, the order was enthusiastically received in West Cork, and at Clonbuig, which is about two and a half miles from Kilbrittain, a training course was held at which selected officers learned something of what life on a column would demand of them, Clonbuig is six miles from Bandon and fifteen miles from Kinsale, two of the West Cork towns held in strength by the 1st Essex Regiment of the British Army under Major Percival. At the end of the course, with a column formally in being, Tom Barry was chosen as its commander. He had joined the British Army at the age of 17, not, as he explained later, to secure Home Rule for Ireland or to fight for little Belgium, but because he wanted to see what war was like, to get a gun, and to feel a grown man. After the war, through reading Irish history, of which before he knew absolutely nothing, and influenced by the post-1916 atmo-sphere, he became an intelligence officer for the IRA in Bandon, and was later asked to take on the training of Volunteers throughout the Brigade area. With his Flying Column he made various fruitless moves to engage the British before it became possible to strike a first blow at Toureen on the main Bandon-Cork Road. It was an uneven fight. The column of thirty-two men ambushed two lorries of soldiers, killing four of them, forcing the surrender of the remainder and then, having collected the arms and equipment and burnt the lorries, letting the survivors go.

The column then marched back to Clonbuig and were disbanded, their rifles and those they had captured being required for other training camps that were being set up. Through these camps some 110 men were available for Flying Column service, and in November forty of them, including only one man who had been at Toureen, were chosen in the Dunmanway area and marched under cover of darkness to a chosen ambush position about a mile and a half south of the village of Kilmichael where the expected target was a convoy of Auxiliaries then operated regularly out of Macroom terrorising the countryside. Among their victims had been the old parish priest of Dunmanway. The Column had a long wait in the cold and rain before the two lorry-loads of Auxiliaries appeared in the half-light. They were immediately attacked with bombs and rifle fire and all eighteen Auxiliaries killed. The ambush and annihilation, coming a week after Dublin's Bloody Sunday, had a numbing effect on the British, and West Cork trembled in anticipation of reprisals (Townshend, 131). It was into this situation, and now with martial law in force on all sides, that Dorothy Stopford entered.

Her lectures, to sixteen girls, given in the open air in the grounds of Ardnacrow House, were no doubt a success, but she startled Cumann na mBan Headquarters when she told them later that from her experience what had principally to be learned by the girls was not the textbook stuff but how to ensure that Active Service Units or Flying Columns had changes of clothes, and that sulphur baths were available for anyone who had a dose of scabies through sleeping rough. In addition, but condensed to two or three talks, she instructed at evening time in neighbourhood farmhouses the officers and men of the Kilbrittain Volunteer company who were sometimes joined by some of the Battalion Officers and by the Medical Officer of the Flying Column. She was accepted as worthy to doctor the IRA of West Cork when she demonstrated to a cynical audience how a tourniquet on the brachial artery, tightened by a pencil, caused the pulse to stop in the toughest arm. On one occasion, a British raiding officer asked her if she would attend a wounded IRA man. 'Of course I would', she said, 'I am a doctor!' He thought he had her. 'Well', he said, 'would you attend a wounded policeman?' 'Of course I would', was her reply, 'I am a doctor – I'll attend anyone who is in need of my services.'

Some of the girls were relaxing in the fields at Maryboro on the last day of their course when someone ran out to say that the Essex Regiment were raiding the Neills' house and wanted to interview Dorothy. 'We stuffed the first-aid notes into a hole in the wall', Dorothy said, 'and I went in. The Captain, Grove-something double-barrelled, but hardly by his behaviour of the old Essex aristocracy, started off with "What was I doing there? Didn't I know that I was in a hot bed of rebels?" "I don't know about that", I replied, "but they're nice people anyway."' Under further questioning she told a story that had been arranged beforehand. 'I was up for the post of Kilbrittain dispensary which was vacant, and had come down to look round, sent by one of the Neill sons who was in Dublin. The story half-went down, but they wanted to know why I had a pipe, showing that they had searched my case. I replied, with perfect truth, "I smoke one, do you want a demonstration?" Some of the soldiers laughed, where-upon the Captain said: "Well, you have orders to clear out of here immediately whatever you are doing." I replied that I was going tomorrow, couldn't go sooner, no train. They then went away, having found nothing more incriminating than the pipe.'

Apropos of that, Denis Lordan told me that he had noticed that Dorothy was an unusually heavy smoker. 'Two of us', said Denis, 'were on the way to do a job during the Tan War, Mick Crowley and myself. She had a problem. She was anxious to smoke a pipe. "I wonder Dinny", she asked me, "what people would think if they saw me smoking a pipe."' They probably advised her not to do so outside the house, and she followed their advice. 'How many times have I listened to words of equal wisdom from the lips of Denis Lordan', she wrote, when he had given her an opinion about the effect on the community of her appearing in riding breeches and a rich red jumper.

'On the day after the visit from the Essex the girls drove

me to Bandon railway station for the Cork train. I had despatches for Dublin. I carried them in a case to the station,
and in the station lavatory transferred them to my person.
The Essex paraded up and down the platform, apparently
indifferent, but eyeing me getting into the train.' The following week she was in Trinity for the conferring and, when a
press photographer took two new M.B.s shaking hands she
saw to it that a false name was given for her. She did not want
the Essex to have a photo of her in their barracks in Bandon.

'After trying without success for various posts in Dublin',
Dorothy recorded in her papers, 'and being quite penniless
by this time, I decided to apply really for the Kilbrittain
dispensary. It was not easy to get the IRA to understand
that I was applying in earnest and not as an alibi again.' There
had been three doctors there in rapid succession. The Black
and Tans, who occupied the police barracks, frightened the
first man out; the second stayed only a short time; and the
third went into residence with the Catholic curate but ran
away in his slippers during a raid by Auxiliaries who took
shots at him as he ran. It was a dangerous place to work in,
obviously; and understandably the dispensary remained
vacant for six months. So, Dorothy said 'I got the post, Anyone was welcome, even a "gurral"!' In the last week of May,
then, she went down to take up duty. Maudie Neill was again
at Bandon Station with a gig, and drove her to Flaxfort, a
bunch of cottages on the arm of a creek of the Timoleague
river, about two miles from the village of Kilbrittain. There
was no dispensary residence, so she stopped with an old
fisherman and his wife, the Wheltons, in their two-storey
council house, taking her meals in the kitchen and sleeping
in the parlour which had been turned into a bedroom. The
family lived upstairs. Their son, Billy Whelton, was out with
the Flying Column.

Dorothy settled in quickly. She loved the place, was seen
to be a jolly person with a capacity to make herself at home
wherever she was, and was the more easily accepted because
some people had heard of her distinguished aunt, while
others 'in the movement' knew of her association with Mary
Spring-Rice, Kathleen Lynn, Dorothy Macardle and Bob

Barton. 'It came, therefore, as no surprise to find me on the national side', Dorothy reported.

The official job should have made immediately for a busy life. The district was large with dispensary centres to be attended on different days of the week and sick people to be visited in their homes. 'The trouble is,' she told Aunt Alice, 'that *no one* gets sick here, so I am very idle.' Her first problem, however, was one of locomotion. The dispensary in Ballinadee was about ten miles away, a distance too far to cycle:

> I intended to buy a motor with my last remaining capital, so some of the girls drove me to Kinsale to look for a military permit, which was necessary for running a car. At the barracks gate I sent in my card to the Colonel, explaining my business. After some delay the Corporal returned with the message that 'There will be no permit for you for a car or anything else on any account.' Good, say I, we know where we are, no need for further camouflage. I'm in the open now and it's much easier. It had been denied in the British House of Commons that motor permits had been refused to doctors in Ireland; so I wrote out a statement of my case, got it witnessed by our good and friendly C. of I. clergyman, and sent it to my sister Edie Stopford in London, who was the Secretary of the Peace with Ireland Council. Thinking the ordinary post unsafe, I sent it by the Republican post underground, but alas it never reached its destination.
>
> At this point the lads provided a horse for transport, a grey cob, from a farm near the Wheltons' cottage. It was foddered from another farm and fetched over to me every morning and evening, thus distributing the expense of its keep. The lads arranged all this; I only had to get on to the horse and off it again. Dr Thomas Watson had given me some leather saddlebags, which you put under the saddle, and these, filled with bottles and instruments, flapped round the horse's middle as he jogged along; on long distance calls and midwifery cases one had to carry a stock of bottles and things. There was a mild sensation the first day I went into Bandon in this position. The first

day at Kilbrittain dispensary no one came, the next day a flock of persons with trumped up complaints came just to have a look at the doctoress and her riding breeches, both novelties in these parts.

It was wonderful hot June weather, the sky a cloudless blue, the furze full out, wayside flowers at their best, the sea blue-green looking out over Courtmacsherry Bay to where the Lusitania sank some five or six years before. Thirsty weather with a glass of milk at every halt, up to six or seven a day. If only there wasn't death waiting round every corner for the lads. The grey cob plodded along with occasional short-cuts across country; I fell off quite a lot, and then some farmer would appear over a hedge and put me on again.

Curfew during that month of June was fixed at 8 p.m. in our parts and a list of the inhabitants of each house had to be pinned up inside the door. It was awfully hot to stay indoors from 8 o'clock on a summer's evening, and we didn't. Major Percival of the Essex had set up his own mobile patrol and scouts who operated between the barracks of Kinsale and Bandon, but we always knew where they were, and we could stay out if they were not in the neighbourhood. Indeed even when they were around I had to go on cases a few times, avoiding them as best I could. There was a volunteer casualty some five miles away who had to be visited every evening for several days. I never had any bother, though in the dark, with the cob's feet clapping, one felt a bit jumpy at times.

Over in Murphy's farm in the townland of Scaife which was the Headquarters of the First Battalion (Bandon) of the Brigade there was a case which Dorothy attended earlier in the day. This was a chap with face burns that had gone septic and which needed continuous dressings. Getting to him was not easy, because of the great discretion required in approaching such a place. She has described the roundabout itinerary: 'I went by horseback from Flaxfort to James O'Mahony's farm at Cloundereen, then Mary O'Mahony, one of the best of the Cumann na mBan, or Ellen, the faithful Jack of all Trades who helped there and about whose courage a volume could be written, escorted me across the fields and open brake to Bawnee. From there I went across the main Timoleague-Bandon road — this the only real danger spot as lorries might be passing — down a deep cutting and up to Murphy's house on the other side of a stream, a matter of two miles or so. By the time I had dressed the wound and got back, a whole afternoon would be gone. I would not dare, of course, to approach by road on horseback.'

She was often held up on the roads, questioned and the saddle bags searched, by soldiers of the Essex Regiment. The Essex's mobile column was not really mobile. Whenever they emerged from the gates of their stronghold, some boy or girl would slip out on a horse or bike and give warning of the road they were taking, to be passed on, in case any of the lads were about, so was time to prepare for them. The local scouts, volunteers and any officers of the First Battalion who were not with the Brigade's Flying Column would be around Flaxfort quite often. Minor engagements such as a flying attack on Kilbrittain police barracks made life exciting. 'Don't come out, Doctor, unless we send for you, if you hear shots,' was their kindly advice to Dorothy before an engagement. She got an embarrassing souvenir in the shape of a Union Jack after the taking of the coastguard station at Howes Strand; but a bad petrol burn had to be dressed in the middle of the night after the station went up in flames.

One of her chief memories of those times was of families living in lofts, cattle sheds, or other makeshift dwellings whilst they scrabbled in the ruins of their burnt houses for belongings. Big houses also went up in flames, but to these Dorothy had not the *entreé*, being only called there on a red ticket to attend to the domestic staff. She was regarded with a certain degree of suspicion by the rich, and by the Protestant community particularly, although she reckoned among her great friends the Church of Ireland Rector in Rathclaren, Mr O'Neill, his wife and numerous offspring, the Barretts of Courtmacsherry, and Dr Whelpley of Bandon who treated the Volunteers in the same way as he did the police and the men of the Essex but 'never told on them'.

This matter of 'telling on them' had painful consequences.

'One day', Denis Lordan told me, 'some of the column was going up for tea to a Protestant house. One of them, we called him Peter, was a deserter from the Argyll and Sutherland Highlanders. They met a local farmer on the way driving his pony and trap, an 'old fellow' and a Protestant. He got talking to Peter and thought from his accent that he was an Auxie. He started to blow the gaffe. 'Is it safe for me to be talking to you, sir', he asked, and was assured that it was. He then told Peter that he had been out walking his land and came across a passage and a dug-out in the middle of the brake. Then, to Peter, he said: 'I'm not like the rest of them round here at all. The Reverend Mr Lord is my man, and I give him the information. You fellows should come round at night I'd show you round.' Peter told his pals and, while Lordan was consulting Tom Barry and Charlie Hurley, the leaders of the column, who were staying with another Protestant nearby, the lads 'made a football of the old fellow on the floor'. He was shot that night; and a cousin of his who had also been giving information died four or five nights later. The clergyman in Bandon, Mr Lord, went unharmed.

That there was a Protestant reaction in the area to the activity of the Volunteers, a sort of anti-independence movement, appears to have been the case; and local Protestant farmers were believed to have been responsible for the shooting of two boys named Coffey. Dorothy was upset by these happenings, and was afraid they might lead to a religious war. One particular incident that occurred during the Civil War positively distressed her. The 'boys' went to a Protestant house to seize a motor car, were fired on, and one of them killed. Then 'our fellows took it out on the Protestants,' Denis Lordan told me ruefully. Dorothy's own position was clear enough. She was a religious person, Denis thought, and went regularly to the Church of Ireland in Rathclaren. If she was late for the Service there, she came to Mass in Kilbrittain. Lordan asked her one day about her church-going in Dublin. 'I hardly ever go in Dublin', she said, 'because I don't see why the Minister should ask for prayers for the King and not for this country'.

The ordinary people liked Dorothy very much as a person —

one of them writing to her called her 'Miss Lady Stopford' —
and thought much of her as a doctor. There were exceptions.
One old farmer sent for her when his wife was ill. When
somebody asked him afterwards how the wife was, he replied
that she wasn't too well. 'It's a man-doctor she wants.' Some
people would not have her on account of her politics, but
they were very few. She loved children, was good with them,
and laughed at their boldness. Nobody commented on her
accent, not even the children to whom it must have sounded
very unusual, but men talked of her habit, when speaking to
them, of doodling with a pen or pencil: as often as not she
was doing a drawing of them.

During the time she was staying with the Wheltons at
Flaxfort the house was raided at least twice. She has left a
vivid record of one of these raids:

We had one visit about 9 o'clock one night, and Percival,
who participated in it, took a look at me round the door
while the subaltern read the list of names. They said that
he never forgot a face, once seen, so we all tried to avoid
meeting his scrutiny. Billy Whelton, the man they were
looking for, was two fields away in a ditch and so escaped.
I was warned about the other raid as I returned on the cob
from my rounds. A boy jumped over a ditch and shouted
that the military were making for Flaxfort. I fairly gallop-
ed back by a short cut ahead of them, hastily seized the
mail which had come in my absence, and had time to burn
certain letters which might have interested them, and was
sitting eating my tea when a detachment of the Essex
rushed in headed by my old friend Captain Grove Whatever
you call him. He leaned over the table and scooping up the
remaining letters lying there proceeded to read them,
without a word. This amused me very much. They then
asked me where I had been and went into my bedroom,
I followed to prevent them stealing anything, and old
Mrs Whelton came in crying 'Shame on yez. Has a young
girl no secrets from the likes of yez?' They would not leave,
and knowing they were certain there was something hidden in the bed under me, I casually moved off it, and the
tore it to bits after three of them making a spring at it.

Such clumsy investigation one could not conceive; a child could have fooled them still one had to have respect for their multiple lethal weapons. . . . After this raid they took to intercepting my letters out of the Kilbrittain Bag in Bandon post office. We knew this from Miss Twomey on the staff there. So I arranged with Dr. Hennessy, the Medical Officer of Health in Bandon, to have letters sent care of him, and rode in twice a week and collected them from that kind old man's Medical Hall.

On the 21 June the Earl of Bandon, an old man, was kidnapped from Castle Bernard which was burned down, and held as a hostage. He was held, at first, in Murphy's house at Scaife, the Adjutant of the battalion headquarters there taking charge of him. He told Dorothy that the 'old boy' grew very fond of his guards. 'Good boys', he used to call them, and he gave the Adjutant a turquoise ring as a souvenir. Later as the search for him intensified, he was shifted about. At one time he was in a farmhouse in Barryroe, a remote headland south of Timoleague. Suddenly the Essex column appeared coming down the road towards the house. The farmer's wife had a nightdress pulled over her clothes and she was popped into the double bed with the Earl in the hope that he might be mistaken for her husband by the soldiers. The lads hid outside. The Column passed by however, little thinking how near they were to their object, and the poor old man to his release. During his captivity, Dorothy reflected, he probably discovered more about his neighbours in County Cork than he had learnt in seventy-odd years living amongst them in his castle.

Whenever she came up to Dublin, Dorothy stayed with her sister Alice Wordsworth at 53 Leinster Road, Rathmines. This was an old terrace house which, on account of the owner being a Protestant with such a patently English name, was regarded as 'safe' for men on the run, and where important meetings could be held. Liam Mellowes and Sean Etchingham, both 'wanted' men, lived there frequently for long periods as did Erskine Childers occasionally. The Army Council of the IRA came together there several times. Mary,

Alice's daughter, then a child of ten, remembers seeing Michael Collins, Dick Mulcahy, and 'Ginger' O'Connell. She told me:

> The first time they met in our house after they had been in session for some little time, my mother happened to look out of the front window and saw that they had left eight men's bicycles propped up along the hedge in the front garden — quite enough to arouse suspicion in any passer-by who happened to notice them. She went into the room where they were, and said aloud 'I think you're all quite mad!' They looked up in some surprise and she said, 'You've left all those bicycles stacked up in the front garden for anyone to see!' Collins leapt to his feet. He was a very big man, and Mother always said she had a vision of small tables and chairs at quite a distance from him falling over when he moved. He rushed out of the front door and down the steps, caught up a bicycle in each hand and carried them up the steps and into the hall and then went back for the rest. They met several times in our house without detection.
>
> One evening there was a ring at the bell, and when my mother opened the door, there was Mary Comerford, Aunt Alice's Secretary, panting with excitement, with blood on her hands and on the front of her dress. My mother said, 'What's the matter, have you had a bicycle accident?' and Mary replied, 'Oh no, there is a young man who has been wounded in an ambush; we can't take him to hospital, and I told the ambulance men to bring him here.' It was the custom of the British forces to search the Dublin hospitals after an ambush and anyone with gunshot wounds was taken to the Castle for investigation. My mother was not pleased by this news as she wanted to avoid doing anything liable to draw attention to our house, but there was no time to argue, the ambulance was at the door and it was almost curfew time, after which anyone seen on the street was liable to be shot. Bobby Childers, a boy of my own age was staying with us as he often did. His father, Erskine Childers, was on the run, and his mother was an invalid. Bobby and I were ignominiously packed off to

bed out of the way, but of course we crept out on to the landing in our pyjamas and watched through the banisters as the stretcher was carried in.

The young man was very badly hurt and quite unconscious, with a bullet hole right through his head. My aunt Dorothy, who was in the house, did what she could for him, but it was clear that he needed specialist treatment if he was to have a chance of life. If he had died in the night, which seemed by no means improbable, our position would have been very awkward, as Dorothy was not yet qualified and could not have signed a Death Certificate. The local parish priest, alerted by Mary Comerford, braved the curfew and came up and gave him the Last Rites of the Catholic Church. By morning he was still alive and the only hope for his life was to get him into hospital despite the danger. Dorothy went to a hospital and arranged for them to take him in, and the ambulance arrived again and sat outside the door while the stretcher was carried out, to the great interest of all the neighbours, and that was all so far as we were concerned. We did not dare to enquire for him, so we never knew if he got better or not — it was safer not to ask. Nor did we ever know for certain whether he was an I.R.A. man or just an ordinary citizen who happened to get caught in an ambush. But it was not long after this that we were raided, and my mother always blamed those ambulances for arousing suspicion of us. Perhaps some of the neighbours gave us away.

One afternoon I was playing with my toys on the drawing-room floor, and my mother was sitting on the sofa writing letters when suddenly there was a loud noise in the front garden. We looked out and saw two lorries drawn up at the gate while the Black and Tans they had carried rushed up the front steps and started hammering on the hall door. Simultaneously a third lorry drove up the lane at the back of the house, and the men from it swarmed over the wall and attacked the back door. My mother opened the front door and the Black and Tans rushed into the hall shouting, 'Where is the owner of this house?' My mother said quietly, 'I'm the owner of this house,' and the officer in charge said, 'Don't be frightened.' This made my mother so angry that she forgot all about being afraid. The officer in charge took her into the drawing-room and questioned her, mostly about Dorothy, who was not in the house at the time. My mother refused to say where she was, and the officer let it go at that and sat down at her desk and started going through all her papers. Then my mother realised that when the raid began she had actually been writing to Dorothy, and that her letter and an addressed envelope was lying on the sofa. She quietly pulled down a cushion on top of them, and called me over to sit beside her, and I sat on the cushion with my little dog, Yetty, on my knee. I don't think I was frightened, just very excited inside.

Meanwhile the Black and Tans had spread all over the house, stripping down all the beds and turning drawers down on the floor, searching for arms. When they found what was obviously a man's room with pyjamas, shaving tackle and such like – both Liam Mellows and Sean Etchingham were staying with us at the time – they became very excited, but my mother told them, what was true that the room belonged to a South African medical student who had just gone to do his hospital's course. They believed her, when they came across his South African passport.

After about an hour, having found nothing of interest to them, they began to re-assemble in the hall. My mother ran upstairs to have a quick look around, and on the floor of her bedroom there was a large revolver. This was a well-known trick. If they found nothing and were still suspicious they would leave a gun behind and come back that night and accuse you of having arms in the house. My mother went up to the officer and said 'One of your men has left something in my room and I don't want it there.' The officer said to the men, 'which of you has left something behind?' and one of the men said, looking rather sheepish. 'Oh, my revolver,' and went up and fetched it. Eventually they left, and my mother and I, and Frances, our gallant old cook (we had a maid in those days, though we weren't at all rich – everybody had) went into the drawing-room to collect ourselves. Then, and not till then, my mother remembered that in her absence earlier in the day, some important papers had been left in for Mr. Doyle, Liam Mellows's *nom de guerre*. She said to Frances, 'Frances, where are those papers that were left in for Mr. Doyle this morning?' Frances gazed all round the room and then collapsed into the nearest chair, pointing dramatically to my mother's desk, and ejaculating 'Jesus, Mary and Joseph' all in one word. The papers, done up in a brown paper parcel, were lying on the top of the desk at which the officer had sat for the entire afternoon going through my mother's papers.

After the raid my mother sent word out that the house was safe no longer, but the members of the Army Council all turned up cheerfully for their next meeting. Mother was terrified that there would be a raid, and a gun fight, for the Army Council men all carried guns. She sent me out to spend the day with friends, much to my indignation. However, nothing untoward happened.

A truce between the British and Irish forces came into effect in July 1921. It was seen as an essential precondition to discussions with the British, and members of the Dáil in prison were released, among them Dorothy's friend Bob Barton. Edie, the work of the Peace with Ireland Council being suspended, came over to Dublin, met Dorothy in Alice's house, and was driven by her down to Kilbrittain. The drive greatly impressed her:

It was an amazing journey. Bridges had been blown up everywhere, and we had long detours; we saw occasional ruins of houses burnt down by the Black and Tans, and of police stations burnt down by the IRA. Owing to the police interdict on cars, there were few to be seen, and since the Truce the police themselves had been confined to barracks. But occasionally we would see a Ford car with a number of trench-coated young men inside who were obviously members of the IRA. They were beginning to emerge from their long periods of anonymity and secrecy and to visit their friends. . . . We eventually reached my sister's house near Kilbrittain where I spent a couple of weeks with her.

One evening we were invited to a 'celebration' *céilí* in a large but remote farm house. We drove there in a pony and trap, and were received with great warmth. As honoured guests, we were not immediately taken to the dance-room, but were asked if we could care to come and have supper with 'some of the lads' who were resting in another room. We entered a large, rather dark room, lit by oil lamps, where we could just make out the figures of five or six young men, all apparently asleep, two stretched on sofas, the rest in armchairs. These were the IRA Headquarters Staff for that area of Co. Cork, anonymous men who had been hunted from pillar to post with prices on their heads and liable to meet death round any corner. Their identity was completely unknown in the countryside, and they were making their first appearance among their neighbours. They were young, sober-minded, responsible and serious, and their Brigadier especially was a fine looking young man full of earnestness and purpose. They were, I presume, still tired from their pre-Truce life of vigil, raids, ambushes and hair-breadth escapes, and so far as I remember they took no part in the subsequent *céilí*, being still shy of publicity. They did not stay long, but soon after supper slipped off from the farm house in their Ford car, silently and mysteriously. Dorothy and I felt that we had been privileged spectators of a very anonymous bit of history.

In the course of the next few weeks, they visited other *céilís* in other farmhouse kitchens, attended by farmers and their families and by other IRA men, who were daily beginning to come out more and more into the open. Dancing was strictly confined to Gaelic dances and singing to Irish patriotic songs, occasionally old melodies, 'Let Erin Remember', 'Danny Boy', or 'Kelly, the Boy from Killann', but usually more topical songs, where new words blended with the old Irish tunes. For instance, to the tune of 'Where the Blarney Roses Grow', they sang 'Could Anybody tell me where did General Lucas Go?' referring to the recent kidnapping of a British General while fishing on the Blackwater as a ransom for Bob Barton who was a prisoner in Portland. The Easter

1916 Rising was commemorated in verses sung to the tune 'The Foggy Dew'; and 'What's the News, said Lloyd George' went to the tune of 'Kitty of Coleraine'. Dorothy kept the words of these ballads among her papers, and of another in praise of the Third West Cork Brigade, whom she personally admired, as did Edie. The general impression of the Cork IRA on Edie was that they were a group of serious-minded and responsible young men, full of patriotic idealism, and with a strong, if rough and ready, sense of justice.

That a truce had been arranged gave Aunt Alice unalloyed pleasure. She did not believe in violence as a means of rectifying anything. 'If people', she would say later, 'have not got the capacity to convince others by argument or fineness of conduct, they should not fall back on the gun and revolution'. She knew, however, that young people found it easier and gayer to shoot and bomb than to read and think. 'I am', she said, 'very near to turning a pacifist, and believing that the methods of a tiger are meant for a tiger and not for a human being.' Her view of the Northern problem was interesting. 'To dispute about the North was perfect folly', she said. 'If it was left alone it would gradually find out that it is more Irish than English. . .'.

The atmosphere in which Dorothy continued in Kilbrittain was, of course, now much more relaxed. She had moved into a rented cottage and was able to entertain Aunt Alice when she came there with Dorothy's sister Alice Wordsworth and her daughter Mary. She took the younger ones out riding with her on horses borrowed from local farmers. She had acquired a second or third-hand motor car. 'It was a regular rattle-box', I was told, 'and there always seemed to be a crowd helping her on with a shove from behind. But she had good fun with it.' It took her round to see her patients, its primary purpose; but she used it also for a run up to Cork now and again. She brought Bridie Crowley with her one evening – she was one of the Crowley family with whom Dorothy had first lodged and became familiar – and insisted that she should share a bottle of hock with her at dinner. The effect of this on Bridie was that she put sugar on the cabbage. Dorothy ventured even farther afield in the jalopy. Having carefully mapped out the route in advance, she drove with Bridie to Lord Monteagle's place in Foynes and had tea on the lawn with Mary Spring-Rice. They went on picnics to the sea nearer home, but what Bridie remembered of those occasions was the problem of getting rid of the prawns that she intensely disliked but of which Dorothy was enormously fond. She would wait until Dorothy had her back turned and then push her share down behind a rock.

During this period of truce many of the men Dorothy had cared for earlier came to visit her in Kilbrittain. Denis Lordan, a particular admirer of hers, was one of these and was invited to stay for lunch. She had a cooked chicken ready but Denis remembering that it was a Friday, told her that if it was all the same with her he would do with a fried egg. Dorothy laughed outright. 'I never can understand you Catholics,' she said, 'You'll eat an egg, but you won't eat the chicken it came from.' She had begun to wear trousers – she may indeed have been the very first woman in that part of the world to do so – and she smoked a lot. She apparently could do nothing without a cigarette in her mouth. More oddly she wore an eye glass for a time – she didn't like spectacles – but the thing dropped out of its socket so often that she gave up wearing it.

She showed off the car to her visitors and drove them over one afternoon to Ballineen to see the Conners, a family that had links, through the United Irish leader Arthur O'Connor, with the French Revolution and the expectation of an Irish Republic. The Conners, like most landowners of substance in that part of Cork, had subsequently presented a solid Unionist face to the world, and that was still the position when the head of the family was Harry Dan Conner, a King's Counsel and an authority on fisheries law. A change came with his son and heir, Henry, who, after his call to the Bar, turned to Sinn Féin and, in a section of the clandestine Department of Agriculture, organised courts for the settlement of land disputes which were in danger of disrupting Dáil Éireann's political programme. A friend and colleague of his at the Bar, William George Price, whom we have met already and of whom we shall learn more, was now pursuing a similar career in the district courts that functioned for a like purpose under the Dáil Department of Home Affairs.

Alice and Mary Wordsworth were again in Kilbrittain for the Christmas of 1921 and Dorothy, wearing a new frock, took them to an IRA *céilí*. They danced right through the night and Mary, then all of eleven years, particularly enjoyed herself. 'My chief dancing partner', she told me, 'was an immensely tall young farm labourer, who was too shy to speak. His name I remember was Jack Mike Aherne. He used to dance with the tips of his fingers just touching my shoulders, and when we came to turn he would swing me up in his arms and off my feet and whirl me round him. The *céilí* ended only with the dawn, and the dancers went to 7 o'clock Mass on the way home. I remember Dorothy driving the trap out of a yard in the cold light with my mother and me, all of us singing out "Thank God we're Protestants," for we, unlike the Catholics, could go straight home to bed. . . '.

On 8 October 1921 a delegation went over to London to discuss the possibility of a settlement of the Irish question with the British, and Alice Wordsworth, her daughter Mary and Aunt Alice were at Westland Row railway station to see them off. 'I talked to Bob for a little while', Alice told Dorothy, 'and to David Robinson and Erskine and Desmond Fitzgerald and Lily O'Brennan. . . . Desmond was asking about Edie and whether she was going to take up work in Dublin. He evidently had his eye on her. At the last moment someone suggested our going to Kingstown with them. There was only time to trundle Aunt Alice into the train as it was moving. Mary and I were left behind with Mary Comerford. . .'.

Dorothy's 'best friend' Bob Barton had become one of the Irish negotiators in extraordinary circumstances as de Valera described later. Though he had personally selected the team, de Valera did not trust Arthur Griffith and Michael Collins, its principal members, and nominated Barton to join them in the belief that 'he would be strong and stubborn enough as a retarding force to any precipitate giving away by the delegation. Childers, an intellectual Republican, as secretary, would give Barton, his relative and close friend, added strength' (*The McGarrity Papers*, 111).

Barton was a member of the Dáil Cabinet since his appointment in September 1921 as Secretary of State for Economic

Affairs, a portfolio which covered Agriculture, Labour, Trade and Commerce and Fisheries as well as the Boycott of Belfast goods, each of which had a director. Ernest Blythe, incidentally, was the director of Trade and Commerce. Towards the end of 1915 it had become clear to him that a Rising was in the wind, and, on St Patrick's Day 1916, Sean MacDermott gave him a strong hint of the part he was expected to play when German guns and a small group of German military men were landed in Kerry. Blythe was arrested beforehand, however, given an exclusion order, and found himself under police surveillance in England when the Rising began. (Michael McInerney in *Irish Times*, 30 Dec. 1932 — 3 Jan. 1933, and Blythe's *Slán le hUltaibh*, 46-7). Subsequently he ceased to be a member of the IRB. But his activities as a Volunteer and Sinn Féin organiser led him to a further spell of imprisonment and a hunger strike. In Dundalk Gaol he wrote for the Volunteer paper, *An tÓglach*, an article on the subject of Conscription, calling on the Volunteers to recognise that the imposition of such an atrocity would be an act of war which merited a ruthless response. He was elected TD in the 1918 General Election.

In a letter to Dorothy in mid-November 1921 from 22 Hans Place, Chelsea, Barton touched upon one of the issues that had come up in the discussions with the British. She was not to pay much attention to rumours about allegiance to the Crown she might have seen in the press. 'It's not for us', he said, and then went on to talk of poor Ulster being in the soup, and how all his sympathies turned to her when he saw the abominable game these blackguard English politicians were playing with her. However, they had made their own bed and must put up with it. 'If there was a ruthless Hun on earth it was Lloyd George. . . .', he said. Then, having written so freely, he warned Dorothy not to publish his letter as it might be considered provocative or even a breach of the Truce. 'These canaille are getting more and more exacting in their claims.' On 6 December he joined his fellow plenipotentiaries in signing a Treaty to establish a Provisional Government leading to an Irish Free State on Dominion lines. He was an apparently confused signatory, but his next letter to Dorothy, dated 27 December, reveals the position he had taken in the split that followed, with de Valera leading opposition to the Treaty in a debate in the Dáil which was suspended over the Christmas. 'The Treaty will go thro', Barton wrote, 'but if Dev. stands clear and firm on Independence another generation will win thro' where we failed. When the unity of the leaders was broken the resistance of the people and their morale must inevitably go to bits. It's a sad story because success was in our grasp at one time; at any rate I believe it was, provided all leaders and people had been prepared to take the gamble and risk all for the ideal. Well the opportunity has gone now and will not return in our lifetimes; that the Provisional Government under the leadership of the pro-ratification party will be either successful, happy or long-lived I doubt. For myself I return to home and oblivion. . . . MacKeon said that this was what he and his comrades fought for; well it was not what I went to gaol for, or the country thought MacKeon fought for.'

On the resumption of the debate after Christmas the motion to ratify the Treaty was carried, but the division was carried into the country, into Sinn Féin and the IRA. It reached down into Kilbrittain, from where, early in February 1922, Dorothy, in a letter to Aunt Alice, said 'It is almost impossible to begin to write when I think of all that's going on, so I will have to leave all the really interesting things aside concerning the changes taking place and write as niece to aunt, not as dispensary doctor to historian, or Irishwoman to Irishwoman. But every day down here we are getting further from the Free State and more republican. At first most were satisfied, but republicanism seems to soak in as time goes on.' A factor in this, no doubt, was the belief spread by men like Liam Deasy, commander of the third West Cork brigade, that they had been decisively winning the war against the British. The conclusion seemed strange in view of the critical arms situation.

Edie returned to Dublin as the Peace with Ireland Council's work came to an end, and joined her sister Alice Wordsworth in her house at Bray outside Dublin. She found that Alice and Aunt Alice like herself were 'Free Staters', that is to say they supported the Treaty, whereas Dorothy was a Republican, and that relations were rather strained as a consequence. 'But', said Aunt Alice, 'though I have argued with her, she remains fond of me, and looks on my house as a haven of refuge' (Pim, 213).

There were rumours of fighting in the city and Edie and Alice went up from Bray to see for themselves. They found a silent city. There was no public transport, and in the air was a singularly sulphurous and ominous feeling, like a thunderstorm. The Republican people had occupied a number of strategic points, with the Four Courts as their principal fortress. They were also defending some street corner houses, whose windows were barricaded with sandbags; and Edie and Alice could occasionally see rifle barrels pointing out from between them. The Kildare Street Club, a former srong-hold of the Protestant Ascendancy, had been occupied, affording some ironic entertainment, Edie thought, to the ordinary Dubliner. There was no incident that day, except that they were personally intrigued to see a Ford car dashing down O'Connell Street and in it, in professional white coat, was Dorothy.

Next day Edie came up to Dublin again and was actually reading in the National Library when there was an outburst of firing. The government attack on the occupied buildings had started. She had lunch with Aunt Alice, and then the two of them decided to stroll down to O'Connell Street where, together with a considerable part of the population of Dublin, they stood watching, from what they held to be a safe distance, the battle of the Four Courts which they could only dimly see. There was a good deal of smoke, and considerable noise of machine gun and rifle fire. Next day the Four Courts fell to the government forces.

On returning to Kilbrittain after her stay in Dublin, Dorothy resumed her normal duties and, forgetful of their political disagreements, Alice and her daughter Mary went down there for holiday. Though sixty years have elapsed, Mary vividly remembers a day when a man who had got his hand caught in a threshing machine was brought in. The hand was in a fearful mess, and he had to be given an anaesthetic before Dorothy could set his fingers and stitch him up. The anaesthetic was given by the District Nurse, who had never given one before and was absolutely terrified: while Alice, who scarcely weighed more than seven stone, was told to sit on the man's legs and keep him quiet! Of course when he was half-conscious he began to struggle violently and finally bucked off the sofa and on to the floor, swearing for all he was worth. The three women tried to control him without any help whatever from the burly fellow who had brought him in. All he could do was to follow the group round the room, repeating over and over again, 'Ah Jer, mind your language, can't ye see there's ladies present.'

Dorothy was never reconciled to the idea of brothers taking up arms against brothers, even on a great matter of principle. She never forgot that she was primarily a doctor, a healer. But she gave herself politically to the anti-Treaty side, subscribed to their funds, and, on returning to Cork from Dublin, brought medical succour to the men of the Third Brigade who had turned their arms against the Provisional Government. Among her patients were Dr Con Lucey of the old Flying Column who suffered a haemorrhage, and Denis Lordan who got a bullet through his shoulder.

Bob Barton had written to her in March to congratulate her 'on having remained a Republican with so many of your relations gone wrong'. Aunt Alice was dreadful, he said, so sure she was right; but he supposed that he and those who thought like him were equally dreadful, so sure that she was wrong. Dick Mulcahy, the new Minister for Defence, was out for war before he and Collins and the Headquarters staff were defeated, but he doubted if they could muster enough Free State soldiers to make a decent battle. The ranks of their own men could not be relied upon and mutinies were occuring almost daily. Poor Eoin O'Duffy, who had succeeded Mulcahy as Chief of Staff was neurotic, he said, and Arthur Griffith, who had led the delegation at the London talks, and was now the President of Dáil Éireann in place of de Valera, wanted to abolish the army because it wanted to support the Republic it had fought for earlier. He, personally, was deeply distressed. 'Many a time I have wished I had died in Portland Gaol', he wrote, 'before I got mixed up with those cursed negotiations. One thing I have learned from them. If you are in a position of leader, you have got to lead and never refer anything to the people. We shall know better where we stand if the Volunteer Convention is brought off despite Griffith. The President [de Valera] is game for any amount of work and is a real tactician. I would back him to beat them any day.'

Barton's expectations were not realised, however. Collins, Mulcahy, and most of the Headquarters staff rapidly built up a national army which had more success in disposing of their opponents than the British had had. In the Kilbrittain area, searches, for one thing, were carried out with greater intensity than before. A letter to Dorothy spoke of a raid on a house she knew well, lasting from three to five in the afternoon. An arrest was made, and her old Cumann na mBan pony and trap taken away. Many of Dorothy's friends, including Bob Barton, found themselves prisoners once more, and she was kept busy answering their letters and sending them parcels of food, clothing and medicines.

Aunt Alice meanwhile was identifying closely with the Treaty side. She admired the young ministers, and with her brother Edward, both of them septuagenarians, distributed pro-Treaty literature in the streets of Dublin. She thought de Valera was sincere but lacked political acumen; he was top-heavy with 'principle', and light-weighted with intelligence (MacDowell, 109). During the Truce she had been at a crowded meeting in the Mansion House at which he was the principal speaker. He was 'a very extraordinary speaker', she told Dorothy at the time, 'with a remarkable power, not of "oratory" but of a white heat of passion which communicates itself amazingly. But argument is lacking. And that is now essential. He leaves every gate open . . . I can't see why there should not be a guard at some of them to ask questions of the whirling driver.'

After the premature deaths of Griffith and Collins, an Irish Free State government under W. T. Cosgrave confronted the vast problems of the hour including the resolution of the Civil War. The Constitution of the Irish Free State, which was enacted in October 1922, provided for an Oireachtas of two Houses, a Dáil to be elected by the people and a Senate, thirty members of which were to be nominated by the government and another thirty to be chosen by the Dáil in a system of proportional representation. When the list of the government-nominated Senators was announced by Cosgrave, on 6 December 1922, sixteen of the thirty were seen to belong to the Anglo-Irish class formerly accepted as being Southern Unionists. Among these were Sir Horace Plunkett, and the Earl of Granard who, unlike his fellow peers in the new House, had never been a Unionist, but rather a Liberal and long-time supporter of the Home Rule movement. The remaining government nominees included representatives of both the old and new nationalism, for example Sir Thomas Esmonde, an Irish Party MP from 1885 to 1919, and Mrs Jennie Wyse Power who had been active in the Ladies Land League in the 1880s and in the Gaelic League, Sinn Féin and Cumann na mBan in later times. The Arts were represented by the poets Yeats and Oliver St John Gogarty.

The large representation of Southern Unionists — sixteen out of sixty — in the Senate fulfilled an undertaking to safeguard minority interest given by Arthur Griffith during the Treaty negotiations. In his capacity as Chairman of the Irish plenipotentiaries Griffith told Lloyd George of this undertaking and promised similar safeguards 'in the case of the minority in the North-East of Ireland'. And, justifying this 'generous adjustment', Kevin O'Higgins spoke of evolution towards completion of nationhood: 'These people, the former Southern Unionists, are regarded, not as alien enemies, not as planters, but as part and parcel of this nation, and we wish them to take their share of its responsibilities'.

And when the election of Senate members by the Dáil took place, it was noted that the first candidate 'to pass the post' was Alice Stopford Green who was described as Ireland's most distinguished historian.

The opponents of the Treaty lost little time in demonstrating what they thought of the Oireachtas, and its members. A Dáil deputy, Sean Hales, whom Dorothy Stopford would have known in West Cork during the Anglo-Irish war, was killed, and Padraic Ó Maille, the Deputy-Chairman of the Dáil, gravely wounded as they drove together in Dublin. As a terrible reprisal and warning, four of the dissident leaders who were at that time imprisoned in Mountjoy were sum-

marily executed. One of these was Liam Mellows whom Alice
Wordsworth had often sheltered in her house on Leinster
Road. Senators were singled out for particular attention; it
was, Yeats said, a particularly unhealthy time to be a senator.
Their property was destroyed. Mrs Green's house escaped,
however. A military guard was placed inside it and, unique
hostess as she always was, she hoped they would be satisfied
with a plain supper. Kilteragh, Horace Plunkett's house, had
a landmine placed in the fire grate of the main hall, and the
resultant explosion practically wrecked the whole building.
The raiders returned later with tins of petrol to complete
their work, and many thousands of pounds worth of pictures
were lost in the fire. Plunkett's love of Ireland remained
unshaken, however. 'He was', it has been well said, 'a very
good example of the pathetic unrequited loyalty which the
Irish aristocrats had for Ireland. They adored the country
that hated them; they idolised the people who ridiculed
them. They never could understand why they were unpop-
ular. They were willing to give devoted service when it was
not wanted. They simply could not understand that their
neighbours despised the idols that they held sacred. Their
own dual loyalty to England and Ireland was incomprehen-
sible to the people by whom they were surrounded. They
were nationalists in a position of their own, their nationalism
set in a wider imperial loyalty. . . . Plunkett not only failed
to understand but positively misunderstood the real values
of his Irish fellow countrymen. But he persisted in serving
their interests according to his lights (Meenan, 112-13).

The fighting ceased in May 1923, and Dorothy Stopford,
having earlier sent in her resignation to the Board of Guar-
dians, left Kilbrittain at the end of June and came up to
Dublin. She continued to attend the Civil War patients there
privately and Denis Lordan brought her to a tenement on
the Quays to treat a fellow who was living there in poor circumstances. When Lordan himself was released from an
internment camp after a hunger strike, she had taken him
into her flat for a fortnight and, feeding him on patent foods,
had brought him back to health. He emigrated later to South
America but, almost thirty years later, when he was back in

Cork, she returned the gold watch to him she had received through him from his comrades for her wedding that he might give it to his daughter for hers.

In 1924, as her private practice developed, she became a visiting physician at St Ultan's Hospital for Children. She maintained her connection with Robert Barton, and, on his behalf invited Liam Deasy and other officers of the West Cork Brigade to visit Anacorre: Deasy in his book *Brother against Brother* describes Dorothy as having been a sterling friend during the Black and Tan war.

Chapter Five

PRIVATE LIVES

It came as a complete surprise to her friends in West Cork when Dorothy married. They did not think she thought of men in that way; she had certainly shown no sign of it when among them. Her friend Dorothy Macardle, the novelist and drama critic, was also taken by surprise. She wrote to her from London 'Me da says you are married!, I'm out of breath! You didn't look in the least as if you were going to be, last time I saw you. Did you take it into your head and propose all of a sudden, or was it premeditated?' Friends in Dublin's medical world, however, had noticed a 'romantic' streak in her. She would wonder aloud whether the person she was talking to didn't think that Doctor so-and-so wasn't awfully good-looking or, if she saw a tender relationship developing, whether the man and woman were really in love. And in her own family it would have come as no surprise had her friendship with Nathan, Robert Barton or other men she knew, led to an engagement. None of this was known in Kilbrittain, of course, where the surprise was all the greater when it was learned that she was to marry a Free Stater. It was indeed worse than that, for Willie Price had been educated in an English Public School, had interrupted his legal studies to take a commission in the British Army, and from a year after the Rising, with one short furlough, had served in the French theatre of war. Nevertheless, a few days before the wedding, Denis Lordan brought Dorothy from the men of 'the old Cork Third Brigade' a gold watch to remind her of their esteem and affection. She had, they said, shared with them the burden of the struggle for the independence of their Motherland and they treasured the memory of the sacrifices she had made for the cause. The accompanying letter was signed by, among others, Sean Buckley, Liam Deasy, Mick Crowley, and Jim Hurley.

On account of his position with the Pay Corps Price was not personally involved in the fighting but was near enough to the 1918 offensives which carried the Germans to within forty miles of Paris to be able to write informative letters to his family about them. This was the time when the British Expeditionary Force had its back to the wall. 'Let's see now if I can tell you something about the battle,' he said in one letter to his sister, Kathleen. 'We knew of course beforehand that it was coming off. . . . Four days before the battle two deserters came in on our front, one of them an Alsatian, and he told us the date. He told us about the trench mortars the Boche had brought up and hidden in shell-holes, how he was going to gas our batteries, and the numbers of men we had. . .'. And, in a few notes he wrote for himself, he described the kind of life he was leading by comparison with what the French people had to endure. Thus: 'There are no signs of our moving. I am too comfortable here to want to move. . . . It is hateful to see all those refugees going through — a big cart piled up, one or two sitting on it, and the rest walking, mostly women; you see the old women with white hair, plodding along behind. It frightens all the civilians here naturally. I tried to cheer up an old woman today, but there is nothing one can say to them.' Next day, he was out of his comfortable quarters and on 'a rotten journey in an open car at midnight sitting on top of the cash. Passed a lot of French troops on the way. . . . We couldn't get any billets . . . Luckily some office furniture had reached our office, so I slept till 7 on a chair and a cash box . . . Have now spent four nights in my clothes . . . We have run 30 or 40 miles in a week.'

He was interested in the political situation at home. By mid-August 1918 it was obvious there was going to be a General Election, and he told an uncle that the government ought to try and bolster up the Nationalists for, as things, stood, the Sinn Féiners would carry most of these seats. He was clearly not a Sinn Féiner himself, nor even a Nationalist, but in about a year, when he returned to Dublin, and was called to the Bar, he began to absorb the atmosphere of the post-Rising Ireland. A change came over himself. For one thing, very significantly the 'William George' with which he had been christened gave way to 'Liam'; as they say nowadays, that was something. This happened apparently through a circle which included Diarmuid Coffey, Henry Conner, Tony Farrington and Ned and Frank Stephens. On the fringe of this circle were less intimate friends like Lionel Smith Gordon, the Englishman Robert Barton had put in charge of the National Land Bank, a Dáil Éireann foundation, and through whom it is likely Liam Price got a clerking job in the Leeson Street branch on his discharge from the Army. His Pay Corps experience would have been considered a qualification. All of these people were by now under Sinn Féin or Irish-Ireland influence, in one way or another they were usually to be found in Coffey's 'communal house' or 'felon's cell' at 51 Pembroke Road, and Liam, to call him by his first name, followed some of the barristers in the group who became justices in the Republican courts.

The people of Kilbrittain would have known none of this and, in the post-Civil War atmosphere, could be excused for wondering how Dorothy could possibly get on with a husband who thought so differently from her on what they regarded as the really fundamental matter of the Treaty. That surely would have affected their thinking on so many issues – on partition in the light of the failure of the Boundary Commission from which so much had been expected, on the division in republican ranks that preceded the creation of the Fianna Fáil party and the manner in which it achieved power, on the Economc War, the Blueshirts, the deal with Britain over the ports, and neutrality – Liam would certainly have had a view on this. How could the two of them traverse such a minefield without danger to their union? The answer is that, neither of them being bitter as so many people at that time were, and agreeing to differ, they traversed it extremely well. It is true that they seemed to be always talking it out on each other about trifling domestic things, but arguments were never pushed too far, and their affection for each other carried them through every difficulty. They had other things, of course, to interest them besides political debate. They had jobs to do, Dorothy with her patients, and Liam, apart from the law, was becoming increasingly interested in aspects of the old Irish world, its antiquities, its folk culture, its place names particularly. And they both knew how to be discreet: when Denis Lordan, for instance, visited the house no mention was made of the Civil War while Liam was around. And Liam behaved similarly, we can be sure, to avoid embarrassing Dorothy, when someone who shared his political views came to the house.

The circle to whom they were attached were all lovers of the Dublin/Wicklow hills: and at week-ends they would go together on what nowadays would be called hikes. Liam had no difficulty in getting along despite his lameness, and his walking improved greatly when, with encouragement from Dorothy, he had an operation which enabled him to dispense with the high boot he had worn since an accident in school at Aldenham. The Stephenses had a cottage just below the Hell Fire Club, the Farringtons another at Brittas Bay, and these were customary rallying points. When motor cars became more plentiful the area of exploration was extended, and the hikers tended to break up into smaller groups. It was in some such fashion that Dorothy and Liam began to see more of each other. They would go out together, sometimes to a place near a river where Dorothy would fish. Liam had no interest in this, but he was happy enough to see Dorothy amusing herself and was mildly proud on one occasion in later years when on an outing she bagged four pike and a perch.

The details of their courtship elude us, but we know that one day at Lugalaw, where a stream joins Lough Dan and Lough Tay, they decided to get married, and hurried to Old Connaught, Bray, where Alice and Mary lived. Dorothy managed to say that 'Liam has got something to say to you,' to break the news. It was obvious when they came in that something unusual had excited them and Liam, very red in the face, had got as far as saying 'It's about ourselves', when Mary ran across the room and embraced Dorothy. That happened in the late autumn or early winter of 1924 and they were married on 8 January 1925 in St Anne's, Dawson Street. It was an early morning wedding, for they wanted to catch the morning mail boat on the first leg of a honeymoon they planned to spend in Italy. Diarmuid Coffey was the best

man, and Mary Wordsworth, who remembers getting a new
coat for the occasion, was the bridesmaid: she was 14 years
of age. Afterwards Diarmuid took her, her mother, grandmother, Aunt Edie and Uncle Robert, along with Liam's
mother and sister, to breakfast. That was all there was to it;
but gradually word of the marriage got round. Aunt Alice
missed the wedding. She was not well enough to attend, and
Dorothy went to Stephen's Green to see her the day before.
In those days nobody bothered to lock their cars, neither did
Dorothy to her cost, for, when she came out of the house,
she found that all the things she had purchased for her
wedding and honeymoon had been stolen. Fortunately, she
had kept the bills, and Alice taking them from her was able
to replace the lost items.

The wedding had brought Edie on one of her rare visits to
Dublin. Afterwards she came less frequently still. She supported herself by taking various odd jobs in England and
abroad. Though possibly the most brilliant of the Stopfords
and always lively and attractive, she seemed somehow to
waste her potential. Aunt Alice Green had hoped she would
follow her into the field of history, her university subject,
but Edie had other ideas including a love of horses and, for
a while a connection with British Labour politics. During a
General Election she was one day driving her car covered
with Party placards and only just avoided collision with a
taxi. The taxi driver, obviously a Labour supporter, leaned
out of his cab and shouted: 'You may be able to vote right,
Miss, but you can't drive.'

Liam was a good-looking man but at first sight somewhat
forbidding, which was perhaps the appearance he presented
on the bench. He could be gruff, even testy at times, and as
a District Justice he was known to have certain prejudices. He
was unbending in the matter of granting extensions for late
night dances which would have meant increased facilities for
drinking; and he was said to be 'hard' in the matter of driving
offences. There was an amusing aspect of this, if true, because
he was a very fast and rather alarming driver himself, so that
when in the car with him, Dorothy was understandably critical.

Going through his district alone, his mind was as often as
not on something other than the road before him. He was
interested in so many things. He might be worrying about a
Court case, of course, or the derivation of a place-name, or
seeking the solution to some conundrum or other he had
encountered in the antiquarian field. Much of his thinking
was about family roots, an interest he shared with the
Stopfords; and his enquiries took him back to the end of the
seventeenth century, to a Joseph Price, a gentleman of the
city of Waterford. Earlier Prices might have come from Wales
or the West Country of England but of these Liam could only
speculate.

However, what he had unearthed was satisfying, Joseph
Price's grandson was an Alderman William Price and, following him, the name William, Liam's originally, appears regularly in the deeds he scrutinised. A William Price in 1816 was
an ordained priest of the Church of Ireland, and the first of
his children was also a William Price. The family thereafter
was established in Dublin, and Liam's researching came on a
reference to the Great Famine and another to the Young
Ireland rebellion of 1848. He discovered that his grandfather
was a Separatist — not a political separatist, however, but a
member of a society that may have had some kinship with
the Quakers of whom at least one Price was a member. Liam's
own father and mother were, however, severely orthodox and
pious which Liam was not.

From his father who was a King's Counsel and Registrar of
the Chancery Division of the Law Courts, he got his second
name, George, and his interest in the law. The thing his spirit
appears to have cried out for was a sharing in the life of the
common Irish people, and this he satisfied in the study of
early history, field archaeology, folklore, but especially place-
names. He had hardly a profound knowledge of the Irish
language, but he knew enough of it for general purposes,
visited its haunts on the Blaskets and Aran Islands, and was
able to rely on the experts among his friends notably Gerard
Murphy, to guide him through difficulties. His name, therefore, and the Irishness it implied, meant a lot to him, but the
Catholic side of Irish life did not attract him at all, it would
seem. He would acknowledge that he was a Protestant though

neither Dorothy nor he showed any interest in formal religion in their married life. He felt, however, that in the new Irish state Protestantism could be a hindrance to material progress, and that he personally might have fared better if he had been a Catholic. So convinced was he of this that he told a relative who had a markedly English name, when he came back from the war, that if he wanted his business in Ireland to prosper, he should get someone with an obviously Irish Catholic name to join him.

In the Senate, Alice Green found herself sharing the company and some of the ideas of William Butler Yeats. She agreed with him that the Senate should not confine itself to the discussion of special subjects only, as W. T. Cosgrave, the President of the Executive Council apparently wished. Yeats was in his element, 'We are a fairly distinguished body', he wrote of his fellow Senators, 'much more so than the lower House, and shall get much government into our hands.' He wanted the Senate, then, to range at least as widely as the Dáil itself would do, and Alice did not see why this should not be so. When it came to practicalities she agreed with Yeats in denouncing an attempt to introduce an amendment to a railways bill making it mandatory on the companies to put all public notices and signs in Irish and to print railway tickets in both languages. Yeats said he would support the government in endowing Irish, but he asked the Senate to turn down the proposal in the interests of the sincerity of the Irish intellect. He had tried to learn Irish, unsuccessfully. What he feared was an irritation against not merely the Irish language, but against all Irish thought, all Irish feeling, which he was sorry to say was already spreading through the country. 'I want to see the country Irish-speaking but I protest emphatically against the histrionics which have crept into the whole Gaelic movement.' He said this when speaking against a resolution to add to the prayers one in Irish. 'This method,' he believed, 'of going through a performance of something we do not know and which we do not intend to learn, will ultimately lead to a reaction against the language.'

With Yeats, Alice Green had a Senate committee set up to prepare for the government a scheme for the editing, indexing and publication of the Irish language manuscripts in the Royal Irish Academy and elsewhere, for the scientific investigation of the living dialects of Irish, and for the compiling and publication of an adequate dictionary of the older language. They were both affected to some degree by the Civil War. Alice could not have avoided seeing the white-washed announcements on the walls of the city that her former secretary Mary Comerford was being ill-treated in Kilmainham while, in the same jail, Yeats was told by Maude Gonne that woman prisoners had to undress in front of windows with no window blinds. He visited the jail, and found that like so much of the propaganda of that time, there was nothing whatever in the complaint: the windows were eight feet off the ground!! (Balliett, *Eire Ireland*, Autumn 1979).

As the Civil War ended, Mrs Green made an appeal for reconciliation between the contending parties. She told her fellow Senators there were masses of inarticulate people who, wearied of the present, were uncertain and fearful of the future, and it was essential to create a new sense of law in the land. Her appreciation of the Senate itself had grown since she entered it and sensed its possibilities. She desired to offer some effective service in return for the honour that had been done to her in making her a member, but as her working days were slipping away, she asked that instead the Senate would accept a casket she had had specially wrought in metal to contain a vellum roll on which the members of that first Senate had signed their names. The casket would be placed on the table at every meeting as a perpetual memorial of the foundation of the House, and a witness of its unceasing service. When it came to the day of presentation, however, she was ill, and the speech she had prepared had to be read for her. In it she laid stress on her belief, that, if an Irish nation was to be revived, roots would have to be dug deep into its soul.

Dorothy and Liam lived at first in a flat in Fitzwilliam Place but were able later to take a whole house, Number Ten, a few doors away, and to employ a cook and several maids. There was therefore nothing in the way of serious housekeeping to be done by Dorothy, which was just as well for she had no illusions about her ability in the kitchen. She would say, when occasionally they had no cook, that she should have married one; that also implied that Liam was not much good in that way either. They were not to have any children, which was the news Dorothy got when a gynaecologist brought her into Portobello House in 1926 for examination. That was a severe blow to her, and she was still lamenting the fact years later that she, who had rather fancied herself handling babies, was to handle none of her own. When she went to the Rotunda Hospital to visit her niece Mary she said to her, 'You managed to do twice what I never managed at all,' and Mary still remembers the sadness in her voice. Liam, too, would have liked to have had children; to have passed on the William or Liam would have meant something to him. Anyhow, the fact that they had no family left friends with the impression that they were always a lonely couple, and that they were forced, more than they might have wished, to occupy their time with personal interests.

What was to be a consuming interest of Dorothy's was St Ultan's Hosptial which had been founded a few years earlier by two remarkable women, Dr Kathleen Lynn and Madeline Ffrench-Mullen. These women had met at lectures on First Aid that Dr Lynn was giving to the Citizen Army; they had themselves participated with the Citizen Army in the Rising, and were briefly interned. They shared a strong concern afterwards to do something about conditions in the city's slums and especially about the death rate of children from preventable diseases. Dorothy's enthusiasm had been aroused by Dr Ella Webb who was associated in St Ultan's with the work of Dr Lynn and Miss Ffrench-Mullen, and was simultaneously running a Children's Sunshine Home for children with rickets. They both admired the daring with which the two founders had started a hospital with two cots in a decaying building and a capital of £70. Dorothy, of course, shared the founder's republicanism and the political ideas they espoused after the Treaty, but not their feminism.

In 1924 – that is, a year before she married – Dorothy became one of the visiting physicians at St Ultan's. It was an honorary unpaid job, for the hospital had no money other than what Dr Lynn could collect on visits to America, and

that remained the position until the Irish Hospital Sweepstakes were started. For nine years Dorothy 'imbibed wisdom'
from another unusual woman doctor, Dr Katherine Maguire
who, to encourage evidence of an enquiring mind, urged
Dorothy to take trouble to find things out for herself, to
read extensively and publish. Dr Maguire herself had a considerable practice in the city and passed it over to Dorothy
when she got too feeble to attend to it. Dorothy was, therefore, doing very well and had some distinguished patients,
when the problem of tuberculosis in children began to
occupy an important position in her thinking, this at a time
when no one regarded the subject as having any relation to
reality. From her reading of the German literature on the
subject, to do which she had to learn German, and from what
she learned on a post-graduate course she attended in
Scheidegg, Dorothy prepared a thesis on the Diagnosis of
Primary Tuberculosis in Children, describing modern con-
tinental theories and practice, and this won for her an MD.
The views which she put forward, like earlier papers to the
Academy of Medicine, were treated with considerable sceptic-
ism, but by 1936 they were generally accepted in response
to the statistical proof she was able to produce of the value
of tubercular testing, and of the use of the Bacillus Calmett
Guerin (BCG) vaccine. A Professor Wallgren in Gottenburg
had been using this for ten years and had brought down the
death rate of tuberculosis in infants from 3.4 to .3 per
thousand. If only something faintly like this could be done
for Ireland!

A beginning had to be made, and Dorothy began in St
Ultan's, using vaccine from an original strain of bovine
tubercle bacilli she obtained from Sweden.

A crisis occurred in 1924 which ended Eoin MacNeill's
political career and as a consequence grieved Alice Green
considerably. An article of the Anglo-Irish Treaty provided
for a Commission of three members to determine the boundaries of Northern Ireland in accordance with the wishes of
the inhabitants, and so far as that might be compatible with
economic and geographic conditions. The popular Nationalist
view was that this meant one thing only, that the Northern

area would be cut into extensively, even perhaps to the extent that the Northern state would become non-viable. But one of a series of conclusions reached by the Commission, was that in determining the boundaries the existing boundary line could be shifted in *either* direction, that there was no more and no less authority to take land from the Northern side and give it to the Free State than there was to take land from the Free State and give it to Northern Ireland. Another conclusion reached by the Commission from studying the article was that Northern Ireland was to survive as a recognisable entity, that the changes in the boundaries were not to be so drastic as to destroy Northern Ireland's identity or make it impossible for it to continue as a separate province of the United Kingdom with its own parliament and government. It appeared to follow, therefore, that rectification of the boundaries should be on a modest scale. There could be transfers from both sides with the balance in favour of the Free State, but the vital areas of Newry and South Down were to be retained in Northern Ireland. News of an agreement on these lines, leaked to an English newspaper, created a sensation. In the Free State the possibility of loss of territory rather than inadequacy of gain was what hurt most. MacNeill resigned from the Commission and later from the government, leaving the Commission's report, signed by the South African Chairman and a third party appointed to represent the Northern Ireland view, politically unenforceable. As a matter of urgency, the British and Free State governments then conferred and agreed to leave the existing boundary as it was, while certain financial adjustments were made in favour of the Free State.

MacNeill was widely criticised. It was said that he had been an unwise choice as Commissioner, and that his judgment was at fault. A recent able study of the whole subject, however, leaves open the possibility that no politician from the southern side of the Border would have survived in similar circumstances. When the Commission was being set up, MacNeill sensed that it would not bring the benefits expected from it, and would damage the political fortune of whoever happened to be the representative of the Irish Free State. He was at pains to ensure that the burden of blame for failure would not fall on a young man at the outset of his political career. To Patrick McGilligan he quoted the line 'the ripest fruit first falls'.

The cause of the trouble within the Commission was the ambiguous character of the relevant Treaty article. MacNeill, moreover, took such a high-minded view of his responsibility as a member of the Commission that he kept his own government in the dark as to what went on inside the Commission, and did not make things easier for himself when he admitted to the Dáil that he had agreed in principle that the Commissioners should present a joint report before knowing what it was going to contain. He had come to realise that his interpretation of the article was quite different from the Chairman's; and that, in consequence, he could not possibly subscribe to the report. His actions, F. S. L. Lyons remarked, were those of an honourable but a much confused and misled man. He was certainly an unhappy man, as he was in the 1930s when he looked at the position of the Irish language in the national life.

At the change-over from a British to an Irish administration a decade or so earlier, Irish had become an essential part of the curriculum of the primary and secondary schools, and was made an obligatory subject for the public services for which Irish-speaking candidates were available. Civil servants and teachers had flocked to language classes, so certain were they that Irish was going to be the thing, and that jobs and promotion prospects would depend on knowing it. But the task of making Ireland an Irish-speaking nation was assumed with more enthusiasm than sense, and one senior inspector of schools had to be reprimanded publicly for declaring that every hog, dog and devil would have to learn the language. The obstacles were of course enormous. The pupils, by and large, were not enthusiastic, the teachers not particularly competent, and over all hung the cloud of political division. For the children Irish became just a subject — at the end of school they could sing the jingle, 'No more Irish, no more French, no more sitting on the hard old bench'. MacNeill would have had it different, He had never favoured compulsory Irish in education, believing that a sense of national duty was infinitely preferable; and to inculcate such a sense he recommended the proper teaching of history. Ignorance on that score, he contended, was the chief cause of the lack of sustained interest in Irish; to anyone who had not a feeling for Irish history or did not identify with Irish history, the learning of Irish was mere philology. In 1932, just as the first Irish government was going out of office, Joseph O'Neill, the Secretary of the Department of Education, admitted that the attainment of easy success was not to be expected, though time was of the essence of the problem. While they were relying on the English-speaking parts of the country to become Irish-speaking, the natural Irish-speaking parts, the Gaeltacht, continued to decline. Would the language as resuscitated by the schools be then a fully living speech with a creative cultural power? It was hard to believe it could be so.

MacNeill had an especially personal interest in this subject. He had often pondered over what had happened since the Dundalk Ard-Fheis of 1915, and had reached the conclusion, which he frankly admitted, that Hyde had been right then and he wrong. The Gaelic League had drawn to its membership many who regarded Irish as a political instrument, while others like MacNeill himself had allowed themselves to become too preoccupied with the critical political situation at that time. The main result of what was then done was that the political aspect of Irish nationality got the upper hand within the League, so that the League became a semi-political organisation. That was a complete departure from its original principles and policy. Ireland was not a political entity only. Enlarging on this statement, MacNeill's son-in-law, Michael Tierney, with whom MacNeill shared many confidences, said that the League suffered fatally when, having become a component of the Sinn Féin movement, it got involved in the politics of the Civil War. To an extent some of the issues that were being debated within the language movement became political. If the government, the government of the Irish Free State, proposed something, that was sometimes enough for it to be condemned in Gaelic League circles. A case in point was that of the Gaelic script and simplified spelling. As early as 1931 Ernest Blythe, as Minister for Finance, directed the attention of the civil service to the system of Irish orthography followed in the Oireachtas translation office, which involved modifications of the spelling given in Dineen's dictionary. He also directed that the Roman script which had been used from the start by the translation office should prevail in an English Irish Dictionary being prepared under the editorship of Father Lambert McKenna, SJ. Father MacKenna was actually working on this direction and paying particular attention to the simplification of the spelling when, with a change of government, he was told to reverse engines. He was to use the Irish script and reinstate Father Dineen's spellings. It was said that that was what the Gaelic League wanted (*Teangeolas*, 17, 15).

In this connection one wonders if Ernest Blythe's work for the revival of Irish was appreciated or, indeed, understood. Even before he became the Vice-President of the Executive Council on the death of Kevin O'Higgins, he as Minister for Finance, and in close collaboration with the Department of Education, initiated a number of schemes that explored the cultural possibilities of the language and aimed at increasing its attractiveness to the general public. He was behind the scheme for the production of books in Irish which set scores of writers to work on original themes or translations, and it was he who subsidised efforts in Dublin and Galway to promote a Gaelic Drama movement. The Galway venture made a most promising start with the help of MacLiammoir and Edwards. He used Irish a great deal, himself, at home and in the office, wrote Irish extensively for the press, and when he came to write his autobiography, three volumes of which had appeared before he died, he did it in Irish. He was probably the most devoted and the most practical of all the Anglo-Irish eccentrics that have fallen under the influence of the Irish language. He also brought an understanding mind to bear on the problem of partition, as a recent historical work has reminded us (Fanning, *Independent Ireland*, 34-6).

Aunt Alice, after a heart attack in 1925, was unable to come downstairs any more. She continued to entertain, however, first receiving her guests in the large upstairs drawing room that overlooked the Green, and then passing them over to her niece Alice Wordsworth who took them to the dining room downstairs. If a party sat too long over the port, Mary, the parlour maid, would be sent down to hurry them up, so that Aunt Alice could take command once more. These dinners were highly thought of in the Dublin of the day; the food was always excellent, and the conversation delightful. Aunt Alice had a very pretty wit, and liked to set the company laughing, as she had done, years before, in Charles Gavan Duffy's house in Nice when the talk turned to Gladstone, who was referred to as 'The Grand Old Man'. This caused Aunt Alice to snort, 'Oh, Mrs Green,' someone said, 'don't you agree with that description of him?' 'Old man certainly,' said Mrs Green, 'Grand? Well, just as my piano is grand, being neither straight nor upright.'

As time passed it became difficult, especially at short notice, to make up a dinner party. This annoyed Aunt Alice greatly. She was heard to say to Thurneysen, the German philologist, and his wife when they came one night that she was sorry she had such a dull party for them — there were so few interesting people left. She did not say it, but there were more exciting things available in Dublin at that time. In the world of the theatre, for instance, everybody was flocking to the Abbey to see Sean O'Casey's plays, *Juno and the Paycock* and *The Plough and the Stars*; there was much talk about the subsidy that Ernest Blythe had given to the theatre, with comments on the fact that Yeats had accepted it as well as a government director on the board. The *Plough* produced disturbances in the pit as the *Playboy* had done, but they only increased the acclaim of the play, and the reputation of the playwright.

As always, Aunt Alice sought the company of men and, if a woman happened to be coming to the house, she resorted to what R. B. McDowell called a little ingenuous social planning to edge her out of the limelight. In this respect she was quite odd. When somebody enquired if there was any woman in Dublin she really liked, she paused before mentioning a name. 'And why', she was asked, 'do you like her?'. 'Because', said Mrs Green, 'she never speaks when her husband is in the room.' In this extraordinary attitude to men she could be rashly trustful. She once gave a visiting journalist she had just met an open cheque, and was lucky to be stung for only a hundred pounds. Her female relatives naturally resented all this, but there were other things about her they did not like either. 'I was never so frightened of anybody as I was of her,' Mary Wordsworth said. 'She could be charming and would say "Nice to see you" when I called, and we could never forget how good to all of us she had been since Grandfather Jemmett's death, but she was just as likely to greet you with a "What do you want?". When I, still a child, came to dine I used to sit silent and eat my way through whatever was put before me, whether I liked it or not. I particularly remember my first encounter with oysters. I didn't like the look of them at all, and had no idea how to eat them but, for fear of Aunt Alice, they had to be eaten, so I watched the grown-ups, and found the oysters were pretty good after all.'

In June 1925 a debate took place in the Senate on an expected government move to prohibit the introduction of Bills into the legislature for divorce *a vincula matrimoni*. Yeats opened the debate with a speech that was considered to have been the most remarkable since the Senate came into existence. He had carefully pondered what he should say while away in Italy, and intended to accuse the government of an assault upon Protestant liberties. It was not a politic speech and was delivered to a very restive audience, some of whom walked out of the chamber protesting. Later he was charged with showing himself, who had been a Fenian, in his true Cromwellian colours. He strayed unnecessarily from the straight line of his thesis and gave particular offence when he referred to the Gospels as devotional not historical documents. In another passage he drew fire by directing the attention of moralists to the private lives of Nelson, Parnell and O'Connell. His attitude to the censorship of books was already well known, but he availed of the divorce issue to make a passionate protest on behalf of the Anglo-Irish from whom he was himself sprung but from whom politically he had almost continuously differed since his earliest days with John O'Leary and the Young Ireland Society. The process led him into what he termed an Anglo-Irish solitude. For many of the Anglo-Irish, lay or ecclesiastic, he had no use whatever, for diverse reasons. It was, therefore, an outlawed solitude (Hone, 223, 369-371). Coming to the end of the speech he said he thought it tragic that within three years of his country gaining its independence, they should be discussing a measure which the minority considered grossly oppressive. He was proud to consider himself a typical member of that minority. He did not ask to control any man's conscience; all he asked for was individual liberty. He was speaking, he contended, on behalf of that small Protestant band which had so often proved itself the chivalry of Ireland. 'We, against whom you have done this thing, are no petty people. We are one of the great stocks of Europe. We are the people of Burke; we are the people of Grattan, we are the people of Swift, the people of Parnell. We have created most of the modern literature of this country. We have created the best of its political intelligence.' And in a piece he wrote subsequently for the *Irish Statesman* he declared 'Ireland is not more theirs than ours. We must glory in our difference, be as proud of it as they are of theirs.'

These declarations would have given great heart to the Anglo-Irish community generally. The Stopfords, the Prices, the Hydes, the Hobsons, and all the others who recognised their special role in the Irish community, would have rejoiced at it, even if some of them would have preferred the occasion of it not to be a debate about divorce. Mrs Green would certainly have agreed to the peroration of the speech in any event.

When Yeats was first a member of the Senate and one of the thirty men nominated by President Cosgrave who, in the latter's view, were plainly the most able and the most educated in Ireland, he attached himself to a small group led by Andrew Jameson, for he knew that he would leave him free to speak his mind. He had no particular regard for the elected Senators, among them were few able persons, though I suppose he would have put Mrs Green in that category. Yeats observed the decline in ability and prestige that occurred as the nominated element began to die out. 'In its early days', wrote Yeats, 'some old banker or lawyer would dominate the House, leaning upon the back of the chair in front, always speaking with undisturbed self-possession as at some table in a boardroom. My imagination sets up against him some typical elected man, emotional as a youthful chimpanzee, hot and vague, always disturbed, always hating something or other (*Explorations*, 412-13).

In her last years Aunt Alice's industry was incessant: it was said that she would tire out people half her age by her sustained intellectual vitality. But there had to be an end to it, and it came in May 1929 after a few months when her fragile health was self-evident, The Stopfords received many messages of sympathy, among them one to Dorothy from Sir Matthew Nathan who was now living in retirement in Somerset. Mrs Green and he had been friends since they foregathered at the beginning of the century to do honour to Mary Kingsley, the explorer and naturalist, and 'she tried to help me', he said, 'when I was in Ireland, and understood the lines of my ineffectual work there. She was a fine person whom it was good to have known.'

Some of the English papers were not so generous. *The Times*, for example, spoke of Mrs Green as the author of works of Irish history whose titles alone were sufficient to show where her sympathies lay; and the *Saturday Review* thought it strange that no tribute to her work had yet been offered by her fellow historians, the implication being that they did not think much of her work. The *Manchester Guardian*, however, dealt with that matter by saying that Mrs Green had broken new ground as a historian by revealing the importance of the Gaelic contribution to Irish medieval civilisation, and that her *Making of Ireland and its Undoing* was a vehement patriotic protest rather than a final judgment of history. It was a protest, however, that was vitally needed in the interests of historic truth. Future research might invalidate some of Mrs Green's conclusions, but Irish history could never be written again as it had been the fashion to write it before her work appeared. As might have been expected, the *Irish Statesman* paid the most comprehensive and warmest tribute of all to her. The unsigned article was undoubtedly written by the editor, George Russell (AE), who claimed a friendship with Alice Stopford Green extending over twenty years during which he came to know her enthusiasms and the spirit in which she laboured for her country. She was, he said, one of the most noble, generous and disinterested Irishwomen of her time. Her affection for Ireland was like a fire illuminating her mind and speech. She had so endowed Irish scholarship that it was no longer necessary for an Irish scholar to become an exile in some European university to gain an exact knowledge of the ancient language and literature of his country. Her *Making of Ireland and Its Undoing* had fascinated Irish readers and brought them to a first interest in their own history. To many the Middle Ages were as blank as the medieval maps where a geographer hid his ignorance by writing over a desert space "Here be lions", and there were even famous scholars who gave it as their opinion that the Irish before the Norman came to civilise them were only a pack of naked savages. The effect of Mrs Green's history was like the cleaning of an ancient wall painting which had been blurred by age or obscured by dark varnishes and dust so that what was painted was invisible. But after its cleansing one could see medieval scholars and craftsmen at their work. What was empty to the imagination became rich and filled up with vivid life. No doubt her histories might be superseded by later research, as scholarship became more exact. But she would always be honoured by the work she inaugurated, and the direction she gave to Irish historical studies. She was a noble representative of the Anglo-Irish, of those who were descendents of settlers, but who became so much in love with the country that they gave their hearts to the Dark Rose as passionately as any of the Gaelic singers.

Aunt Alice left most of her considerable fortune — a matter of £20,000 in the old money — to Robert, her only nephew and executor. That, too, looked as if she was singling out the man for special treatment. However, all the others got a share, and Alice Wordsworth used hers to send Mary to Cambridge where she did a good degree in Modern Languages, and to do a world tour, herself. Robert had returned to Cambridge after the war and taken a degree in economics before embarking on a career that lived up to his aunt's expectations. Beginning with a post in the British Overseas Bank in London, he went on political missions with his cousin Sir John Simon, first to Canada and then to India to organise the British withdrawal. From India Simon told Aunt Alice that her nephew had turned out 'quite first rate in devotion, good sense and tact; he would contribute something worthy of the Stopford name. Afterwards, he was with Lord Runciman in seeking a settlement between the Czechs and the Sudeten Germans. He was involved in the problem of international private debts in Austria and Hungary and when that work folded up under the Hitler regime, he stayed on in Budapest and organised for the British Embassy the escape of influential Jews, with their money, to England. In 1939 he went to Washington as financial advisor to the British Embassy and, after the liberation of the Netherlands, he worked from England on the relief of distress in Holland and Belgium.

Two things of converging interest occurred early in 1932. The Cosgrave government went out of office on 9 March before the votes of a combination of parties and individuals, and Eamon de Valera became the President of the Executive Council and the head of a Fianna Fáil administration. This, as we shall see, gave no pleasure to the Anglo-Irish, some of whom emigrated to Britain as so many more had done at the time of the Treaty. The new government, which stressed its republican objective, set out at an increased tempo to continue the removal of the obnoxious elements in the Treaty and took full advantage, of course, of the Statute of Westminster of 1931 which the brilliant young men of the first government had materially helped to promulgate. De Valera's first target was the Oath of Allegiance which was embodied in the Constitution of the Free State; simultaneously he suspended payment of land annuities into the United Kingdom Exchequer. The action on the annuities and the retaliation that followed constituted what was known as the Economic War which ended in a de Valera-Chamberlain compromise that preceded the outbreak of the Second World War.

More significant, perhaps, in the context of this book, was the death, also in March 1932, of Lady Gregory at the age of 80. Right up to 1930 when her health began to fail, she had continued to come regularly to Dublin to keep a proprietorial eye on the Abbey Theatre, and it was realised that no one would ever again nurse the Theatre as she had done since its inception. To those who were young when she was old she tended to appear a formidable person. She was so like Queen Victoria, some thought, that they almost called her Your Majesty. MacLiammoir spoke of her as having a gentle frosty dignity as of some royal personage. Her best and oldest friend was Yeats. He had spent some part of each summer at Coole, but necessarily she saw less of him after he married and she was lonely without him. With the passage of time also, she had ceased writing plays, but, as long as she could, she kept herself in touch with the theatre's play-producing policy, and had at last made the friendship of Sean O'Casey, the greatest of the post-1916 Irish dramatists. It had grieved her particularly when, on account of a controversy about his *Silver Tassie* he refused to receive her in London when she wanted to meet his wife and baby son.

When AE heard of Lady Gregory's death he wrote, appropriately to Yeats. 'Though you must have expected this for a long time, a passing of one who had been your best friend for the best years of your life cannot but move you deeply, and I am sorry for you that from this on your life must be lonelier. She was a very noble old lady. The generation to which she belonged was I think a rarer and finer breed of life than those who came after. I think of her, of Horace Plunkett, of Mrs Green, and others like them who thought in the noblest and most disinterested way about their country. . . . My own acquaintance with Lady Gregory was comparatively slight . . . but I always appreciated a workman doing beautiful things. . .'. And then he echoed what was being widely said in his circles, as de Valera came to power, 'The Anglo-Irish were the best Irish but I can see very little future for them, as the present belongs to that half-crazy Gaeldom which is growing dominant about us. I am very sorry for the loss of your friend.'

Gaeldom might be said to have triumphed when in 1937 a new Constitution was enacted in which Irish was declared to be the first official language with English *recognised* as the second official language. There was a large element of make-believe in this declaration, of course, for the Irish-speaking areas continued to shrink, few monoglot speakers of Irish had survived, and the acquisition of Irish as a vernacular was having very limited success. The political parties still professed to believe, however, in the possibility of halting the decline at least, and may in a sense have given expression to that belief by electing Douglas Hyde to the presidency of the state for which the new Constitution made provision. He had retired from the UCD chair in 1932 strangely believing that the language was saved (Dillon, 60), and left Dublin to live permanently at Ratra Park in Roscommon. He was enjoying his retirement, returning, as Yeats had done in a different way, to early enthusiasms. He began to re-read, and to translate into English verse, some of the Irish legends, and to amuse himself as he liked to do as a country squire. In 1938, when he became President of Ireland, he was a distinguished figurehead nevertheless, and his election was a belated tribute to the great enterprise to which he had in early life committed himself. Perhaps he saw it, too, as an *amende* for the unhappy circumstances in which he had left another presidency in 1915, and the 'Pope' O'Mahony, one of the great characters of the time, gave him a national anthem on the English model:

> God save our gracious Hyde
> Long live our noble Hyde
> God save our Hyde
> When Dev and Cosgrave clash
> He will do nothing rash
> More power to his old moustache
> God save our Hyde.

When his term of office expired in 1945, his successor was Sean T. O'Kelly, 'the gentlemanly' little man' who had been among the advance IRB party that forced him out of the Gaelic League.

Incidentally, MacNeill in May 1937 accepted an invitation from de Valera to chair a committee whose task was to examine the draft constitution with a view to simplifying the spelling of the Irish language version. This was a thorny subject but, as the work had to be done in great haste, the committee somehow managed to tender a report within a month. It was not signed, however, by four members who were known to have advanced ideas about simplification (Colm Ó Murchú who was the Clerk of Dáil Éireann, Shán Ó Cuív, Osborn Bergin and Tomás Ó Raithile). The current version of the Constitution, however, conforms to the spelling standards of the Translation Branch of the Office of the Houses of the Oireachtas.

Hyde died in 1949. By then all the men who had shared greatness with him were dead, AE since 1935, Yeats since 1939, and MacNeill since 1945. Of the men of the next generation Ernest Blythe, who died in 1975, and who had had his Yeats-admiring friend Desmond Fitzgerald in government with him, became the managing director of the Abbey Theatre on retiring from politics. While he was still a government minister, he had other earlier associates with him in the persons of Bulmer Hobson and Sean Lester, both in the civil service, the former in the office of the Revenue Commissioners, the latter in charge of publicity in the Department of External Affairs and subsequently the Irish representative in Geneva. Hobson ceased to be active in national politics after 1916, but he made his ideas on economic issues known in a group that produced a minority report for the 1933 Banking Commission.

Lester's international career was meteoric and brought lustre to the name of Ireland. He settled a dispute for the League of Nations between Peru and Columbia, before becoming the League's high commissioner in Danzig where it was his duty to watch over the democratic operation of the constitution. When the Nazis obtained a majority in the Danzig parliament they embarked on a brutal persecution of the minority and particularly of its Jewish elements. Lester made vigorous protests and efforts were made to intimidate him, but his complete disregard of his own safety in the face of anti-League demonstrations seriously worried the Nazi leaders who feared that it might not suit Hitler's book if the League's high commissioner were physically assaulted in the streets.

Subsequently as deputy secretary-general of the League he found himself in direct conflict with Joseph Avenol, the secretary-general. In Lester's view any compromise between Nazi doctrines and the principles of the League was unthinkable. He was therefore horrified to discover that, after the collapse of France, Avenol was contemplating that the palace of the League in Geneva might become the co-ordinating centre of the New Europe he believed was emerging. He wrote to the Vichy Government putting himself at its disposal; he endeavoured to get control of the League's funds;

and made every effort to secure Lester's resignation. The President of the League's Council sided with Lester, however, forced Avenol's resignation, and installed Lester as acting secretary-general. The victory of the Allies came as a welcome relief but it was followed by a profound disappointment. The meeting at San Francisco to lay the foundations of the new world order deliberately ignored the League, and it became Lester's melancholy duty to arrange for its dissolution. The task completed, he retired to his house in Connemara (D. M. Gageby, Stephen Barcroft; and Edward Phelan in *DNB*).

De Valera retired from public life in 1973 having been head of government for twenty-one years and President for another fourteen. This long period of office was by no means untroubled. It covered the years of the Second World War when Irish neutrality was asserted and maintained. De Valera insisted that the revival of Irish was the state's most urgent objective, more important even than the restoration of national unity. He spoke about it endlessly on public occasions; and used it himself as often as he could but, as the years went by, he was assailed by doubts about the Gaelicising role of the State, and whether the Irish people were themselves able and willing to do what was required of them. He began to emphasise that, while the State and public institutions generally could do much to *assist*, the inclination, willpower, persuasion and efforts of the people were what really mattered. Without widespread popular support the language movement could not succeed. You could bring a horse to the water, he said, but you could not make it drink.

People spoke disparagingly to him as if the cause was already lost, but he refused to believe that. However, he failed to carry the people with him. The decline of the Gaeltacht continued. There was an outcry against compulsory Irish in the schools and public service, and teachers complained that all aspects of education were being subordinated to the language question. The policy was therefore modified; and the national aim was re-stated to be the restoration of Irish as a means of communication so that the population of the country would be truly bilingual. But even on those terms the doubt remained as to whether Irish could be restored.

The satirist Myles na Gopaleen, himself the product of revival-ist parents, declared that there was an immense body of proof that Irish could not be revived at all. He did not think, generally speaking, that it was possible to learn Irish. Cer-tainly few people had mastered it, he said, 'Mr de Valera's Irish is bad and laborious, and Douglas Hyde's downright bad.'

We conclude our kaleidoscope with Dorothy Stopford, whose story we have intermittently told since the first chapter. She had started to write a book in 1937 about the forms of TB that affected children but the pressure of accumulating work, both private and in St Ultan's, made this a slow process. She had added to her responsibilities the role of consultant physician to several hospitals including the Newcastle Sana-torium, so that it was usually late at night before she could settle down to write anything. The holidays she had taken, either alone or with a medical colleague, between 1934 and 1937 were for the purpose of improving her knowledge. In August 1938 she went to Denmark with Liam, the first holiday she had shared with him since 1931, and they spent a few days together in Paris in 1939. She was all this time bur-ning the candle at both ends and endangering her health. Yet the book had to be written, and she compromised with Liam by agreeing to go that year to a little hotel in Glenmalure among the Wicklow hills where she thought she could ease the strain by continuing a little writing with some fishing. The compromise did not work. She got an attack of muscular rheumatism which confined her crippled to bed at home for the rest of the year. However, she finished the final draft as a new question arose with the outbreak of the war; would she be able to get the book published? She was told on all sides that it would be impossible, but a publisher in Bristol turned up and, despite his works being bombed practically out of existence by the Germans, managed to produce a thousand copies of *Tuberculosis in Childhood*.

She could speak optimistically about the achievements of the TB unit in St Ultan's, which was about to be enlarged by the addition of twenty cots for children up to 5 years. 'I am using sulphropyridine during initial fever in primary TB'; the mortality rate had been reduced from 77 per cent to

23 per cent in six years. She gave these statistics to the Minister for Health and emphasised that the clinical work in St Ultan's, based on the experience gained notably from Scandinavia, was far in advance of what was being done in England. She said this in the hope of being given the money for a new unit, and this was promised. But from the time the Minister asked the hospital to send their plans, it took three and a half years before the additional beds became available. This was a form of frustration she found hard to endure. There would be other forms.

One arose out of a proposal to form a national Anti-TB League on the lines of what was being done in other countries. The objects in view were the stimulation of a popular interest in the campaign to control the spread of the disease, which was declining everywhere except in Ireland, to make propaganda for the removal of the 'stigma' of TB, and to press for increased X-Ray facilities, sanatorium beds and after-care. The proposal was discussed at a meeting in the College of Surgeons in April 1942, and Dorothy, when she spoke, struck several notes which were bound to be regarded as controversial. She said she did not want over-representation of local public bodies in the direction of the League. She was opposed to using sweepstakes as a means of raising revenue; and she made a particular point of the League not being affiliated with the Red Cross or being in any way under the control of the Local Government Department. Following this meeting all sorts of contacts were made and in April 1943 everything appeared to be ready to establish the League formally when the Catholic Archbishop of Dublin Dr John Charles McQuaid intervened to say that a campaign such as was contemplated should be carried out by the Red Cross Society which operated under government patronage and which he considered to be a *sine qua non* for success. This bombshell left Dorothy utterly indignant, but realist that she was, and after 'some very dark weeks' and discussions and consultations, she told a friend that 'We have gone into the Red Cross. We have got very little except that we have kept our own organising committee together, and I think that we will have a free hand to do some sort of modified campaign against TB.' She became a member of the Red Cross Anti-TB

Committee when it was formed but resigned when the committee ruled that all members should be members of the Irish
Red Cross Society. She saw this as a breach of the compromise
that had been reached earlier.

The war had prevented the importation of the BCG vaccine
but when the war was over supplies commenced to arrive
again and she used them, first, on the infants of TB parents,
vaccinating them a few days after they were born. She wrote
more papers for the medical journals, lectured, and entertained overseas experts she had encouraged to visit Ireland.
One of these, after seeing St Ultan's, told her that 'Your Unit
is quite unique; I could not imagine anything better than
what you have arranged.'

The state of her own health was causing Liam concern.
Visitors to the house thought he had become 'terribly growly
and difficult', but he was really only trying to get Dorothy
to cut down on her work, on seeing so many people, and on
sitting up late at night reading and writing. He induced her
to take a longish holiday in 1948 on a mountain farm he had
bought at Castleruddery in Co. Wicklow, and which was to
have been their hide-out in the event of Dublin being bombed,
but from March to September 1946 she was ill again. This
forced her to give up all private practice and the work she
had been doing for children for years in the Royal City of
Dublin Hospital in Baggot Street.

She read a paper at the inaugural meeting of an Irish TB
Society in October 1946 on the subject of the large-scale
employment of BCG, a subject in which the government was
expressing interest. But there were frustrations and she told
a Norwegian friend that she had never put in a more work-
like period, 'I got Herpes Opthalmicus out of it, and went
down to a conference with a red scarf over one eye, looking
like a sinister female pirate. I am sure your Government
departments are not so stupid.' She continued to press her
point of view and, eventually, in 1948, what she originally
recommended was approved. But it was another year and a
half before a building for a separate BCG unit was ready for
use; and other dificulties were raised about licences for the
importation of vaccine. The Department of Health was a
hell-hole, she said.

The picture improved significantly with a change of government and the appointment of Noel Browne as Minister for Health. Browne was an old friend and had been in touch with her after the inauguration of an Irish TB Society for which he had strenuously campaigned. He lost no time in tackling the problem, as he saw it. Regional sanatoria were to be built and, while waiting for them, arrangements were to be made to provide more beds at once. He appointed Dorothy to be the Chairman of a Consultative Council on TB, and gave the Council a list of subjects on which he wished to have their advice. The Council held a long series of meetings and Dorothy kept an eager eye on these and on the detailed work of sub-committees. These meetings often ran until near midnight, and on top of her work in St Ultan's and much consultative activity, they brought the threat of a breakdown. She was told by her doctor that she must take things easier, especially that she must cut out night work. She followed this advice for a time, but her eagerness to get things done was always driving her on. On the day of the formal opening of the new BCG Unit at St Ultan's, at which the Minister for Health announced that Dorothy would chair the Central Committee, she got an attack of faintness, and barely contrived to finish a speech of thanks. Within a fortnight she called the first meeting of the Committee and outlined a policy of expansion. Vaccinators were appointed, county schemes initiated and a post-graduate course held in University College, Dublin. 'There is at present a wave of enthusiasm for BCG,' she said. 'All doctors want to be doing it at once, but of course they will be all tired of the new craze in two years time. I expect to be thrown out any day as too conservative. I am having an awful time, up in the skies one day, and plunged into the prospect of immediate dissolution the next. Yet we make progress.'

The prospect of dissolution came nearer in mid-January 1950 when, as the inevitable result of all the strain and overwork, she suffered a stroke which caused partial paralysis and temporary loss of speech. She was taken to a nursing home in Herbert Street which was directed by a former Alexandra Nurse who always wore her uniform and decorations, a practice Dorothy disliked. She would talk of 'that woman!' She liked even less the picture of Winston Churchill on the wall opposite her bed; the idea of having to live with 'that thing', she murmured. She survived everything, however, and at the end of a month went home, though obviously enfeebled. 'It is worth it to get BCG across', she told Liam but he was not so sure. He would loudly argue with her. Her concern to save lives was killing herself. Did she not realise this? 'Let them die,' he was heard to say. 'You have done enough for them.'

To make it easier for her to move around on the flat, Liam moved to 1 Herbert Park and there she fought off the boredom by writing an occasional scientific paper or book review for the *Irish Journal of Medical Science*. In that fashion she continued to live on until 28 January 1954, when she got another stroke and died without recovering consciousness two days later. She was buried on a cold snowy morning in St Maelruen's graveyard in Tallaght, leaving Liam greatly distressed. Edie died in 1960 and Alice in the following year. Robert lived on until 1978.

Liam faced up to his sorrow courageously and, practical man that he was, had by 1955 prepared an account of Dorothy's fight against tuberculosis, and had it published privately with a photograph of her which shows how little in the way of outward appearance she had. Not to put a tooth in it, she was a rather plain woman, and seems to have cared nothing for clothes or make-up, so that Liam had to prompt her to get something new to wear on an important occasion. However the book, rather than the picture, was the important thing, and Liam must have been pleased with the reception it got from close acquaintances of Dorothy he sent copies to.

Walter Paget of the Middlesex Hospital considered Dorothy's work was an important piece of Irish history and on that account he regretted the book was for private circulation only. But the last thing Dorothy would have wanted, Liam knew, was to give offence to people who had been involved in the battle now that it was won; nevertheless the book, though written with restraint, was to remind some people of offensive aspects of the anti-tuberculosis campaign. One Dublin doctor, when he read it, told Liam he was particularly glad to be reminded of that disgraceful episode when

Dr McQuaid so nearly 'managed to stop all preventive work against tuberculosis'. Equally exaggerated was the declaration of another doctor that 'much of Dorothy's struggle as a pioneer was against that curse in this country, Roman Catholicism', a statement that overlooked the fact that some of Dorothy's closest collaborators were Roman Catholics. Comments of that sectarian kind would certainly have displeased Dorothy, about whom, as somebody said, the most wonderful thing was her lack of bitterness. Bob Barton commended Liam's wisdom in restricting the circulation of what Surgeon William Doolin called 'a sad but exquisite memoir'. It was obvious to Barton that Liam and Dorothy had consulted together about things over the years, otherwise Liam could not have written so intimately of her struggle, disappointments and final success.

That was true, and Liam for the rest of his life emulated Dorothy, by giving even more of himself to the varied areas of research in which he was interested. This led to a stream of articles and notes for the *Journal of the Royal Society of Antiquaries* whose editor he was to become on field monuments, prehistoric burials, finds of archaeological objects, place-names and local history. To the *Proceedings of the Royal Irish Academy* he contributed a further series of papers, including an important corpus of archaeological material on the ages of stone and bronze in Wicklow. In the Society of Antiquaries whose President he was during Dorothy's last year, he was recognised as the most modest of men, abhorring vanity, pomposity and humbug. The National University of Ireland honoured him with a degree, and when he died in 1967, a special volume was published by the Society 'as a tribute to a great Irishman'.

So, in their different ways, Liam Price and Dorothy Stopford out of their Anglo-Irish backgrounds gave of their best to Ireland. Aunt Alice would have praised their work and recognised its significance in the national context, as she recognised and esteemed the contribution of so many other Anglo-Irish families. It was this she had in her mind when, in her speech to the Senate on the day her silver casket was presented she said that if an Irish Nation was to be revived — and she implied that an Irish parliament had no other *raison d'être* — roots would have to be dug deep into its soul. She saw the nation, as Eoin MacNeill saw it earlier, as a brotherhood of adoption as well as of blood. Ireland had given hospitality to men of good-will coming within her borders, and to that generosity the newcomers had responded honourably. They had become faithful members of the Irish people. Strangers at first, they had felt the wonder of the land and the quality of its people, and had entered into her commonwealth. Whether of ancient Irish descent, or of later Irish birth, they were united as one people, and were bound by a lofty obligation to complete the building of a common nation. They had lived under the breadth of Ireland's skies, been fed by the fatness of her fields, and nourished by the civilisation of her dead. Their people lay in her earth, and would in that earth await their destiny.

BIBLIOGRAPHY

Unpublished Sources

Diarmuid Coffey's Statement on the Irish Volunteers for the Bureau of Military History (In possession of Saive Coffey).

Hyde Memoir, Folklore Department, University College, Dublin.

Douglas Hyde Papers, National Library of Ireland.

Nathan Papers, Bodleian Library, Oxford.

Liam Price Papers (In possession of R. J. Going).

Liam Price, *Dr Dorothy Price* (For private circulation only), Oxford 1957.

Mary K. Smith (Mary Wordsworth), Miscellaneous Notes.

Dorothy Stopford Diaries 1908-1910 (In possession of Mary K. Smith).

Dorothy Stopford-Price Papers, National Library of Ireland.

Alice Stopford-Green Papers, National Library of Ireland.

Robert J. Stopford Papers, National Library of Ireland.

Robert J. Stopford Papers, Imperial War Museum, London.

Published Sources

Akenson, Donald Harman, *The Church of Ireland: Ecclesiastical Reform and Revolution*, Yale 1971.

Barry, Tom, *Guerilla Days in Ireland* (repr. Tralee 1962).

Bolger, Patrick, *The Irish Co-Operative Movement*, Dublin 1977.

Bowman, John, *De Valera and the Ulster Question*, Oxford 1982.

Boyce, D. G., *Englishmen and Irish Troubles*, London 1972.

Boyle, Andrew, *The Riddle of Erskine Childers*, London 1977.

Daly, Dominic, *The Young Douglas Hyde*, Dublin 1974.

De hIde, Dubhghlas, *Mise agus an Connradh*, Dublin 1937.

Denson, Alan, ed., *Letters from AE*, (London, 1961).

Digby, Margaret, *Horace Plunkett, An Anglo-American Irishman*, London 1949.

Dillon, Myles, *Douglas Hyde in The Shaping of Modern Ireland*, London 1960.

Donoghue, Denis, *Yeats*, London 1971.

Donoghue, Denis, ed., *William Butler Yeats, Memoirs*, New York 1973

Edwards, Ruth Dudley, *Patrick Pearse, The Triumph of Failure*, London 1977.

Fanning, Ronan, *Independent Ireland*, Dublin 1983.

Gaughan, J. Anthony, *Memoirs of Constable Jeremiah Mee*, Dublin 1975.

Gregory, Lady A., ed., *Ideals in Ireland*, London 1901.

Griffith, Kenneth, and O'Grady, Timothy E., *Curious Journey*, London 1982.

Gwynn, Denis, 'Thomas M. Kettle', in *Studies*, Winter 1966.

Hayden, Anthony P., *Sir Matthew Nathan*, Queensland 1976.

Headlam, Maurice, *Irish Reminiscences*, London 1947.

Hobson, Bulmer, *Ireland Yesterday and Tomorrow*, Tralee 1968.

Horgan, John J., *From Parnell to Pearse*, Dublin 1948.

Hone, Joseph, *W. B. Yeats 1865-1939*, London 1965.

Inglis, Brian, *Roger Casement*, London 1973.

Lyons, F. S. L., *Ireland since the Famine*, revised edn., London 1973.

Macardle, Dorothy, *The Irish Republic*, revised, London 1968.

Marreco, Anne, *The Rebel Countess*, London 1967.

Martin, F. X., *Howth Gun-Running 1914*, Dublin 1964.

Martin, F. X., '1916 — Myth, Fact and Mystery' in *Studia Hibernica*, No. 1, 1967.

Martin, F. X. ed., *The Easter Rising and University College, Dublin*, Dublin 1966.

McDowell, R. B., *The Irish Convention*, London 1970.

McDowell, R. B., *Alice Stopford-Green: A Passionate Historian*, Dublin 1967.

Meenan, James, *George O'Brien*, Dublin 1980.

Nowlan, K. B. ed., *The Making of 1916*, Dublin 1969.

Ó Broin, León, *Charles Gavan Duffy, Patriot and Statesman*, Dublin 1966.

Ó Broin, León, *Dublin Castle and the 1916 Rising*, revised edn., London 1970.

Ó Broin, León, *The Chief Secretary: Augustine Birrell in Ireland*, London 1969.

Ó Broin, León, 'Maurice Moore and the National Volunteers' in *The Irish Sword*, Winter 1979.

Ó Broin, León, *Revolutionary Underground*, Dublin 1976.

Ó Conluain, Proinsias, *Sean T.*, Dublin 1963.

Ó Lúing, Seán, *Art Ó Gríofa*, Dublin 1953.

O'Hegarty, P. S., *A History of Ireland Under the Union, 1801-1922*, London 1952.

Ó Mordha, Muiris, *Tús agus Fás Oglach na hÉireann*, Dublin 1936.

O'Sullivan, Donal, *The Irish Free State and its Senate*, London 1940.

Pim, Sheila, *The Wood and the Trees: A biography of Augustine Henry*, London 1966.

Ryan, Desmond, *The Rising*, Dublin 1949.

Rodgers, W. R., *Irish Literary Portraits*, London 1972.

Stanford, W. B., and McDowell, R. B., *Mahaffy: A Biography of an Anglo-Irishman*, London 1971.

Stephens, James, *The Insurrection in Dublin*, Dublin 1916.

Tierney, Michael, *Eoin MacNeill, Scholar and Man of Action 1867-1945*, London 1980.

Townshend, Charles, *The British Campaign in Ireland 1919-1921*, London 1975.

Tuohy, Frank, *Yeats*, Dublin 1976.

Webb, Beatrice, *Diary, 1. Glitter around and Darkness within*, ed. Norman and Jeanne MacKenzie, London 1982.

Webb, Beatrice, *Diary, 2. All the good things of Life*, ed. Norman and Jeanne MacKenzie, London 1983.

Williamson, Burke, *The Zeal of the Convert*, London 1976.

Yeats, W. B., *Autobiographies*, London 1955.

Yeats, W. B., *Essays and Introductions*, London 1961.

Yeats, W. B., *Explorations*, London 1962.

Yeats, W. B., *The Senate Speeches*, ed. Donald R. Pearce, London 1961.

INDEX

Alphabetical arrangement is word-by-word. Passim indicates that the references are scattered throughout the pages mentioned.

AE *see* Russell, George

Abbey Theatre (Dublin), 58, 69, 108, 210

Ancient Order of Hibernians, 35, 44, 62

Anglo-Irish community, 12-13, 17-18, 211-12, 215, 216, 225-6

Ard-Fheis, Dundalk, 1915, 71-3

Ashe, Tom, 140

Asquith, Henry Herbert, 6, 111, 116

Barry, Tom, 170-1

Barton, Robert, 152, 153, 183, 225; in Irish delegation to London, 187-9; on the Civil War, 191-2

Bayly, Admiral Sir Lewis, 122, 125

Bentinck, Lord Henry, 164

Berkeley, George Fitzhardinge, 62, 164

Bewley, Charles, 90

Birrel, Augustine: as Chief Secretary in Ireland, 57; his Irish Universities Bill, 58; warns Nathan of Alice Green, 65-6; informed of Rising, 87; condemned by Plunkett, 96; arrives in Dublin, 98; resignation of, 110; at Royal Commission of Enquiry, 120, 125-6

Black and Tans, 155, 163, 166, 181-2

Blythe, Ernest: joins IRB, 39; learns Irish, 40-1; imprisoned with Pim, 44-5; resigns from IRB, 119; director of Trade & Commerce, 188; his work for the revival of Irish, 208-9; at the Abbey Theatre, 218

Boundary Commission, 1924, 205-6

Brade, P. H., 122-3

Browne, Noel (Minister for Health), 223

Campbell, J. H. (Attorney General), 96, 151

Carson, Sir Edward, 60-1, 111, 112, 144

Casement, Roger, 32, 35; supports Fianna Eireann, 36; friendship with Alice Green, 46-7; produces anti-enlistment leaflets, 47; in search of arms for Irish Volunteers, 62; goes to Germany, 64, 68; arrested for landing ammunition, 78; imprisoned in Tower, 133; trial of, 134-5; execution of, 135

Childers, Erskine, 167, 187; goes to Germany to buy ammunition, 62-3; works for the Irish Convention, 150

Civil War, 190-4

Clann na Gael, 40, 67, 68, 76, 77, 120

Clarke, Tom, 46, 90; presides over IRB meeting, 67, 68; prepares for Rising, 75-6; execution of, 105

Coffey, Diarmuid, 88, 198, 199

Collins, Michael, 166, 180, 187; vindicates MacNeill, 118; intelligence gathering of, 161-2; visits Alice Green, 167-8

Colum, Padraic, 21, 49

Comerford, Mary, secretary to Alice Green, 146, 167-8, 180, 181, 203

Connolly, James, 19, 40, 67, 81, 90; and the Irish Citizen Army, 59, 60, 75; advocates rebellion, 68, 76; calls out Citizen Army, 86; execution of, 109-10

Connor, Henry, 186, 198

conscription, 148, 150

Constitution of Ireland, 1922, 192-3

Constitution of Ireland, 1937, 216-17

Conyngham, Lady Freddy, 100

Cope, Alfred, 167

Cosgrave, W. T., 136, 192, 193

Crowley, Bridie, 185-6

Crozier, Brigadier General E. F., 165

Culverwell, Ann Beatrice, her views on the Rising, 113-14

Cumann na mBan, 44, 68, 160, 169, 171

Dáil Éireann, 153, 161, 166-7, 191, 193

Daly, Edward, 105

de Valera, Eamon, 120, 143, 161, 187; background of, 136-7; opposed to 1921 Treaty, 189, 192; becomes President, 215; importance of Irish language to him, 219

Deasy, Liam, 189, 195

Devoy, John, 63, 76, 107, 124

Dickinson, Charles, 102, 103, 104

Dillon, John, 74, 77, 120, 127

Dillon, Myles, on *Cathleen Ni Houlihan*, 41

Donovan, John, 157

Douglas, Lord Alfred, 45

Dublin, civilians killed at Bachelor's Walk, 63, 77

Dublin Castle attacked by Citizen Army, 83-4, 87, 89

Duffy, Charles Gavan, 10-11

Duffy, George (son of C G), 35, 167

Dungannon Clubs, 35, 47

Dunlop, Robert, 23